Scent of Saffron

Rouhi Shafii

Scent of Saffron

Three generations of an Iranian family

Scarlet Press

Published by Scarlet Press
5 Montague Road, London E8 2HN

The author asserts her moral right to be identified as the
author of this work in accordance with the Copyright,
Design and Patents Act 1988

British Library Cataloguing-in-Publication Data
A catalogue record for this book is available from
the British Library
ISBN 1 85727 088 6 pb

Designed and produced for Scarlet Press by
Chase Production Services, Chadlington, Oxford, OX7 3LN
Typeset from the author's disk by
Stanford DTP Services, Milton Keynes
Printed in the EC

To the dear memory of my grandmother Bibi Attieh and my mother Afagh Khanum, to whom I owe the substance of my survival.

Contents

Acknowledgements

I would like to express my gratitude to Avis Lewallen of Scarlet Press who took up my project and helped me to materialise what I had long had in mind. My children, Parham and Parastou, showed great affection and support by constructively criticising my work and offering comments. Parham's pride in me and Parastou's sense of prefectionism and artistic talent were the backbone that gave me the strength to continue. I am grateful to my brother Mehdi who encouraged me to go ahead with the writing of our family's history, although it was at some stages very painful for him to remember the past. He also translated some of the poems used at the beginning of chapters and offered his own poems to be quoted as well. I express my love to Alex, my sister-in-law, who gave me a free hand to write what I wanted about her and did not restrict me in any way. I am indebted to all my relatives and friends back home, who polished my memory and offered help.

My deep gratitude to Mr Khonji for reading the background history and correcting me all the way through. Shadab Vajdi, contemporary poet, permitted me to quote extracts from her work and showed sincere interest in my project. My love to Dr Paul Weeks, who took the time to read my epilogue and comment on it. The Library for Iranian Studies was my main source of information and background reading. I would like to thank all the staff, especially Dr Ajudani, whose extensive insight helped me all the way through my reading.

My mother, Afagh Khanum, was a very private person. I hope she forgives me for exposing her life to *namahram* (strangers). I also hope that I have not done any injustice to the people I have mentioned in the book, be it my own family or others.

Rouhi Shafii
London, 1997

Prologue, 1995

A townhouse in Middlesex, England

I gave my heart to the river
So that it takes my heart away from the town
From a town whose inhabitants
Talk to themselves
Because they have no one to talk to.
      Shadab Vajdi, 'Let the Heart Go'

It is an autumn morning. I wake up early as usual. In Iran, because of the heat, the day starts very early, with most schools and offices opening from seven in the morning. But now I lie in bed for a few more minutes. Often I dream; in Persian or in English. Sometimes my dreams are mixed. I may be back in Iran with the friends I have made in England. A strange spirit of unity dominates. Sometimes I wake up totally confused. Where did I travel to last night? To the valleys of the villages where I spent my childhood summers, or to my aunt's orange orchards, where I spent my teen years? Sometimes I dream of the last turbulent years I was in Iran and that is when I get a headache and wake up frightened.

I sometimes envy the cats for the way they enjoy spreading their relaxed bodies on comfortable beds, as if that is the only moment that exists; no past, no future. My white Persian kitten did the same when she slept on my bed in my home in the southern province of Kerman. There most families kept cats as pets. These beautiful creatures have long, white hair and gleaming eyes. I have kept cats ever since.

I peep at my clock–radio. Too early to get up yet. Suddenly, I feel the warm sunshine through the net curtains. This is an occasion I relish. Morning sunshine in October, so pleasant and full of sweetness. I feel a different person when the sun is shining. In England I live every moment of a sunny day. In autumn it is uncommon for the weather to be so generous, to drive away the clouds, letting me feel at home.

I now get up, go downstairs, pull the curtains open and the sun rushes into my living-room. I wonder where home really is. Is home the city where I spent my first nine years of life, or is it where my mother wasted her youth and suffered so much to raise her six children? Is home Tehran, where I went to college, worked for two decades, lived a happy life? Rationally, this townhouse in Middlesex could best be described as my home. I go to the door and pick up the letters the postwoman has delivered. One of the good things about this country is the amount of mail one receives every day. Back in Iran I received only an occasional letter.

I go through the letters and open the one that has my name spelt correctly. Normally, as my name seems difficult to pronounce or write, very few bother to spell it correctly. I cannot recall all the spellings used of my name. I open the letter. It is about my National Insurance payments, reminding me that I am getting close to pensionable age but have not yet made enough contributions.

The sun hides herself behind the scattered clouds and I feel a chill. Why couldn't such a letter come on a cloudy, perhaps rainy day, when possibly I would have been depressed anyway? I become anxious before thinking rationally. Am I going to grow old away from home? After all those years that I worked in Iran, what happened to the money I paid into the pension schemes back there? Gone with the wind? Gone along with everything else that withered away? The home that I spent two years building near the Alborz mountains. My thousands of books that went up in flames because they were banned. My neighbours who emigrated before me and whom I never heard of again. My pride in being part of a great nation that suddenly fragmented. Gone is the glittering sunshine. I close my eyes and nostalgia invades my mind. I drift back in time, in search of my past.

I feel an urge to share my past with you. I want to tell you my story. It is a story with a difference. It is not a tale of kings and queens or of heroes and heroines. My story is about ordinary women like myself, whose lives were transformed by events in the late twentieth century. My story is about Iran, or Persia, and the women of Iran whose popular history barely exists. We have had thousands of poets, writers and historians who across the centuries have left a rich cultural heritage. None the less, women are rarely mentioned as creators and mentors of the society. They are hidden behind curtains and high walls. In modern Iran a woman must be a hero, a member of an upper-class family, or a prominent figure for whatever reason, to be written about or be heard of. My story is dedicated to those millions who are not allowed to speak about their lives or articulate their inner thoughts. I share my life with you, hoping it will make a difference in your perception of us, alien women in the West. It is a tribute to the lives, loves, joys and sorrows of those whom you might have seen on your TV screens or have come across in the street.

Now that I live in England, free of many constraints, I am able to write. In Iran, women are discouraged from talking frankly about their feelings, thoughts, beliefs or ambitions. We are brought up to be reserved, to be considerate, to observe the strict rules of society and to conform. Disobeying the rules is not acceptable and the penalty is severe. Your 'sin' will be punished by being advised, blamed, scorned, limited, excluded, marginalised, penalised, criminalised, imprisoned, tortured, or even executed. I was brought up to conform, but rarely did. I was brought up in the spirit of self-censorship. We censor our thoughts, emotions, feelings, aspirations, and who we really are. Censorship is part of our literature, history, education and social upbringing. We have never been an open society and possibly never will be. If we don't self-censor, we come to harm. We may not talk frankly with our parents, it is rude and disrespectful. We are not allowed to ask questions in the classroom. We are not allowed to talk about our beliefs in public. We might open up to a degree, depending on the political mood, but we will never say what we really want to. In three thousand years of written history it has always been this way. Moments of complete freedom of thought are rare and hidden from our history. Eradicated. In writing this small history of women's lives, I will observe some of the rules. I cannot ignore them, no matter how much I want to. Therefore, my story is 'the truth but not the whole truth'. Nevertheless, I will share some secrets with you, for in our culture, it is believed that women are 'cunning and conspicuous'[1] and get their way, no matter how they are restricted.

I will open a window onto my past, through which you will see the efforts and struggles of ordinary women as they reject their subordinate position and push for a hidden agenda which will give them the power they have long lost. I will walk down memory lane, taking you with me to the land of lovers and poets, the land of A Thousand and One Nights.[2] I will take you to the villages of southern Iran, through the streets surrounded by tall eucalyptus trees and rose gardens. You will travel with me, on horseback, into the unknown, feel the hot winds of summer-time that rush towards the Indian Ocean and the cold winter breeze across the snows of the Alborz mountains. I will take you to the subterranean waters that irrigate the farmlands in the middle of the deserts. I will pick the reddest rose and the prettiest of white daffodils to give to you for being my companion on this journey. Let me take your hand and whisper in your ear what our great twelfth-century poet and philosopher Sa'adi[3] said:

> *As created from the same essence,*
> *Children of Adam are one body,*
> *And mind,*
> *Restless are other organs,*
> *When one is not well and in pain.*
>
> Sa'adi, *Golestan*

Iran, a brief history

Persia or Ancient Iran, 7000 BC–1775 AD

Iran is in the Middle East, in western Asia, part of the Iranian plateau which comprises many countries including Afghanistan, Tajikistan and Georgia. Iran covers an area of 636,300 square miles, more than six times that of the UK. It is bordered to the north by three republics of the former Soviet Union (Azarbaijan, Turkamenestan and Armenia) and the Caspian Sea, to the west by Turkey and Iraq, to the east by Afghanistan and Pakistan, and to the south by the Persian Gulf and the Gulf of Oman. The climate ranges from sub-tropical to sub-polar. At the beginning of the twentieth century, Iran's population was about 12 million, now it is more than 65 million. Different peoples and cultures have lived there side by side for thousands of years: Persians, Azaris, Arabs, Kurds, Baluchis, Turkamens and many other smaller nationalities.

Iran's strategic position has long made it a target of invasion. Iran has been invaded by Greeks (Macedonians), Arabs, Mongols and Turkic peoples and has suffered continual interference in its internal affairs. During the nineteenth and twentieth centuries, Iran has been the scene of constant rivalries between the modern states of Britain, Russia and America.

Iran is one of the oldest countries in the world. Iran's civilisation dates back to 7000 BC when settlements were engaged in agriculture, cattle raising, weaving and clay-making. By 5000–4000 BC the people of Khorasan and Kerman were using copper to make tools. From 4000 BC onwards the textile and copper industries developed. Some of the copper was exported to other countries. Elamite tribes are the first communities known to have existed on the Iranian plateau, where they developed cities and urban civilisation. They are known to have invented the Elamite cuneiform script, one of the earliest forms of writing. Elamite tribes lived in Khuzistan, Pars and Kerman. Along with agriculture they invented the irrigation system and they were among the first to domesticate animals.

Elamites ruled parts of the Iranian plateau for thousands of years. The paintings and sculptures which remain indicate that women had a high status within these settlements. In excavations in Shush, an ancient town in southern Iran, the first family units who lived in houses have been found: a few rooms, a stock-room, and a kitchen. A house has been excavated in Shush containing fifty rooms. Its owner, Tamtay Varash, owned thousands of cattle and his business dealings went as far as Bahrain. Excavations in the south-west have revealed brass utensils and arms made of different types of metal. In Luristan, the wealthy were buried with their gold and silver.

A form of government headed by the Elamite settlements has been traced as far back as 3000 BC. Apart from a strong central kingdom, smaller kingdoms also existed. From 2000 BC, economic growth and consequently class society emerged among the Elamite community. The growth of urban societies and the emergence of a class society entrenched male dominance and a patriarchal family system, which had been until then mainly matriarchal. As cities developed and laws to enable the governing of the more complex society were ratified, more restrictions and harsher codes were placed on the family unit and its members. Under the Babylonians, who had inherited the western regions of the Elamite Empire, the Code of Hammurabi[1] (1752 BC) limited the time for which a man could pawn his wife or children to three years and expressly forbade beating or oppressing these debt-pawns. The Hammurabi Code also states that men could easily divorce their wives, particularly if they had not borne children.

It was only in the last millennium BC that the Elamites were defeated by the Assyrians, Babylonians and other peoples from Mesopotamia, who took over most parts of the Iranian plateau and established their own kingdoms. Numerous battles between the kingdoms resulted in the destruction of the Elamite civilisation. Around 2000 BC the Aryan tribes entered the plateau from north Europe, and after many battles, established their domination over parts of the indigenous Elamite kingdom. The Elamite kingdom survived until 1200 BC. Parts of the indigenous Iranian population of the present time are the descendants of those Aryan tribes.

The establishment of the Persian Empire 550 BC–640 AD

The Persian Empire was established during the rule of the Achaemenid Dynasty, which dates back to 550 BC. The empire extended as far as Egypt, Macedonia, India and the Black Sea. During this dynasty coins made of gold, silver and copper went into circulation. Decrees, and regulations documented on thousands of petroglyphs (rock carvings), reveal women's involvement in high-status professions, especially in the treasury and finance. Unlike other parts of the world, there is no trace of slave labour in ancient Persia and equal wages were always paid to male labourers and women employees alike. Interestingly, overtime for women was rewarded not by coins but in the form of wine and beer. The kings, in doing their kingly duties, were also salaried. During the Achaemenid Dynasty an army consisting of thousands of officers and soldiers was established. The cities of Persepolis and Pasargadae[2] were built by the Achaemenid emperors. Cyrus the Great (558 BC) made Pasargadae the official capital of the empire, where he himself held ceremonies and celebrations. His grave is located in this city; a huge monument depicting the grandeur of that historical era.

By 500 BC some of the nations ruled by the Persian Empire had rebelled against it. There were also numerous wars between the Persians and the Macedonians. Finally, Alexander of Macedonia defeated King Darius III and conquered Persia, overthrowing the Achaemenid Empire in 330 BC. After a century of rule by the descendants of Alexander (the Selucides), Partians (or Ashkanians) re-established Iranian rule. Many centuries of Partian rule was followed by an equally long period of rule by another Iranian dynasty, the Sassanids, until the Arab invasion and the Muslim conquest of 640 AD.

The Persian Empire as the dominant civilisation with established cultural mores had a great influence on the ancient world. By the time of the Sassanid Dynasty, feudalistic relations had replaced the commune system, and class rigidification and social hierarchy had come into existence. Due to the influence of the Zoroastrians' high-ranking clergy, who encouraged patriarchal gender relations, women gradually lost their high social status. Women attached to the nobility, and the courtiers, became imprisoned in the harems and were hidden from the public.

However, even from the earliest times, up to the Arab invasion, incestuous marriages (in which men were permitted to marry their sisters, daughters or mothers) and polygamy were widely practised, especially among the king's courtiers and the nobility. When Alexander defeated King Darius III in 330 BC, the harem captured from Darius consisted of his mother and wives, who travelled in their own carriages and were attended by their own troops of women on horseback. Fifteen carriages carried the king's children, their nurses and a crowd of eunuchs. More carriages carried Darius's 365 concubines.

The emergence of the Zoroastrian religion

The first known religion is Zoroastrianism, perhaps dating as far back as the first millennium BC. The holy scriptures of the Zoroastrians are referred to as Avesta. The basis of Zoroaster's teachings has the complex eschatology characteristic of Near Eastern religions, with two opposing elements: the angel and the devil, with evil spirits, heaven and hell and the day of judgement. The god Ohrmazda, who stood for good thinking, good speaking and good behaviour, was involved in constant battles with evil.

Zoroastrianism was adopted as the state religion by the Sassanid Dynasty. This religion gained much support among the nobility and created a hierarchical social structure. Zoroastrianism grew in power as the state cult and its rulings on family and male-female relationships became indisputable. The patriarchal family, which was by then well established within the emerging feudal society, demanded the wife's total obedience. Now, praying to Ohrmazda every morning on rising and obeying her husband became a woman's paramount duty. The extent to which Zoroastrians were able to infiltrate Mediterranean countries depended on the relations of the Sassanid Empire with its arch rival, the Byzantine Empire, which had adopted Christianity in 330 AD. Christianity was thus already established in many parts of Europe. Spreading chiefly among the Aramaean and the Arab populations of Syria and Iraq, Christianity was later adopted by some Iranian kings. King Khosrau Parviz, for example, looked on it favourably and took two Christian wives.

Next to the Zoroastrian religion, two other major religions emerged and their teachings and influences continue to this date. The Manichean religion was founded by the Iranian Mani, who lived between 216-277 AD, and who integrated different elements of other religions (Zoroastrianism, Christianity, Judaism, Paulician and Bogomil), in order to establish a religion of wide appeal. Manicheanism formed a point of identification for the intellectual and bureaucratic classes, more than the official Zoroastrianism. The second major pre-Islamic religion with a social content was Mazdakism, founded by Mazdak during the Sassanid Dynasty in the fifth century AD. Mazdak believed in communal ownership and the elimination of social classes. Mazdakism appealed to the lower and non-official classes and was considered a danger by the Sassanid Dynasty.

The Arab invasion of Iran, 640 AD

It was around 570 AD that the Prophet Mohammed emerged in the Arabian deserts. After he defeated his enemies and established himself in Mecca, he sent messengers around the world, inviting kings and emperors to convert to Islam. It is known that when his messenger reached the Sassanid court and delivered the Prophet's message to King Khosrau Parviz, he tore the letter up and threw the messenger out. He then ordered the governor of Yemen, which was part of his empire, to kill the Prophet. Years later, after the Prophet's death, Muslims conquered parts of Africa and Asia and set out for Iran. The Iranian Empire was in a state of civil war and was also engaged in prolonged battles with the Byzantine Empire. In addition, the increasing power and influence of the Zoroastrian clergy, and the exploitation of the lower classes by the kings, had turned the people against the ruling elite. The last Sassanid king, Yazdegerd the Third, who was unable to reign his vast kingdom, was easily defeated. When the Arabs attacked Iran little resistance was offered. Towns and villages were rapidly captured by the new aggressive army, which was aided by religion, economic force and the superior mobility of its camels and cavalry. Social dissatisfaction and the weakness of the Byzantine and the Persian Empires facilitated the Arab conquests.

Although at the beginning many welcomed the new religion and converted to Islam voluntarily, over time the limitations put on them and discrimination between the Arab Muslims and Iranians (Ajams) created a new form of oppression. The Arabs ruined the long-lasting Persian civilisation. Palaces, historic buildings, colleges, schools and libraries were destroyed. The Persian language was replaced by Arabic. As a result, a mass exodus began and thousands of Iranian intellectuals fled to India. Nevertheless, over a period of around two centuries, Iranian mores and culture, preserved by generations, influenced the invaders. Iranian politicians, scientists, writers and philosophers became masters of the Arabic language and enriched the Arab Bedouin[3] culture.

Gradually Iranians infiltrated the Calipha's[4] courts and attained high office. Some became prominent even in the Islamic jurisprudence. They were then able to revive the Persian culture and bring back a degree of freedom to the Iranian people. Those Arabs who remained in Iran were integrated into the indigenous population and Iranians could carry on with what was left of their traditions and customs from the pre-Islamic eras. Over time, opposition to the Umayyed[5] (661–749) Caliphas grew among those Iranians who had sided with the minority branch of Islam, i.e. Shi'at.[6] The Umayyed Caliphas were accused of discriminating against the non-Arab converts in favour of Muslim Arabs. Some of the Shi'at Imams who were under persecution by the grand Calipha in Baghdad sought refuge in Iran. For example, Imam Reza, the eighth Imam after the Prophet Mohammed, fled to northern Iran from the Calipha's persecution. His mausoleum in the city of Mashed is a holy shrine for millions of Shi'at Muslims.

Although before the Arabs Iran had repeatedly been invaded by other powers, none left as lasting an effect as the Muslim Arabs did. Over the centuries, Islam as a religion and a way of life dominated the Iranian culture. However, after nearly two centuries of Arab rule, great dynastic rules were again revived in Iran. The Seljukes Dynasty (1040–1194) created an empire stretching from the Mediterranean to Xin Diang in China. Unfortunately, the Mongol invasion of the twelfth century, which laid waste to most parts of the country, dealt a severe blow to Iran's infrastructure. Nevertheless, Mongol rulers gradually became 'Persianised'. They became Muslims and spoke Persian as their first language. A great branch of them ruled India as Muslim-Persian speaking kings until the advent of the British colonial rule in India in the eighteenth century. Over the centuries, numerous movements and upheavals emerged; Babak Khoramdin in Azarbaijan and Sarbedaran in Khorasan were among the many who fought for the liberation of Iran from foreign rule.

Even when there was no spectacular upheaval, such as the Mongol invasion, post-Islamic Iran was seldom ruled by a single dynasty. One of the notable exceptions to this fragmentation was the Safavid Dynasty (1501-1722). Shi'aism gained force during the Safavid and a system which placed the religious leaders, or *mujtahids*,[7] above the kings in religious matters was established. In socio-political terms, this doctrine laid the foundations for a Muslim institution, which claimed to lead secular groups and people on non-religious matters, while the state too, took its guidance from this institution. While the kings and the rulers ignored this stand, the populace increasingly turned to mujtahids for guidance and support, especially against unpopular kings, a tradition which still survives today.

After centuries of invasions, destruction and massacre, Iranians became sceptical of their neighbours and other nations and kept to themselves, leaving change and destiny in God's hands. Over the centuries, Iran went into a deep sleep. The wave of revolutions which swept Europe after the Middle Ages had little effect on Iran. Although some enlightened individuals tried to wake the nation to the European Renaissance, little changed.

Art and culture in ancient Persia

Peoples of the Iranian plateau have been creators of a rich civilisation since ancient times. Inevitably, most works of art were destroyed during the invasions but miniatures, sculptures and paintings found in the ruins of ancient Persia indicate the grandeur of those eras. Over the centuries, in literature, poetry prevailed at the expense of other forms because kings and emperors traditionally supported the poets. Post-Islamic Persian poetry was born during the ninth century in the north-east region of Khorasan. With the emergence of Ferdowsi in the tenth century, the golden era of Persian poetry began. Ferdowsi, a patriotic poet from the town of Touse in the north-east province of Khorasan, began the task of reviving the ancient Iranian epic and historical legends (and to some extent, historical facts) through his poetry. He spent thirty years writing thousands of lines of poetry, through which Iranians learnt of their past, which had been eradicated from their oral history. He wrote *Shah Nameh*[8] in a unique, simple but eloquent language that everyone could read and understand. After Ferdowsi, Iran witnessed the emergence of prominent poets and philosophers such as Omar Khayyam, Hafiz, Sa'adi, Rumi, Nezami and many others.

From the Safavid Dynasty until the beginning of the twentieth century, no great poet emerged in Iran. The Safavids, who were pioneers of the new school of Shi'aism in Islam, encouraged and supported only religious art and poetry. As a result, Persian poets emigrated to other countries such as the Ottoman Empire and India and established the so-called 'Indian style' in Persian poetry, which survived until the nineteenth century.

Women in art and literature

From the archaeological excavations and historical documents, we understand that women had an equal role to men and a prominent position in ancient Persia. There is a rug in the Hermitage Museum in St Petersburg, Russia, with the name of a woman – Aria Dokht – woven on it, as the treasurer of the fourth king of the Achaemenid Dynasty. In the seventh century AD two women, Azarmin Dokht and Pouran Dokht, sisters of King Khosrau Parviz of the Sassanid dynasty, reigned the kingdom in turn after his death.[9] Throughout Iranian history we have had women poets, sculptors, painters and musicians, as well as politicians. Nevertheless, women have rarely been mentioned in the history books. In a recently published book (*Famous Iranian and Persian-Speaking Women*), the name and a brief history of approximately 740 such women are described.

In the work of famous poets, such as Ferdowsi, women have often played a strong, prominent role. However, it must be said that women in Persian literature are generally portrayed as submissive lovers, unfaithful, cold-hearted and conspicuous. Persian literature is full of nostalgic descriptions of the woman's body. Hair, eyes and eyebrows have played an important part in shaping male fantasies. In those writings where women have been praised, they have attracted praise for their role as obedient wives, mothers, and virtuous members of the clan and are seen as being in constant need of protection.

Contemporary Iran, 1775–1925

The Qajar Dynasty, founded by Agha Mohammed Khan, marks the arrival of Europeans in Persia. From then on, contact with Europeans, foreign travellers, merchants and diplomats increased. In 1835 Americans established the first Western-style school in Urumieh, in the north-west of the country. Muslim children were not allowed to attend this school. In the big cities, religious *madrases*,[10] which had been established since the eleventh century (almost a hundred years before the establishment of the European universities), catered exclusively for the education of boys. Families who wanted their daughters to learn the Quoran, had to recruit private tutors. After the American school, missionaries followed the same path and a number of schools were established in other major cities. These establishments played a significant role in shaping personalities and developing modern thinking among young Iranians. Suddenly, information about the outside world was infiltrating through the closed doors.

Although foreign states had sent ambassadors to Iran during the Safavid Dynasty in the fifteenth century, it was not until the eighteenth and nineteenth centuries that countries such as Tsarist Russia, Britain, France and later the United States targeted Iran, seeking privileges in competition with each other.

Iran's economic history

Unlike other Middle Eastern countries, Iran's steps towards progress and modernisation were slow, with intermittent interruptions. Iran, having a vast mountainous terrain with long distances between populated centres, remained nomadic and dominated by tribes and large landowners. The Qajar Dynasty lacked a solid central administration and the few attempts at reforms met with opposition from the *ulama*[11] and large landowners. Although by the end of the nineteenth century the power of the central government had increased, the ulama were still influential and the tribal leaders powerful. The balance of power among these, and foreign interference, kept Iran free from any dramatic developments.

Among the foreign powers, the British Empire and Tsarist Russia had a significant role in the politics of nineteenth- and twentieth-century Iran. Widespread interference and prolonged armed aggression (especially by Russia), which had started during Fath-Ali Shah's (1791–1834) reign, continued during the reigns of Mohammed Shah and Naser a-din Shah. From 1848, during the reign of Naser a-din Shah, numerous contracts were signed with foreign companies. Previously, the only contract had been that of Sir John Malkom of Britain and Fath-Ali Shah.

Naser a-din Shah signed an agreement with Baron Julius de Reuter (1872) of Britain, giving him the sole right to build a railway from the Persian Gulf in the south to the Caspian Sea in the north. In exchange, Reuter was granted exclusive rights to nearly all the economic resources of the country to exploit for seventy years. This agreement was cancelled because of Russia's opposition. For this, Britain blocked Russia's attempts to build the railway. Although in some instances these rivalries coincided with the anti-foreign sentiments of the people, enterprises which could truly help Iran to modernise its infrastructure were also blocked.

A significant development drew the people into politics when Naser a-din Shah signed an agreement with Major Talbot, giving Iran's tobacco industry to the sole authority of a British company. Traditionally in Iran, pipe smoking of tobacco, especially hubble bubble (*ghelian*), had been popular among all classes of people. Both the people and the ulama opposed the tobacco concession and made protests which took the form of street demonstrations in major cities, demanding the cancellation of the agreement. Among the ulama Haji Mirza Hassan Shirazi and Jamal Aldin Afghani, prominent clergymen, issued a decree declaring a ban on the use of tobacco, on religious grounds. This resulted in a universal boycott of tobacco, forcing Major Talbot into bankruptcy. The movement against this initial foreign intervention through investment involved thousands of women, including Naser a-din Shah's own wives, who refused to smoke the pipe. Finally, the Shah was forced to cancel the agreement and pay damages to the British company.

During the Qajar Dynasty the main government income was taxation collected from the peasantry. The bureaucrats, landowners, high-ranking ulama and merchants were almost tax exempt. The majority of the population, who lived in rural areas, paid for the principal officials of the royal household and religious establishments. In order to afford this taxation, peasants were often forced to sell their crops at very low prices before the harvest. Needless to say, the income from taxation, apart from a small amount for security measures, was not used for public purposes. Throughout the nineteenth century the value of currency declined and agricultural prices rose. This augmented the landowners' incomes and brought forth a rise in government taxes. New investments in land and growth of land ownership resulted in further exploitation of the peasants.

Due to difficulties in public transport and the lack of protective tariffs efforts to establish modern industries were unsuccessful. Apart from the concessions which did not take off for various reasons, there were a few which did, including an Indo-European telegraph line, which connected major cities to the capital. This in turn brought about some foreign investment and helped the central government to gain control over the provinces. Investment projects, such as a British company's navigation on the River Karun in Khuzistan and the British Imperial Bank of Persia (Bank Shahi), which had the exclusive right of issuing banknotes, faced partial opposition by Iranian investors, the ulama and small traders, but were successful.

Oil, the early phases

In 1901 an Australian-born British subject, William Knox d'Arcy, obtained a concession to drill for oil in the south of Iran.

Understandably, Iranian oil was not taken seriously until its discovery in 1908. Soon after, the British government took an active role in purchasing the majority of the shares in d'Arcy's company and the Anglo–Persian Oil Company was established.

To facilitate the production and export of oil the British government built up relations with heads of tribes who were influential in the south-western regions of Iran. As a result, special treaties were signed between the British government and Sheikh Khaz'al, the head of the Arab tribes and the leaders of the Bakhtiari tribes. According to these treaties, the British could install pipelines to export the oil. In exchange, the tribes received a combination of payment and protection by the British government. As for the Iranian government, according to the original concession of 1901, the actual royalty was only 16 per cent of net profits, but in reality other expenses were also deducted from this figure. In years to come, the oil became a vital energy resource for Western countries and played a major role in international politics. Against this, Iran became more dependent on the income generated from the oil and hence was dragged into international politics because of its rich resources.

The role of the clergy

In the first part of the nineteenth century the mujtahid's political power, which had been firmly established during the Safavid Dynasty, remained reactionary and xenophobic to Western-style reforms. Any change initiated by the Qajar Dynasty often faced fierce opposition.

This period marks the emergence of a new Islamic cult, the Babi, which was an outgrowth of the Sheikhi[12] school of Islam. Seyyed Ali Mohammed, a Sheikh from Shiraz, announced in 1844 that he was the Bab, or the gate to the Hidden Imam. Faced with the ulama's opposition, the Bab broke from the Islamic orthodoxy and declared himself a new prophet. Babism retained some elements of the past Shi'aism, while having new social features. In particular, the Bab called for women's equality and part of his programmes discouraged polygamy. Babi's most prominent preacher was a woman, Qurratol' ayn,[13] who is known to have appeared unveiled when giving her sermons.

Babism found followers among the tradesmen by encouraging new economic attitudes; charging interest on loans[14] and forbidding begging and idleness. Shortly afterwards, Bab started being persecuted and he was finally executed by Amir Kabir, Naser a-din Shah's prime minister. In the 1850s a number of Babis moved to the Ottoman Empire in Turkey. Those who remained in Iran adopted an old Shi'at practice of hiding their faith (*teghyeh*).[15] By the 1860s the majority of Babis chose to follow the new dispensation of Baha'ullah, who claimed to be the new prophet predicted by the Bab. His followers took the name of Bahais. Bahaism spread among the middle-class intellectuals, often advocating Western culture.

Naser a-din Shah's reign lasted fifty years. A corrupt, autocratic king, he wasted Iran's wealth and resources by travelling frequently to the West and keeping a lavish life-style. During his reign the British, who by then had their contacts in the ruling circle, strengthened their power base. In 1854 the first Freemason (free thinkers)[16] Society opened in Iran. Thereafter, most politicians and important personalities became members of this society, hence advocating the British interest in Iran.

The Qajar Dynasty, which lasted 150 years, did little to change Iran. Corruption, economic stagnation and slow development mark the period 1775–1925. Amongst a handful of the royal family, only Prince Abass Mirza and one notable premier, Amir Kabir, Naser a-din Shah's son-in-law, initiated development and reform. Amir Kabir's premiership, lasting only three years, was a golden era for Iran. Being well educated and well informed, he aimed at bringing Iran up to modern times by initiating reforms in the judicial and tax system and founded the Dar-Al Phonon School, which pioneered modern thinking. His intelligence service reduced corruption and prevented foreign intervention in the country's affairs. Amir Kabir's reforms were halted by his assassination by Naser a-din Shah. The king himself was also assassinated by an opponent in 1896. Mozaffar a-din Shah replaced him.

Music, dance and wine

Until the fifteenth century and the emergence of the Safavid Dynasty, entertainment in the form of music and dance was part of the popular culture throughout the Iranian plateau. Among the many who were the founders of art and music Abu ali-ibn-Sina (Avizenna),[17] Farabi and Barbad were famous. In portraits, miniatures and paintings remaining from ancient Persia, the harp (*chang*) is seen being played by women at royal receptions. The Safavid Dynasty discouraged music and dance and instead promoted religious music and art, including mourning processions to commemorate the martyrdom of Imam Hossein.[18] Popular music, however, continued to exist and a number of prominent musicians emerged after this period. The town of Jolfa in Isfahan, which was built by the Safavids to settle the Armenians who were under persecution elsewhere, became the centre of entertainment. Here, women worked as bar tenders and appeared in public unveiled.

Although drinking is banned by Islam, wine never lost its popularity in Iran. People often drank it in secret. After Islam established its power and banned drinking, taverns (maykhaneh) moved to the outskirts of towns into rundown buildings where they did not attract much attention. Famous poets such as Khayyam, Hafiz and others have often described a rundown, remote building (kharabat), where wine was served by young attractive girls (saghi) who danced around the room, offering the drink in blue ceramic bottles. The girls and sometimes young boys who worked in these taverns were not necessarily prostitutes. Nevertheless, in the poets' fantasies, flirting with them and love-making are often mentioned.

From the eighteenth century onwards, Iran witnessed an emergence of a new literary movement, especially in Isfahan. The country at this time was free from invasion and Karim Khan Zand, the founder of the Zand Dynasty (1759–73), encouraged art and the establishment of cultural associations. The second king of the Qajar Dynasty, Fath-Ali Shah (1791–1834) was the patron of literature, art, music and dance and during his reign Iran witnessed a creative upsurge in these areas. Literary groups formed to revive the golden eras of Ferdowsi and Hafiz. Music bands (motrebs), often members of one family, formed in major cities, especially in Tehran. Women and sometimes young boys performed the dances. Women also formed their own bands and played in the royal courts. In Fath-Ali Shah's court there were two prominent female musicians who had their own band; Mina and Zohreh were renowned players of Persian musical instruments and often competed with each other at royal receptions.

Eugene Flanden, who had accompanied the French ambassador to Iran in 1840, noted that wealthy Iranian receptions were often accompanied by an orchestra which played 'monotonous songs about love, wine and bravery'. Edward Brown, the famous orientalist who spent many years in Iran, noted that 'the honourable guests sit at the top of the Sofreh,[19] while musicians, dancers and singers were also allowed to eat with the guests.'

Apart from the formal bands which played exclusively in royal courts and wealthy households and harems, popular Jewish bands existed in almost all cities. Most women musicians and dancers were either Jewish or Armenian. Musicians did not enjoy a high social status, because their profession was regarded as vulgar by the general public. Music was not to be followed as a profession among the Muslims. In the rural areas, from ancient times, weddings and public feasts had often been accompanied by popular folk music, whose instruments were different from those played in the urban areas. Here, musicians were often groups of gypsies who played their drums (*dohol*) and pipes (*soma*) in the open air.

It was not until the constitutional revolution at the beginning of the twentieth century that art (in the form of music, dance and song) gained social respect and schools of music were established to train the talented.

Constitutional revolution, 1905–11

A greeting to
And a handshake with
The dawn
A salute to the sun.
  Shadab Vajdi, 'Greeting'

Until the nineteenth century Iran was one of the most backward countries of the Middle East. Revolutions and mass revolts rarely threatened its kingdom. Although limited reforms were carried out by Crown Prince Abass Mirza early in the nineteenth century and later by Amir Kabir in the mid-nineteenth century, the social and economic situation did not change dramatically. It was only at the end of the century, as political, social and economic crisis crippled the old, outmoded system, that Iran witnessed a movement which had the features of a classic revolution.

Iran had been under the influence of the religious leaders for centuries. The clergy's economic independence had allowed them to act against the kings whenever they found it necessary. During the Qajar reign, the ulama, who by tradition had their headquarters in the holy cities of Ottoman Iraq, away from the Persian kings' rule, began to campaign against foreign domination which they believed would eventually destroy Islam. In the second part of the nineteenth century, with the establishment of Western-style schools, the clerical power, which so far had had the madrases and the whole education system under its monopoly, declined. Also, administrative and legal reforms reduced the role of Shari'at.[20] Among the renowned clergy who opposed change were four pan-Islamists: Seyyed Jamal a-din Asadabadi, known as Afghani; Mirza Agha Khan Kermani; Sheikh Ahamed Ruhi; and Mirza Reza Kermani, who assassinated Naser a-din Shah in 1896.

During the last decade of the nineteenth century many writers, poets and journalists, inside and outside the country, began a campaign of consciousness-raising to bring Iran into line with modern times. Among these were Seyyed Hassan Taghizadeh, Malek al Shoarai Bahar, Iraj Mirza, Mirzadeh Eshghi and Malekoll Motekalemin, an enlightened clergyman.

During the first years of Mozaffar a-din Shah's reign (1896–1905) waves of demonstrations, strikes and sabotage swept Tehran. Groups of intellectuals, merchants and factions of the clergy demanded an end to the king's arbitrary rule. This was the first time that enlightened Iranians made a loose alliance with the ulama. Telegraphic communication and the underground network of the religious establishment, through mosques and the clergy's regular sermons, were the crucial tools of spreading revolutionary ideas.

Within a short period after the start of Mozaffar a-din Shah's reign, due to the mismanagement of the economy, prices rose and food shortages spread dissatisfaction among the people. As a result, radicalisation of the movement took the masses onto the streets. The ulama through their popular speeches, the intellectuals through the publication of magazines, newspapers, poetry, music and songs, members of the secret societies and merchants, concerted an all-out mass mobilisation. Women, who had become partially politicised by participating in protests during the tobacco concession a few decades earlier, took to the streets and eventually formed their own clubs and societies.

Demands went as far as the creation of a parliament, justice department, freedom of speech and democratisation of the country. Finally, in 1905 Mozaffar a-din Shah was compelled to sign the constitutional order and call for elections. In the period 1905–8 the liberals and the ulama worked together to form a parliament and draft a constitution, in which the power of the king was limited. Also any agreement with a foreign country had to be ratified by the parliament. In the first phase of the parliamentary elections, the right to vote was only granted to men with a certain amount of property and social status: nobility, the clergy and large landowners.

Shortly after the constitutional movement, Mozaffar a-din Shah died and his tyrant son, Mohammed-Ali Shah, replaced him. Mohammed-Ali Shah was against all reforms and, after a coup, ordered the army to close down the parliament and to shoot those who demonstrated on the streets.

The constitutional movement was initially an act of liberation by the urban middle class and its demands did not go further than the parliamentary liberalisation. However, after Mohammed-Ali Shah's coup, the public, who by then had hopes of gaining political freedom, became agitated.

Tabriz, a city in the north-west, became the centre of the next wave of struggle. Two heroic figures, Satar Khan and Bagher Khan, emerged to lead the movement. They began an armed struggle and within a short period Tabriz fell into their hands. By 1909 many other cities, including Tehran, had fallen into the hands of the armed revolutionaries. The king abdicated and took refuge in the Russian embassy. Ahmed Shah, Mohammed-Ali Shah's young son, was appointed as the new king. The parliament re-opened and members were elected. At this point, the Russians and the British, foreseeing the collapse of the dynasty, increased their presence in the north and south of the country. These two countries, with the cooperation of the reactionary forces, suppressed the people's movement and prevented it from further radicalisation. Unfortunately the group of revolutionaries, who were once united against the Qajar kings, split over political matters.

By 1911 the constitutionalists still held office and, in an attempt to reduce British and Russian involvement in the running of the country, invited the Americans to help them to regulate the country's finances. Morgan Shuster[21] arrived in Iran in 1911 as adviser to the Iranian government. During his short stay (only 9 months), Shuster established an efficient finance system and put the financial affairs of the country in order. The British and the Russians, who did not see Shuster's honest efforts as being in their interest, objected to his presence and forced the government to cancel Shuster's contract. Shortly afterwards they signed a contract with the Iranian government by which the recruitment of foreign expertise had to be under the direct supervision of either Britain or Russia.

World War One put a halt to the increasing interference of Britain and Russia in Iran, although the British admitted that Iranian oil was extremely important for winning the war. After the war the British once again turned their attention to Iran. In an agreement initiated by Lord Curzon, the then British Foreign Secretary, the Anglo–Persian treaty was signed in 1919, making Iran a virtual British protectorate. The Iranian people opposed this treaty and as a result it was never ratified by the Iranian parliament. In 1919 Iran was made to sign another treaty with Britain, giving her supervision over the Iranian army. General Dixon came to Iran to take control of the army's high command. At the same time plans were put forward to abort constitutionalist aspirations and to establish a powerful central government by way of a coup.

The role of women in the constitutional revolution

The constitutional revolution was a landmark in the awakening of the Iranian society from its centuries of deep sleep. During the years of upheaval rigid social structures broke down and men and women formed new ideas. Active participation in demonstrations raised people's awareness. Women, who until then had been confined to harems and behind closed doors, began to speak of liberation and freedom. In 1907 Mirza Hossein Khan Edalat, who had returned from abroad, wrote an article in an Azarbaijani newspaper criticising the situation of women and arguing the need for reform. He emphasised the necessity of unveiling. The clergy and the public became infuriated at his suggestions, his newspaper was closed down and he was tried and sentenced to jail. Outside Iran, along the northern borders, Iranian writers and thinkers also campaigned against the oppression of women.

During the constitutional movement women were as active as their awareness and limitations permitted. Ivanov, a Russian observer, wrote that, 'On January 20, 1907, women convened a meeting during which they demanded the establishment of girls' schools.' During the upheavals, a photo showing some sixty women patrolling an area under siege in Tabriz was taken. In the battle between Satar Khan, the head of the Tabriz revolutionaries, and government troops, the bodies of twenty women, disguised as men, were found among the dead. Ahmed Kasravi, the prominent Iranian historian, has noted that in 1905 about 500 women gathered in Baharestan Square to demonstrate. According to Morgan Shuster clandestine women's clubs and associations in Tehran had vowed to stop the government borrowing money from the British and the Russians.

Intellectuals who fought against the arbitrary rule of the Qajar kings often wrote articles defending women's participation in public life. Dehkhoda, a journalist and writer, wrote articles in magazines and newspapers denouncing polygamy, parental pressure on daughters and general prejudices against women. During the revolutionary years the number of women who published women's magazines increased. In 1911 the first women's magazine, *Knowledge*, was published in Tehran. Mrs Sedigheh Dowlat Abadi also published a magazine in Isfahan, called *The Language of Women*. Isfahanis were outraged, Mrs Dowlat Abadi's house was stoned and she was forced to leave for Tehran, where she continued publishing her magazine. Other women, in Rasht in the north of the country and Tabriz, followed her path.

In fact the first women's association had been established during Naser a-din Shah's reign and, although it was clandestine, even some of the king's daughters attended its meetings. During the constitutional movement numerous societies and associations emerged. Some survived for a long time, others were closed down immediately, either by the clergy establishment or by pressure from men generally.

After the first parliament was closed, thousands of women, covered in black *chadors*,[22] gathered in front of the parliament building to protest. During the constitutional revolution and after World War One reforms concerning the situation of women entered official debates. During 1918–19, two Azarbaijani writers published a series of articles under the bogus names of 'Feminist' and 'Feminia' in the *Tajadod (Modernity)* newspaper, which was the organ of the Azarbaijan Democrat Party. Poets such as Lahuti, Eshghi and Bahar put women's liberation in the forefront of their campaigns. Although women became active in forming societies, associations and schools, it was enlightened men who wrote about women's liberation and proposed reforms. Aref Qazvini, the poet and composer of revolutionary songs, passionately supported the women's cause. Kasravi, the historian, wrote verses about women's liberation and persuaded the Dervishes[23] to recite them on the streets of Tabriz, instead of the usual religious songs. Popular songs about women's liberation were written by poets and recorded on the newly arrived gramophones. People were able to listen to these songs in their houses or in the traditional cafés. In 1932 the Congress of Women of the East convened in Tehran and hundreds of women attended it.

Reza Shah, founder of the Pahlavi dynasty, 1925–41

Our era
Is the era of execution of infants yet unborn
Of the changing of breath
Of man's fear of his own shadow
Shadab Vajdi, 'Our Era'

During the Qajar Dynasty constant foreign intervention, arbitrary rule, corruption and Iran's general backwardness hampered modernisation and change. The discovery of oil not only did not improve Iran's economy, it made the country prey to foreign powers. During the fifteen years after the constitutional revolution, until 1921, Iran plunged into chaos and changed cabinets fifty-four times. Rivalry between Britain and Russia produced instability, and leaders of the liberation movement found it impossible to fulfil their promises.

Fortunately, the October Revolution in Russia changed the political scene of the Middle East, especially Iran. There were groups of intellectuals in the north of the country who looked to the Soviet changes with great hope. Lenin's government did not pursue the imperialistic notions of Tsarist Russia and shortly afterwards he withdrew Russian troops from Iran and cancelled oppressive treaties.

The British, on the other hand, were frightened that the radicalisation of the people and democratisation of Iran would lead it towards communism and therefore decided to consolidate their power by arranging a *coup d'état*. They believed that a dictator would put an end to the constitutional movement and protect their interests against the growing power of Lenin's socialist state in the Soviet Union. In the early 1920s General Ironside arrived in Iran. In 1919 General Dixon had arrived to take control of the army and preparations for a coup were coordinated between the two generals and the British Foreign Office.

Two figures emerged as potential candidates: Seyyed Zia Tabatabai, an influential journalist, and Reza Khan, the chief officer of the Cossack army. Iran had regiments of Cossacks which had been formed on the Russian model and were in fact the only trained and disciplined section of the army. The coup happened in March 1921, when Seyyed Zia and Reza Khan seized power by bringing the Cossacks into Tehran and taking over strategic points. Politicians, some members of the parliament, and old statesmen were arrested. A number of people were also killed in street fights. A group of 53

communists who, inspired by the October Revolution, aimed to
push Iran towards socialism, were the first to be jailed. Their leader,
Dr Taghi Arani, later died in prison in suspicious circumstances.

Initially after the coup Seyyed Zia Tabatabai was appointed prime
minister and Reza Khan head of the army. Shortly afterwards Reza
Khan removed Tabatabai from his post and he himself became
prime minister. In 1925 Reza Khan attempted to declare a republic
based on the Turkish model, but the ulama opposed his plan. In 1926
Reza Khan finally had the last Qajar king, Ahmed Shah, who was
nominally reigning but in fact lived in Europe for most of the time,
removed and declared himself the king and founder of the
Pahlavi Dynasty.

Reza Shah was given a free hand to establish a strong central
government. Although an illiterate Cossack it soon became apparent
that he was an ambitious man. He understood that Iran needed
modernisation, without which no reforms were possible. Reza Shah
did not have a concrete strategy for modernisation, but the fraction
of the oil revenue he had and the collection of taxes enabled him
to establish a central government, regular army, navy, police force,
finance and a banking system. Building roads, hospitals and schools,
including girls' schools, were among Reza Shah's top priorities.
Tehran University opened in 1934, along with some other colleges
of higher education. He organised the training of thousands of
people for administrative positions and recruited the young and the
educated in the newly established state departments. Middle-class
families encouraged their sons to join the civil service rather than
to continue in their father's profession.

In 1933 Reza Shah renegotiated the oil concession with the
Anglo–Persian Oil Company, raising Iran's share of the profits to
25 per cent. Despite this, the British succeeded in keeping the terms
of the original contract of 1901 for another thirty years. Foreign
investment, as well as money from a group of domestic investors,
helped Reza Shah to fulfil some of his ambitions. Reza Shah's
interest in the army, which he saw as instrumental in warding off
foreign control and suppressing internal unrest, gained privileges for
the high-ranking officers and even lower-ranking personnel. Although
the bureaucracy had expanded and became modernised, corruption
and favouritism persisted alongside it.

Among Reza Shah's priorities were controlling the tribal
movements and challenging the ulama's power. Although he managed
to weaken the ulama to a great extent, he did not go as far as Kamal
Ataturk in Turkey. Unlike the Qajar kings, who had been religious

and therefore had given the *mullahs* their support, Reza Shah confiscated most of the fertile lands of the religious establishments and prevented the clergy from getting involved in politics. In addition, he sent the rebel clergy into exile. As a result of the policy of centralisation, the power of the ulama, the landowners, tribal leaders and provincial governors weakened, and control became increasingly concentrated in Tehran and in the hands of the government.

However, democracy and social freedoms were absent under Reza Shah's dictatorial rule. Reza Shah felt free to suppress any opposition. By the late 1930s few constitutionalists or democratic figures remained in politics. Nevertheless, the idea of modernity entered the official debates and some European-educated personalities paved the way for the establishment of a modern state.

Like his counterpart, Ataturk of Turkey, Reza Shah also considered himself the symbol of nationalism. He paid a visit to Turkey in the early 1930s and was impressed by the developments in that country: men wearing European clothes, women unveiled. Most of all, he understood that he could not truly open Iran to capitalism and foreign investment unless women entered the job market. He encouraged women to come out from behind their high walls and their harems and play a greater role in public life. Women were given the chance to go into higher education and to become teachers, nurses, doctors and lawyers. Few answered his call though. Women, who for thousands of years had been kept in harems and behind closed doors, supervised by the patriarchal system, did not understand what was expected of them.

After Reza Shah came to power, in line with building a modern state, a number of public institutions were established. A campaign, which had begun during the constitutional revolution, to eradicate Arabic words from the Persian language was re-run. The media was encouraged to write in simple language and to abandon the old-style language which was accessible only to the elite. The Ministry of Culture and Education and the Academy of Languages were established. The country's name, which had previously been Persia, was changed to Iran, in order to give it more identification with its people's origin from the Aryan tribes. However, inside Iran (or Persia) itself, the country had always been referred to as 'Iran'.

The first few years before Reza Shah consolidated his arbitrary rule, newspapers and magazines flourished, a radio station was established and cinemas and theatres opened in major cities. The performance of comedies, including those of Western playwrights such as Molière and Chekhov, became popular. Although Reza Shah's reign was accompanied by the imprisonment, detention and execution of many writers and intellectuals who had emerged during and after the constitutional movement, the impact of the revolutionary years and contacts with the Soviet Union as well as Europe resulted in Iranian society emerging out of the Middle Ages. However, modern thought expanded only among the urban middle class. Out in the vast country of Iran the majority were unaware of these developments.

Unveiling women, oppression or liberation

The campaign waged by the intellectuals to free women from their centuries of oppression in Turkey, by removing their *hejab*,[24] convinced Reza Shah that the veil must have been the prime barrier to women's liberation and their participation in public life. Unveiling had already been implemented in Turkey and from what he saw, had had positive outcomes. Unveiling women was a blasphemous act and vehemently opposed by the clergy. It required long-term work and an enormous effort.

To begin with, consciousness-raising publicity campaigns began in schools and offices. Trained agents travelled around the country, talking about the benefits of women's involvement in public life. To give legitimacy to the act Reza Shah asked his own wives (he had three) and daughters to appear in public unveiled. On January 7, 1934, accompanied by the Queen (the mother of the Crown Prince was officially the Queen) and his two daughters, Ashraf and Shams, who were wearing long coats and hats, looking extremely uneasy and embarrassed, Reza Shah attended a ceremony at The Girls' College of Higher Education officially to mark the unveiling. Mrs Hajar Tarbiat, the college principal, had made preparations for the occasion. The students and some of the mothers welcomed the royal family. Reza Shah made a speech in which he wished 'half of the population, who until now have been deprived of using their natural talents and capabilities, to actively participate in society and train future generations with more awareness'. After the ceremony, women participants put their chadors back on once outside the college gates.

Celebrations, official ceremonies and state banquets followed throughout the country. In Tehran a famous female singer, Ghamar, wearing evening dress and a diadem, appeared in front of hundreds of guests in the Grand Hotel's main reception hall to give a concert.

A few women singers had already gained official state honours and entered the upper-class banquets and receptions. These were the new generation of artists who were distinguished from the former outcast groups (motrebs). They were trained to gain music an honourable place in the society.

Enlightened women welcomed the unveiling. Feminists who had campaigned for women's rights and had already founded numerous associations and societies, women who had travelled abroad, men who advocated women's rights and poets and writers who considered women as prisoners under their black cover, were among the many to welcome the unveiling. A wealth of literature on the subject which emerged during this period was initiated by men. Not too many women writers or poets existed to promote modern ideas among themselves. Parvin Etesami was the only woman poet who wrote about the need to educate women and free them from the dark ages. Parvin's unfortunate death in 1941 did not give her much time to contribute to the liberation of women.

Shortly after women's unveiling the Shah issued a decree for men to abandon the old-style dress code and wear European attire. The only exception were the clergy who kept their traditional religious outfit.

Unveiling was welcomed among the minority of educated, urban women, but compared to millions of illiterate women who were kept in the darkness, they were just a small number. Throughout the country many families opposed the unveiling and refused to send their women out in public. After an initial phase, Reza Shah turned to force. The newly established police force and gendarmes were ordered to attack veiled women and tear off their hejab.

Throughout the thousands of years of Iranian history, especially after Islam, women had worn some type of hejab. They could not possibly imagine going onto the streets without their heads covered to be seen by namahram.[25] Women were frightened and screamed whenever their chadors or head scarves were pulled down and piled in a corner of the street. Many fought with the police and some decided to imprison themselves inside their homes. Those women who fought were often arrested and, for the first time in history, 'women's prisons' were established in Iran.

State functionaries were ordered to bring female members of their families to the 'receptions' held to mark the occasion of unveiling. Many preferred to divorce their wives and some resigned from their posts. Documents remaining from that period demonstrate how the unveiling was carried out. The implementation and the reaction of the people differed from area to area. In Kerman, for example, soon after the government relaxed its policy, women went back under the chador. In Tehran, Tabriz, Oroomieh, and Rasht, where there were more educated women, they stayed unveiled. However, modern women were outnumbered by the majority of people who believed women should be kept hidden from the public. For millions of women who knew nothing of the world outside and were frightened of going out without covering themselves, unveiling was a shameful act. The disastrous consequences of forced unveiling among women were felt 45 years later, when women were forced to re-veil using similar aggressive methods.

Chapter One

Kerman, my mother's birthplace

Kerman is a city amid the deserts of south-east Iran. The province of the same name comprises many towns and villages which sprawl along the desert plateau. The name Karamania or Kerman goes back to the seventh century BC. It is mentioned on the oldest maps as having been a part of the Persian Empire. Kerman city is the centre of the province and is encircled by dry, barren mountains. Ancient customs and traditions still pervade everyday life, as the people of this region are most resistant to change. Until the beginning of the twentieth century many Zoroastrians lived in this city, following their own unique religious rituals and customs. Zoroastrians were a very close-knit community before the majority of them migrated from Kerman. The people's language is Persian, although it is spoken with a dialect that makes it different from the Persian spoken in Tehran. It has a tenderness and warmth, blended with humbleness and kindness. Kermanis are famous for their hospitality and generosity.

The weather in Kerman is cold and dry in winter and hot in the summer. Being in the desert Kerman is understandably not the greenest city; nevertheless, there exist thousands of ancient gardens with plane, poplar and pine trees, tall and grand. If you travel to Kerman by air you will see for miles the sands of the desert, then a sudden glitter of greenery. There are thousands of small towns, villages and plantations around Kerman which have survived the desert for centuries. Networks of subterranean waterways, which were built centuries ago, irrigate plantations. Kerman was once a strategic city, used as a stop-over point when travelling to the waters of the Persian Gulf. It is close to the borders of Pakistan and Afghanistan and has been used by merchants and smugglers alike.

Although Kermanis are famous for their hospitality, they are at first wary of strangers. This is not surprising, as Gengis Khan of Mongolia and in recent history Agha-Mohammed Khan (founder of the Qajar dynasty) have both invaded Kerman, killing Kermanis in their thousands. It is said that Mohammed Khan made a pyramid of seventy thousand gouged eyes. Consequently, people of Kerman have become very secretive and rarely open up to strangers. They are in general very religious. Although Kerman is said to be the birthplace of the Zoroastrian faith, Islam established itself firmly among the middle and the lower classes. The people of Kerman, however, are also very superstitious and so religious rituals are often blended with ancient traditions.

Politically, Kerman has had its own statespersons elected by the people. Although women of Kerman have traditionally been excluded from politics and public life, women from the upper classes did participate in politics in the mid-twentieth century. In the past 70 years Kerman has elected two women to parliament: Mrs Nezhat Nafisi and Mrs Atefeh Ibrahimi. In addition, in the 1970s, the first Minister of Women's Affairs, Mrs Mahnaz Afkhami, was from Kerman.

The bazaar

Kerman has an abundance of historic sites, one of which is the grand mosque (Masjid Jame'e), at the far end of Shahpoor Street and the bazaar. The bazaar plays a central role in daily life. It is comprised of a lengthy covered passage with narrow alleyways branching off on either side. The main entrance to the bazaar is from a spacious square. In the old days small inns (*caravanserai*) with stables and stock-rooms existed around this square. These were mainly owned by Zoroastrian merchants who used the front section as a *hojreh* (shop) for trade. Nowadays, although new shops have replaced the hojrehs, the old architecture has been conserved.

A few hundred yards from the entrance to the Kerman bazaar you find a circular clearing, a high ceiling with a skylight. Rays of light penetrate through the glass porthole, illuminating the dusty atmosphere of constant bustle. The main feature of this hazy circle is a shop which sells herbs, dried fruit and vegetables. On the right, tiny shops and stalls crowd the narrow, dimly lit passage. On the left, a passage leads to the coppersmiths' bazaar. Here, tens of shops display pans, pots and copper ornaments. The cacophonous noise of the coppersmiths' hammering is almost deafening. Facing the coppersmiths' bazaar is yet another large square. People from the surrounding villages can often be seen lazing on the benches around this square. At the far end of the coppersmiths' bazaar two narrow alleyways lead into the gold and silver bazaar, full of jewellery and silverware. Kerman is famous for its quality gold and silver and copper, and has the second largest copper mine in the world, after Chile. Its copper industry is a main contributor to Iran's economy. Further in the centre of the bazaar there is the historical Ganj-Ali Khan public bath. This was built by Ganj-Ali Khan, Kerman's governor-general in the sixteenth century and is now preserved as part of the national heritage.

The main part of the bazaar is, however, its mile-long passage. On either side of this cramped passage hundreds of shops sell their goods: food, herbs, dried fruit and vegetables, tea, coffee and spices. Shopkeepers kindly invite the shoppers to examine their goods and to taste their herbs, dried fruit or exotic spices. A famous feature of the bazaar is its two tea houses, just off the passage-way. Instead of serving tea or coffee these shops serve ice cream and a cool sherbet called *Faloudeh Kermani*. Faloudeh is cooked starch, drained in cold water and mixed with sugar and rose water and served in deep dishes with plenty of ice. In the tea houses men and women are separated by a curtain. Women who are tired from walking around the bazaar go to these tea houses to eat the delicious cold Faloudeh and rest for a while. A long table is shared by all customers. Here women find the time to chat and exchange ideas. The bazaar is also characterised by its regular crowds of shoppers, peddler porters, errand boys, beggars and idle window shoppers who do not hesitate to push you aside. Porters who carry sacks of goods, vats of dye or bales of cloth shout loudly to the people to give way.

Kerman has undergone many changes throughout the present century. However, many old features of the city are intact. Until recently, the main industry in the city and its surrounding villages was carpet-weaving. There existed hundreds of workshops and factories, where thousands of girls as young as six were employed to weave carpets. Kerman's carpets were once famous throughout the world. In recent decades they have lost their advantage due to intense competition from other cities. Pistachio-growing is the second biggest industry and in Rafsanjan, one of Kerman's biggest towns, there are thousands of pistachio gardens.

My grandparents' house

My grandparents' house in Kerman was typical of desert houses. The rooms, all surrounding a central courtyard, were spacious and bright, with high ceilings and colourful glass at the top of the door frame. The biggest room, with two doors opening to the veranda, was kept spotlessly tidy and always locked, ready for guests. Carpets covered the entire floor area of all the rooms. Mattresses were spread on the floors, on the top of the carpets, from wall to wall, and hand-made cushions were laid against each wall for guests to lean on. Curtains were embroidered with lace, and oil lamps, colourful crystal and glasswork decorated the shelves. The courtyard was bordered by cypress and pine trees and all types of flower beds. A pond stocked with goldfish was located in the middle of the courtyard and vases of geraniums were laid around it. Summer evenings began by the splashing of cool water over the hot stones of the courtyard. Water would spread on the wide verandas, in front of the rooms and across and over to the *pashuyeh* (borders of the pond). Moist air would fill the courtyard. The carpets were spread around and cushions laid against the walls on the veranda. Dinner was placed on a white sofreh, on the floor. The family shared such summer evenings, sitting around the sofreh, cross-legged, eating and conversing. The main evening entertainment was story-telling by the elders, poetry reading or talking about ordinary events of the day.

The house had a thick wooden gate at the entrance which opened onto a long, enclosed corridor. The courtyard appeared at the end of this corridor. The gates had big metal handles, with which people had to knock hard in order to be heard. Most houses were shared by more than one generation. Couples had their own quarters but the kitchen and the guest room were shared by all. Sometimes a widowed aunt, mother-in-law or a single uncle lived in the same household. Servants had their own rooms, usually located near the gate.

Sleeping on the rooftops under the desert sky

Because of the heat, on summer nights, almost everyone slept on the rooftops. Roofs were accessible by narrow stairways. Part of the roofs were flat, apart from the ceilings of the big rooms which were dome-shaped. Most of Kerman's houses were connected through their rooftops. The houses had high walls around them which hid them from view, but only low walls separated each roof from the next. One could jump from one roof to the next and travel to another street. Rooftops were an ideal place for secret meetings and lovers' rendezvous. Young boys and girls would jump from roof to roof to meet their sweetheart. In summer evenings women gathered on the roofs to gossip with neighbours and their giggles could be heard from all around.

At the beginning of summer extra rugs, mattresses and blankets were carried to the rooftops and stayed there until it was too cold to sleep under the blanket of the sky. In the morning the bedding would be rolled and wrapped in *chadorshab* (large, square, thick woollen fabric) and covered by the rugs. Poets and writers have often mentioned the skies and the bright stars over Kerman. On cloudless nights the sky seemed so close that you could imagine stretching out a hand and touching the stars. The nights when I slept with my grandmother on the rooftop and counted the stars are unforgettable. She would hold me in her arms and talk to me in her sweet voice. I refused to sleep on a separate bed when she was around, until I was eighteen and went away to university.

Almost all the houses had dark, cool cellars where food was preserved. There were no refrigerators. These cellars were also used for storing bottles of distilled herbs and vegetable extracts. Rose, mint, rosemary, oregano and many other herbs were distilled each season and kept in bottles to be used either as sherbet on hot days or as medicine. For example, a mixture of mint extract in a glass of water and sugar was best for heartburn. Home-made jams, marmalades and pickles were also stored in the cellars. There were no bakeries in those days and storing home-made bread in the cellars kept it fresh for almost a month.

In each house an *abanbar* or water reservoir kept clean water, usually taken from the household's well or purchased from the carts that toured the streets selling fresh spring water to the inhabitants. At the beginning of the spring, depending on the weather, labourers appeared on the streets, offering to clean the abanbars. These labourers offered other services as well; spring cleaning and taking the rubbish out. Duvets and mattresses made of cotton became heavy and awkward after a while. They had to be undone and the cotton beaten. Cotton-beaters were on the streets from dawn to dusk singing out their services.

In the summer there was no cooling system. Instead, the house had a *howzkhouneh* (a room with a huge *badgir* [wind-turret]). The wind circled through the openings of the turret and travelled down into the room. In the middle of the room a round pond was filled with cool water. Rugs were laid around the pond with mattresses and cushions. Melons and watermelons floated in the pond throughout the summer. After lunch everyone had an afternoon nap around the pond, away from the heat. Some, however, took refuge in the surrounding gardens, whose tall trees kept the heat away and some went as far as the mountainous villages nearby.

Walking down to the payabs

A network of underground water ran for hundreds of miles from outside the city through the big houses and out onto the streets. Sometime in the past *payabs*, or narrow stairs, had been built through a tunnel which led down to these streams. Once you had climbed some hundred stairs down, it would take a few minutes just to get used to the shadowy space which was only lit by the dim light coming from the entrance high above. Although the water was warm and shallow, the darkness gave it a mysterious depth and gravity. Women often went down in groups to do their washing or to take drinking water. The houses were mostly connected through this underground water system and one could walk through them for long distances. Once in a while, when congested by mud and dirt, labourers would sweep it all away with their thick brooms.

The desert weather

Kerman has cold, dry winters that people used to endure with no central heating. They warmed their rooms by traditional means; mainly by *korsi*. A sunny room was allocated for the korsi. In the middle, a big, low table would be covered with a huge cotton quilt or blankets. Mattresses were laid on the floor and cushions against the walls. Under the table, a charcoal brazier would burn slowly. Families would spend the whole winter under the korsi. At night everyone stretched out and slept side by side. The top of the korsi was used to eat meals or junkets: nuts, roasted watermelon and melon seeds and dried fruits. When you sat around the korsi, feet and arms were put under the blanket to keep warm. It was hard to come out from under the warmth of the korsi to go to the toilet or enter other rooms. After the introduction of oil stoves, the use of the korsi reduced. Nowadays central heating is installed in almost every house.

Kerman's streets were narrow, muddy in the winter and dusty in the summer. When it rained, the mud would stick to shoes and made walking an effort. In the summer, desert dust storms and cyclones were not unusual. The only transportation available were *doroshky* (carriages) drawn by horses. The automobile did not arrive until the late 1940s. People were used to walking long distances and did not expect to ride in a carriage unless there was an elderly or a sick person to be transported. Women wore flat shoes which made it easy to walk. High-heeled shoes were not introduced until the 1950s. It was a custom for women to walk in pairs or in groups. This way they could chat while walking long distances. Very rarely would a lone figure be seen walking on her own. At night women were always accompanied by male relatives.

Moin al-Towdjar family, 1900–35

My story begins with my grandmother's family. Moin al-Towdjar was a well-respected merchant in the city of Kerman. He imported goods from India and China and traded them in his hojreh which was located in the square, facing the bazaar. In the early twentieth century, Moin al-Towdjar married a 13-year-old girl. Because of her beauty everyone called her Bibi Aroose (the bride lady). She bore seven children; three daughters and four sons. The sons went to school for seven years and received the formal education that was available at the time. The youngest daughter, Bibi Attieh, my grandmother, was the only female who attended school and finished six years of elementary education. The two older girls were restricted to what they learnt reading the Quoran. Bibi Aroose died at a young age, leaving her seven children behind. My mother's grandfather never remarried, and his single sister moved in to take care of the children.

In Kerman, like other provinces, young men aspired to work for the newly established government organisations. That was the only secure yet prestigious profession. In the family of Moin al-Towdjar all four sons were recruited by the government. The eldest son went into banking and was employed by Bank Shahi (the first Iranian bank), the second became a police inspector and the two remaining sons went into the services of the Public Notary offices. All three daughters of Moin al-Towdjar married young. The eldest was married to a man from a village in the north of Kerman and thereafter rarely visited the city. The second daughter married a man from Rafsanjan, a city far from Kerman. In later years, when I was about eight years old, she moved back to Kerman, where I remember visiting her regularly.

Bibi Attieh, my grandmother and the youngest daughter, was married off to an educated man, seven years her senior. His name was Ibrahim Sa'id. He was kind and gentle and although my grandmother was only 13 when she married, he treated her with much love and respect.

Bibi Attieh was surrounded by her four brothers for most of the time. Two of them were very close to her. The youngest brother, Abdol Karim Khan, lived with her for years before he married. Nobody in the family approved of his marriage because the girl belonged to a lower social class. His marriage was not even a 'proper' one but a temporary one (*moteh*) with no contract. Not having a permanent marriage contract was considered absurd, according to the family tradition. They never accepted the bride as a wife although she bore five children, some of whom now live in America.

In those days, women were not allowed to choose their husbands. They couldn't even aspire to going out on their own. They were not allowed to walk on the same pavement as men and if a woman wished to cross the street where men were, she had to ask the police to accompany her hurriedly to safety. The worlds of men and women were completely different. Men had their own life and dealt with what was known as the 'outside world'. Women were mainly engaged in domestic matters, taking care of the children and the household. Visiting relatives, going to the holy shrines, attending religious ceremonies and going to the *hamam* (public bath) were their main entertainment.

My grandparents

Grandfather Ibrahim was a poet. His given name as a poet was Paysepar. He wrote many poems, some of which were published years after his death. My grandfather Paysepar was an intellectual, modern man for his time. He let my grandmother play the Iranian musical instrument, the tar, an unusual act for a man. Shortly after the birth of two lovely daughters, my mother Afagh (the horizons) and her sister Iran, grandfather established a separate house for his small family. The daughters were sent to a well-known primary school where the teachers were foreign missionaries. Grandfather was not ashamed of having two daughters and no sons and aimed to give them the best education available. Little Afagh was his favourite and he often gave her special treatment.

My grandfather was a senior civil servant in Reza Shah's modern state of the early 1930s. Reza Shah's modernisation plans needed an accurate census. Birth certificates did not exist at the time. People were simply called after their fathers. Reza Shah ordered national birth certificates for every Iranian. Grandfather was assigned to supervise this process in Kerman and travelled throughout the province. It was difficult to convince people to give correct information about themselves. They were frightened that their sons would be drafted into the army. They were often confused as to what surname they should choose and left it to the clerk to put whatever name he wished. Ironically, my grandfather issued a certificate to a young man in Jiroft, a small town in the south of the province, who did not hesitate to choose his ancestor's name: Shafii. Grandfather never knew what future relations his family were to have with this aggressive tribe leader.

The shadow of grief

I am thinking of the logic of the wind
That tore flowers into petal
For no reason.
   Shadab Vajdi, 'What has been left?'

Happiness withered away from this small family when my grandfather suddenly became ill. No one was able to diagnose his ailment. He started having severe pains in his chest. Doctors could do nothing. Was it cancer or perhaps tuberculosis? Nobody knew. After a short while he died at the aged of 33, leaving his young wife and two daughters devastated. Much later in 1979, when my mother Afagh passed away, we discovered her brief diary. It was only six pages long. At the beginning she wrote: 'I was 12 when God took my father. I was very sensitive and his death struck me hard. My sister was younger. My mother cried all day and night and we visited his grave every Friday. Alas! It was useless. He was not in this world any more.'

Grandfather was buried in a cemetery on the outskirts of the city. I myself remember accompanying my grandmother, my mother and Aunt Iran to his grave every Friday until we all moved away from Kerman city. My grandmother often said that on the holy days of Thursday and Friday the souls of the dead get hungry and wander around relatives' homes in search of food. I often looked in dark corners, hoping to find my grandfather. On holy days special cookies were made to be taken to the grave. A mixture of dough with dates and walnut, shaped into a ball and roasted in oil, was the favourite of the dead. It took my grandmother the whole of Thursday to prepare for the visit. She cried while making the cookies and murmured prayers. On early Thursday or Friday afternoons the whole family, sometimes accompanied by other relatives, would visit the cemetery. It was a sombre occasion and we children were not allowed to misbehave.

Upon approaching the grave, which was in a dusty, gloomy open space with no trees or greenery, my grandmother, my mother and Aunt Iran would start crying. They would throw themselves on the grave as if embracing their loved one. They would not stop until someone pulled them away from the cold stone. Then they would calm down, bring some water and wash the stone, put the food on it and look for a *ghari* (mullahs who came to the cemeteries to recite the Quoran by the graves). Then each adult would sit down around the grave, putting two fingers on the stone, murmuring verses and asking God to forgive the dead and to rest their soul in *Behesht* (heaven). On such days the cemetery was always full of people who had a loved one buried. After the brief ceremony, cookies were offered to everyone who was around. Instead of thanking us for offering them cookies, people who took a piece said loudly: 'May God have mercy on the dead and forgive all their sins.' The children, who had been ignored until then, were allowed to eat some as well. The ghari was given a few coins as well as the remaining cookies.

When my grandfather Paysepar died Bibi Attieh, his widow, was only twenty seven, Afagh twelve and Iran ten. The immediate impact on this small family, apart from the loss of a beloved husband and father, was also a financial one. There was no pension or money left, except a tiny piece of land in Bardsir, a village in the north of Kerman. The land was supervised by my grandfather's brother. The income from the cultivation of this land was not enough to maintain the family. My grandmother was young and inexperienced. She did not see herself as being in a position to take control of the land and, although she had finished elementary school and could teach at the primary school, the thought did not occur to her. No woman in her family had ever worked outside the house. Her family could not help her financially. Grandfather's relatives, mainly his brother, came to visit but they did not offer any financial help either. Hard times lay ahead. Although Bibi Attieh was an attractive young woman and could have remarried, she chose instead to live with the sweet memories of her dead husband and refused proposals of marriage by other men.

Three years passed in hardship. The girls became adolescents. Afagh grew into a lively girl who was about to finish middle school and enter high school. She loved to play in the courtyard with her friends and cousins and her laughter filled the house. Finally, poverty forced my grandmother to sacrifice a member of her family. Suddenly, Afagh noticed frequent visits by some of her father's relatives. One day, while in the courtyard with her friends, she was summoned into the living-room and told that she was to be married. The man was a distant relative, twice her age and wealthy. Afagh's uncle (on her father's side) had convinced my grandmother that this was the only way she could protect her family. Afagh hated the idea of getting married at such a young age. It meant that she would not be allowed to attend school any more and all her plans for a bright future would be ruined. She would be confined to household chores and would lose her friends. In her diary she wrote: 'I was fifteen and fairly pretty but it was too soon for me to get married. My mother did not let me continue my studies because she thought by marrying me off she would be able to allow my sister Iran to complete her education. I was sacrificed for my sister.' I believe my mother always envied Aunt Iran and never forgave her.

It was 1936 and the beginning of the unveiling. Afagh loved to dress nicely and accompany her young uncles to the 'receptions' that were held in the public offices in celebration of the unveiling of the women. At the time, Kerman had two girls' high schools and six elementary schools with just under a thousand students and forty-eight female teachers in all. The schools had been given the responsibility of teaching and publicising the benefits of women's emancipation. However, shortly after the forced imposition period relaxed, the majority of teachers and students went back to their traditional way of wearing the chador, although covering the face never returned. My grandmother, Bibi Attieh, like thousands of women, did not step outside the house for a good two years. Although women in her family were not brought up to hide themselves from male relatives indoors, as some women did, the idea of appearing in public unveiled seemed absurd. Sometimes in the cover of night and accompanied by one of her brothers grandmother went out to visit a relative or a friend. It was only the wife of her eldest brother, by then the head of Bank Shahi, who was herself from a wealthy and well-known family, who appeared in public unveiled.

The unhappy bride

My mother's wedding was grand. The groom spent lots of money, inviting many people for the reception. In those days couples did not meet before the wedding night. Girls were not expected to have prior sexual knowledge. Older women gave them a brief talk on the subject, once it was certain they were to be married. For this reason, young married girls were forbidden to see their former friends. They were expected to associate with older women and leave their inexperienced, innocent friends behind. In fact, if a girl married while still at school she was expelled immediately, as there was a danger that she might pass her sexual information to other girls. As the day approached, some talked to the bride about sexual matters and what was expected of her. And so my innocent mother, who had until then been busy with school and plans for a future, as her father had wished, became a bride before she knew its meaning. She was taken to the hamam, accompanied by some of her own relatives and the groom's family. The wedding bath lasted for hours. Women were singing and dancing all the time and distributing sweets, fruit and money to the workers who washed, scrubbed and massaged the bride. Afterwards she was taken home to be dressed and made-up.

The religious ceremony, as was the custom, took place in my grandmother's house. A room was decorated with lace and flowers. A hand-made, ornately embroidered sofreh was spread on the floor and decorated with a silver framed mirror, candlesticks, a long bread covered with seeds, plates full of sweets and coloured walnuts, flowers and other ornaments, and a Quoran. My mother, whose face was hidden under a veil of lace, was brought into the room amongst the cheers, clapping and singing of the women. A mullah was summoned to perform the religious ceremony. He preached about the benefits of marriage and how God and the Prophet encouraged it. Finally, he recited some sentences in Arabic and asked my mother if he was allowed to marry her on her behalf.[1] My mother did not want to give her consent but the presence of so many people, all holding their breath, waiting, did not permit her to refuse. After her announcement of consent, there were cheers and jubilation. She was given many presents by members of her husband's family as well as her own uncles and aunts. The wedding party started. Men and women celebrated separately. Dinner was served and the guests stayed through the night enjoying themselves.

At midnight, among the music and cheers of the women, my mother was taken into the *hejleh* (bridal room). The groom followed later. He was in his best clothes. The hejleh was decorated with lace and flowers for the couple to consummate their marriage in a special bridal bed. During the first night some members of the groom's family, along with some other women, stayed outside the hejleh, waiting for the groom to finish the job. Clean white handkerchiefs were put under the pillows to be used and shown to the groom's relatives as a sign of the bride's virginity. Sometimes the newly married would stay in the room for as long as three days and on the third day a big party welcomed them back into the outside world. This was of course if they wanted to stay for that length of time away from curious eyes.

The minute my mother was alone with her husband and saw him for the first time, she felt hatred. She was frightened of him. She would not let him touch her. She wrote in her diary: 'I did not like this husband. He loved me but I wanted to kill myself. When he came home at nights I was very distressed. Several times I wanted to commit suicide and I was taken away from the well by members of the family.'

Nearly all houses in Kerman had their own well. They were deep and frightening. Children were warned not to approach the wells in case they fell into them, in which case death or severe injury was inevitable.

My mother blamed my grandmother and her own uncle for the unwanted marriage, although she wrote in her diary that there was nothing she could do except to reject him. The man was apparently a nice man, very much in love with her. He bought her lots of presents and tried hard to seek her affection. Nevertheless, she hated him. He travelled a lot and so she was happy when he was away, but her miseries began when on his return she had to act the part of the wife. Older women convinced my mother to see a fortune-teller and a sorceress to find out why she did not love her husband.

On an unforgettable occasion, her husband asked her to accompany him for a visit to his aunt. When they arrived at the house, he sent my mother away to see a local fortune-teller. She came back in the evening to notice a huge crowd in the alleyway and around the aunt's house. She managed to enter the house and witnessed a horrifying scene. People had just pulled her husband out of the well. He was covered in blood and the police were questioning everyone. She started screaming and did not know what to do. The police were questioning her but her husband managed to obtain her release by saying she had nothing to do with his decision to commit suicide.

This incident added to her miseries. Her husband was taken home where my mother nursed him for a while. To the family's horror they found out that the man had problems with his sanity. Doctors examined him and in the end decided that it was best to send him somewhere quiet, where the weather was good. His brother rented an orchard outside the city and Afagh accompanied him, hoping he might recover. After a couple of months his situation deteriorated and he became dangerous. Afagh refused to stay with him any longer, so his brother took him to their village, where he died six months later, which was how my mother became a widow at the age of sixteen. She never knew the cause of his insanity or sudden death. She was relieved that she did not have to put up with an unwanted husband. She began school again and took a private tutor to teach her to play the tar. She left this marriage behind her and never spoke of it to anyone. Years later I heard some of the details from my aunt but never disclosed it to any of my siblings. They found out after her death when my mother's brief diary was discovered.

My mother longed to become a teacher, the only job girls were permitted to engage in. Aunt Iran did continue her studies and received her high school diploma. She became a teacher at a primary school in the late 1930s. At this time, my mother and my aunt, together with my grandmother and her youngest brother, Abdol Karim Khan, lived in the same household.

Chapter Two

Jiroft, my father's birthplace

Jiroft is located to the south of Kerman and stretches between two mountain ranges. It is a narrow plateau, some hundred miles long. The plateau starts from the town of Baft in the north of the province and stretches down to the port of Bandar Abbas in the Persian Gulf. In the mountainous valleys of Jiroft the weather is cold in the winter and cool in the summer. In the plateau, it is mild in the winter and sub-tropical in the summer.

At the beginning of the century orchards, springs and pastures covered the valleys. Nomads and people who had settled in the valleys for centuries used the pastures to raise cattle and cultivate the lowlands. When urbanisation began in Jiroft, people migrated to the town. One had to travel on horseback and mules through dangerous mountains to arrive at the highlands and valleys which hid closed communities. One such community existed in Raman, in the highlands that were full of gigantic pine trees, north of Jiroft. Settlers of different tribes had inhabited these valleys since the Middle Ages. In order to survive, one of the tribal chiefs had ordered his people to slice a giant pine tree and to carve it deep enough for a reasonable amount of water to be held. He placed this on the top of two valleys to lead the water down to the lowlands. The settlers were then able to cultivate the lands and to grow orchards. This was in the early eighteenth century. The man was called Ghasem Shafii, who is the first known ancestor on my father's side.

There was also another deep folded valley by the name of Dalfard. Mountains shielded Dalfard from the outside world. In the spring, herb bushes covered a large area of the mountains. Women collected the herbs to use as medicine, for distilling or in food. In addition, wild daffodils and cumin bushes covered the lowlands. Dalfard was a long stretch of beautiful landscape. At the beginning of the century, when clans had their own territories, the Shafii clan owned some plots of land and orchards in Dalfard as well as in Raman. Huge plane and walnut trees and figs, cherry, peach, pomegranate and wild pear trees covered their orchards.

Two rivers divided the valley into narrower stretches. One of the rivers passed through the Shafiis' orchards on the west side of the valley. If you walked about a mile upwards along this river, you entered the narrow valley of Kouhsir (the garlic mountain). The roaring of water could be heard from around the corner. A waterfall would then suddenly appear in front of you. The water poured with a continuous, fierce roar. The pond was deep, blue and cool. Underneath the rocks, shielded from the main force of the waterfall, maidenhair herbs engaged in a continuous dance with the water that splashed over them. You climbed the sides of this fall to get to a second and a third. The last pond had a frightening depth. Locals told stories of girls having drowned in the dark pond, their bodies never found. That was the reason the ponds were called 'the girls' killer'.

There was another river on the eastern side of the valley. In winter and spring, when it flooded, villages were cut off for a few days. If it rained in the highlands, flooding soon followed. The roaring of the flood, which swept everything in its way, could be heard from miles away. Huge piles of wood, rubbish or whatever was in its path would be swept down through the valley and some twenty miles further into the plateau. It was believed that if you stood in front of the flooding river, even before it reached you you would be frozen by its magnetic power and swept away. And so when people expected flooding, they kept well away from the river bank.

Where the valley of Dalfard ended, a wide and hazy plateau, surrounded by grey and white mountains, came into sight. Twenty miles away the town of Jiroft could be seen through the haze. At the beginning of this century Jiroft was more like a big village than a town. It had been built on the ruins of the ancient and prosperous town of Daghianus. Marco Polo, the Venetian traveller, mentioned Daghianus in his diary: 'In the south of Godar-o-zia (or Jiroft) a prosperous town with golden soil existed.' According to historical evidence, in the twelfth century AD the people of Daghianus were clay-makers and merchants who traded with other regions. It is not known why the town literally disappeared from the face of the earth. Local people believed that it was either an earthquake or the flooding of the main river, Helil, that buried the town. The ruins can still be seen on the western side of the Helil, where they have recently been preserved as part of the national heritage. When we were young we would often browse in these ruins to find a piece of ornament, a broken jar or painted bricks, tiles and sometimes women's jewellery.

At the beginning of this century the population of Jiroft consisted mainly of nomads who migrated with their cattle into the mountainous valleys in the summer and returned to the outskirts of Jiroft in winter. The rest of the population consisted of people of African origin, or those who came from Baluchistan on the borders of Pakistan or the western regions of Persia: Kurdistan, Loristan and Yazd. The language spoken is Persian, although it is difficult to understand the dialect of those in the highlands.

Until the mid-twentieth century, parts of Jiroft, depending on location (mountain, desert or sea coast), were ruled by warlords, tribal chiefs or groups of bandits. Large areas were out of local government control. The governor-general of Kerman was given the sanction to rule these areas. Tax collection, drafting the young for the army and buying crops from the farmers were the main ways in which the governor tried to impose his rule. Very few people were literate in Jiroft and cultural mores and religious rituals were carried out as they had been for centuries. Villages lacked modern facilities; education and health care were unheard of. Twentieth-century modernisation had yet to reach this area. It was not until the late 1930s that Reza Shah, in pursuit of establishing a one-nation state, established state departments in the area and sent the army to bring the warlords, bandits and tribal leaders under his control.

The Shafii clan, 1900–40

Salar Tajmorad was the head of the Shafii clan. His first known ancestor was Ghasem Shafii who had settled in the highlands of Raman. Tajmorad married twice. His first wife bore four children, a daughter and three sons. After her death, while the children were still young, he remarried. Tajmorad's second wife, Safieh, was the daughter of a wealthy family. She bore two sons: Hassan and Akbar.

Although Tajmorad was the clan chief, it did not mean he was financially well off. People were generally very poor in the area and it was not easy to raise a family. Salar Tajmorad lived most of his life in the highlands of Raman, where he owned some orchards and raised cattle. He was also surrounded by his clan members, whom he had the responsibility of supporting, advising, settling their disputes, giving them permission to marry off their children and defending them against any injustice outside the clan. In return, he would receive small presents along with a great deal of respect. After the death of his first wife and his remarriage, he brought all the children under one roof. Safieh was a kind woman and took care of all the children. In the rural areas life was uncomplicated. Boys took care of the flocks of sheep, horses and the crops and girls helped with weaving carpets and *khorjins* (saddle bags), milking the sheep, making bread and dairy products. In the summer, they dried fruits and prepared syrups from dates or grapes.

Salar Tajmorad, like any other person in the tribe, lived under spacious black tents, which were made of horse hair. The opening to the tent was drawn and fastened at night. Inside the tent big colourful khorjins, full of the family's belongings and food stocks, were placed in rows against the tent walls. Khorjins were woven out of the most colourful threads and decorated with ornaments which hung from their sides. When the tribes migrated from one place to the other, khorjins were placed on mules and donkeys, their colourful sight adding to the jingle of ornaments which filled the air. The arrangement of khorjins around the tent protected the inhabitants from the cold and any outside interference. The more khorjins the family wove and filled with goods, the wealthier they became.

In the middle of the tent an *ojagh* (fireplace) was located, where tea was made and the food kept warm. The head of the family sat at the top of the tent, leaning on several big cushions while his back was protected against the mattresses and duvets that were carefully wrapped in chadorshabs. The rest of the family, the wife, children or other members, sat around the ojagh, eating or just passing the time. At night the only light came from the fire burning in the ojagh. Sometimes branches of a certain bush, which grew in the highlands and contained oil, were used as lamps. Mattresses were laid on the floor and the whole family slept close to each other. If a man had more than one wife, he allocated two tents for his household. Normally the whole clan lived together.

Tribal life was uncomplicated but hard. Women woke up at four o'clock in the morning to milk the sheep and prepare bread. The sheep were then taken for grazing by the shepherds. The household chores were carried out outside the tents in a communal manner. The tents were raised in a circle or rows and the animals were kept a few yards behind each tent in temporary stables. Tribal life was community life, where there were no secrets and all members shared a degree of responsibility. Life outside the tribe was scarcely known to women. There were no schools or doctors and so the mortality rate was high. The sick were treated by local herbs that women kept in their small *mafrash* (first aid kit). Mafrash were made of pieces of colourful materials stitched into a big, round bag, tightened at the opening by a strong thread. Inside, white bags preserved and separated different herbs, seeds and roots. Women hung the mafrash from the tent pole and knew the use of each herb in case of an illness.

The Shafii clan used to move to the outskirts of Jiroft in winter, where they owned some plots of land and cultivated grains and other crops. In the second month of spring, when Jiroft was beginning to get hot, they moved to the highlands. Among other chores women had the responsibility of packing for the journey. Sometimes it would take days before they arrived at their destination. They moved with the cattle, carrying their belongings on donkeys and mules. Men rode horses, while women sat on the top of the loaded donkeys. Sometimes women walked alongside the caravan. If a woman was pregnant and had to give birth, the caravan would stop for the child to be born and then set off again after a short while. Older women acted as midwives. After the birth, a mixture of butter, different seeds, herbs and sugar was prepared for the mother. She ate it for three days, during which time her energy was revived. She was then ready to continue with the journey.

According to my uncle, who is now in his mid-eighties, Salar Tajmorad was a very religious man. He used to say his prayers loudly and fast during the holy month of Ramadan. The two children from his second wife were his favourites while the other children were almost ignored and left on their own. Hassan quickly learnt his father's ways in order to be able to follow him as chief, while Akbar was sent to the only primary school in the nearby village of Jiroft to learn to read and write.

Tajmorad believed that he would die a sudden death. When he was in his eighties one evening, he called everyone into the tent and told them that he was about to die. To their surprise, he said his prayers loudly, then lay on the floor of the tent and passed away. At the time the family was living in Jiroft near a holy shrine. The shrine of one of the Imams (Shoeyb) lay at the top of a hill. Salar Tajmorad was buried at the foot of the hill, where his wife Safieh joined him later. Although most of the graveyard has been destroyed, their graves are still there after almost 75 years.

The clan were devastated by their chief's death, but Hassan quickly took over and proved to be capable of running their affairs.

Hassan was young, clever and very aggressive. He was the best fighter and nobody could beat him in mountain-climbing at night. This was a necessity for survival in those days. If a fight broke out, the men, fearing reprisal, would flee to the mountains and lie low until the dust settled. After Tajmorad's death Hassan became head of the family and now his mother Safieh had to obey him. In the patriarchal rural families, upon the father's death, supremacy transferred to the older son or brother. Sons often used to beat their sisters or mothers if they did not obey them. Since the older brothers from Tajmorad's first wife did not have Hassan's ability, courage and aggressiveness, they accepted his supremacy. The first action taken by Hassan was to confiscate most of the plots of land and orchards that were under his father's name. Instead of dividing them among all the children, he registered them under his own name, depriving others of their inheritance. Although Hassan was illiterate, one did not notice this shortcoming. He had a fuming temper and would not hesitate to beat on those who opposed him.

After Salar Tajmorad's death the family became even poorer. Hassan began trading with the Zoroastrian merchants in Kerman. He often took dried fruit, sheepskins and grains and traded them for fabrics, sugar and other necessary goods. There were no cars or trucks at that time and goods had to be carried on mule and horseback some 200 miles. It took people weeks to travel while facing many dangers on the roads.

When Hassan fell in love with a girl from another tribe he ordered his mother to move to the girl's neighbourhood. Safieh cried and protested, but it was no use. The children from Tajmorad's first wife were left on their own. The daughter Halimeh was the only one they took with them.

In the late 1920s, at the start of a bad winter, Hassan had to take a consignment of goods to Kerman. Safieh warned him that she might not be in this world when he returned. In Kerman, Hassan dreamt that his mother was seriously ill. His dreams often turned out to be true so he became worried and left his goods with the Zoroastrian merchant and returned to Jiroft in haste. He arrived in the village and rushed to their tent, only to find it empty. His mother had died of an unknown illness. They had buried her at the foot of the holy shrine, close to her husband. Until his old age, Hassan used to visit his parents' graves every once in a while.

Hassan and Akbar were left to manage on their own. Their relatives, especially their cousin Shahnessa, often came to help and they somehow managed to pull through the hard years. They married the sister Halimeh off to the first person who proposed. Hassan only had to take care of Akbar for a few years. Akbar was a clever, hard-working young man. He began his independent life, fell in love with a woman some years his senior and married her. Shortly after his marriage Akbar was drafted into military service, leaving behind his wife and a new-born son. Akbar's wife, Bibi Fatemeh, went through lots of hardships while he was away. After more than half a century, they still recall those years. In later years Akbar improved his financial situation by working for wealthy landowners, managing their plantations to the south of Jiroft. He acquired plots of land for himself and became a respected, wealthy man. Akbar had five children and a prosperous life.

Hassan had lots of romantic encounters. He finally married a village girl in his early thirties but soon divorced her. It was easy for men to divorce their wives at that time. He simply asked the mullah to annul his marriage. Hassan had high ambitions for himself. The city life had attracted him and he thus aimed to marry a city girl. My mother happened to be that girl. Later she called herself 'the most unfortunate woman'.

Hamams: hunting for brides in the steam-filled chambers

Although houses in Kerman were big and spacious they did not have any baths. Hamams were public baths built in almost every neighbourhood. According to Islamic teachings one had to take a bath and clean oneself after sexual intercourse. Thursday was the appropriate night for men to spend with their wives and so on Friday mornings, before dawn, men could often be seen with bundles of clothes under their arms, rushing to the hamams. It was different with women. Preparation for the hamam took a whole day and so women went to the hamam either once a week or once every two weeks. They had to prepare their henna and the herbal mixture which they used as shampoo. Packing a big bundle along with different sizes of copper bowls, towels, a headscarf and a loincloth took many hours. They also took with them lots of fruits and sherbets, since they stayed inside the steamy, hot rooms for many hours and became thirsty. Women of higher status did not carry their bundles with them. Rather, they sent them by a servant who informed the attendant of their arrival. Women spent hours in the hamam, chatting, gossiping and generally having a nice time.

The architecture of the hamam was itself very interesting. Big hamams had a wooden outer door which opened on to a corridor, leading to a large hexagonal changing room which had stone platforms all around. A small pond with Persian blue tiles and a fountain lay in the middle. Women left their bundles on the platforms, took off their clothes, wrapped the loincloth, called *lowng*, around their waist and took the copper bowls, trays, henna and herbal shampoos through a second corridor and into the main chamber. Here they settled in a corner, sitting on the big copper trays. The corners were assigned according to the women's social status; that of their male relatives. The actual hamams were big chambers with brick walls, blue paisley and flowery tiles, and domes with glass portholes at the apex, to let the sun into the otherwise windowless, steamy chamber. Plenty of pairs of hot and cold water taps were scattered around and at the far end of the room, a few steps up, a hot pond called *khazineh* was the main feature of this chamber. Women went into the khazineh as the last act of cleansing. The hot water in the pond, however, smelt like rotten eggs. I imagine that was because they rarely drained it. The khazineh itself was deep and dark and nightmarish for children.

While growing up I went to the hamam either with my mother or grandmother and was always frightened of going into the khazineh. The stench of the rotten water and its depth scared me. I wonder how women did not contract infectious diseases. One memory which I still hold is that when I finally was dressed, and went out of the hamam, back into the streets after all the scrubbings, my cheeks looked like two fresh radishes!

Women *dalaks* (workers) had the job of shampooing, rubbing, scrubbing and massaging the customers. Dalaks were hard-working women who spent most of their lives in the dampness of the baths. They inevitably suffered from rheumatism and bone defects in later stages of life. Dalaks were often good-natured, simple people who chatted non-stop. They knew everyone and all the town's gossip and hence were a good source of information. Every woman had her own dalak whom she would use for years. Once the women's eyes got used to the steam, they looked around in search of familiar faces and the chatting started. Children were allowed to play around and enjoy themselves. Boys were only allowed to go to the hamam with their mothers until six or seven years of age.

Going to the hamam was one of women's enjoyments. It was a social gathering. Those who were in search of a bride for their male relatives went to the hamams to look for the 'proper' girl. Once the family had heard of an unmarried girl they would try to find out her hamam day. They often sent a matchmaker, or an older family member, to the hamam to scrutinise the girl and approve of her beauty. These women were to report any deformity. In addition, the girl's behaviour was under close observation. Sometimes women saw a girl by chance, who might be a suitable candidate for the families that happened to be looking for a bride. Women exchanged ideas and information, gossiped and released themselves from their monotonous daily lives inside the closed doors. Dalaks were the women's confidantes. Every year, on New Year's Day, dalaks were the first to visit their customers' houses to receive tips and sweets and fruits for their services throughout the year.

Hamams were often built by wealthy people whose names were engraved on the tiles at the entrance arch. The most famous of these hamams in Kerman were Ganj-ali Khan and Vakil, both located at the heart of the bazaar. Later, Ganj-ali Khan hamam was turned into a museum.

The chosen bride

On one of his trips to Kerman Hassan told some women confidantes of his desire to marry a city girl. He said he wanted a wife who was virtuous, attractive and from a well-respected family. He convinced the women acquaintances that he was wealthy and the head of a big clan. They were keen to find him the girl he was looking for. Suggestions were made of several girls whom he refused for various reasons. Then one day one of these women friends saw my mother in the hamam and took a liking to her. She visited Hassan and told him about my mother. Hassan acted quickly and sent a matchmaker around to my mother's household to make inquiries. On hearing about my mother's uncles and their status and her father, whom he had met years before, Hassan decided to approach the family. Men often preferred to marry virgin women and so my mother's previous marriage was a negative mark. This, however, did not belittle my mother in Hassan's eyes. He sent a message to one of my mother's uncles and asked his permission to visit them. All the male members of the family were present at this first meeting and although some of them did not like Hassan, they agreed to proceed with the marriage. There were no investigations into his life. Jiroft was far away. My mother, after her previous failed marriage, had just restarted school. She was seventeen. Hassan went to the school to

have a look at her. It was 1937, the unveiling period and girls went
to school in uniforms.

Kerman, my grandmother's household, 1939

Your fate is written on your forehead before birth.
                                    A Persian proverb

My mother did not object to this marriage. She knew that it was
her fate not to continue her studies. Her second marriage took place
with the least of ceremonies. The wedding gown was a simple dress
with a collar and a bow-tie. A photograph of their wedding day shows
the bride and groom, on a stool, hand in hand, expressionless. My
father, with his Hitler-style moustache and wearing his best suit,
frowning. After the wedding, Hassan moved into my grandmother's
household, where Aunt Iran and the youngest uncle lived as well.

A few months into the marriage my mother began to discover
Hassan's true nature. Although he did not have a regular job in
Kerman, he sneaked out of the house and disappeared for most of
the day, without explaining his whereabouts. Mother suspected he
was having an affair and attempted to follow him around the town.
She even went to some women fortune-tellers and asked them to
give her advice on how to deal with this problem. A woman wrote
spells and drew a chart in the middle of a white fabric to scare away
all the devil in him. I still have that cloth. Another woman took a
piece of a sheep's joint that looked like a small oval face, painted it,
and gave it to my mother to throw over the wall of her house to
send the evil away. However, Hassan continued his sneaking around
without any explanation.

Finally, and upon my mother's insistence, he confessed that he
was addicted to opium and since he did not want to smoke at
home, he went to friends' houses. In addition, she found out that
he was illiterate and had a fuming temper. This devastated my
mother. She wrote in her diary: 'The man that became my husband
was an addict and very bad-tempered. He made me bad-tempered
as well.' Afagh tried hard to keep a brave face. The sensitive young
girl, whose father had been a poet and who herself played the tar
beautifully, suddenly faced the reality of her wasted life. She eventually
taught her husband how to read but could not convince him to give
up his addiction. He was a long-term addict and could not give it
up so easily.

At the beginning of the twentieth century opium poppies were grown in many parts of Iran and Jiroft, with its fertile land, was a suitable place. People made quality opium and often exported it to other areas. Addiction was widespread throughout the province of Kerman. Men were the main addicts, while women generally objected to it. My mother hated it.

Born of love, joys and sorrows, 1940

My mother became pregnant when she was 19. Madame Sheikhi, an educated midwife, came to deliver me. In each family when they expected a new-born, preparations were made for months before. Cookies and sweets were made. Herbal seeds, like cumin and coriander, and coffee, coconut and roasted chick peas were ground and mixed with sugar to make smooth powders. These were served in special silver bowls throughout the ten days after birth. There were celebrations and relatives and friends came to visit. When a child was born, women observed a few things. Round-the-clock nursing of the mother and the baby was the duty of the women in the family. It was believed that up to ten days after the birth, an evil genie (*a'al*), who was capable of killing the mother and taking the baby away, would wander around the house. In the villages women protected the mother and the baby by putting ropes around their bed. In addition, a lamp was kept burning throughout the night and women relatives kept guard by staying awake.

In the urban areas the mother had to rest for ten days after the birth. On the tenth day a mixture of eggs, honey and ground seeds were massaged into the mother's lower back, to strengthen her spine. She had to keep it on for a few hours until she was taken to the hamam, where the dalaks washed her, and gave her a good massage. While in the hamam she was given lots of sherbets, made of distilled herbs. In celebration of the newly born, the dalaks received extra tips and sweets were distributed among the customers.

Naming me amid disagreements

Six nights after my birth a celebration was held for my naming. Lots of friends and relatives were invited. A band of motrebs with a popular singer and their dancers were invited to perform for the guests. Among others father had invited one of his friends who was an army general. He was from Tabriz, a modern city in the north-west of the country. Apart from the general's wife, his two nieces, who were attractive

young women, accompanied him. Although my mother did not like
them, she did not voice her dislike. My mother had a notion that
father flirted with other women and was suspicious of all his women
acquaintances. The party went on throughout the night.

Traditional music and dance has always existed in Iran. After the
unveiling, Western-style dance and music, along with drinking
alcohol, were overtly adopted by the upper-class families and
government senior servants, especially the army officers. In modern
Iran the armed forces became a vehicle of social mobility. Many of
these officers came from underprivileged backgrounds and their
rise introduced a new component into the upper-middle classes. These
army officers were known for their wild parties, where men and
women drank and danced together. Rumours about the infidelity
of their wives were widespread. At my naming celebration, the
general's nieces drank a lot and started dancing with the band. The
women dancers were offended and refused to perform.

During the night a list of names, written on separate pieces of paper,
was handed to my mother's elder uncle. He brought the Quoran
and put them inside one of the pages. Everyone was silent. He pulled
a name from the list which was meant to be my name: *what the holy
Quoran had chosen.* In addition, he wrote my date of birth and the
chosen name on the back of the holy book.

In the meantime, one of the general's nieces, while dancing and
flirting with my father, suggested that I'd be named after her;
Rouhina, so that my father would remember her thereafter. The
next day, my father, without consulting my mother, went to the
notary office and registered me as Rouhina. My mother was furious
and refused to call me by that name. Instead, she chose the other
name: Aghdas. I did not like the name my mother chose. It was old-
fashioned and ugly. When I was eighteen and had finished high school,
I asked everyone to call me Rouhi. The fury over my naming
remained between my parents for as long as I can remember. And
so I began life amongst lots of love and affection from my mother,
my grandmother and Aunt Iran.

The end of Reza Shah, 1941

Although Iran was not directly involved in World War Two, things
were scarce in the cities and life became hard. Reza Shah had
declared the country's neutrality but his pro-German tendencies had
made Iran a target of the Allied forces. Reza Shah collaborated with

the Germans. The Germans had helped to build the main railway, some factories and other industries throughout Iran. They had also strengthened their presence by building hospitals and other establishments in the big cities. In Kerman, for example, a fully equipped hospital was built and German doctors ran it for many years. It became apparent that the link between Reza Shah and Hitler's Reich stemmed from the issue of race and the racial origin of the Aryan tribes, some of whom had emigrated to Iran and Germany thousands of years ago. Radio Berlin often broadcast lengthy Persian programmes, publicising the bonds between the two countries.

The British and the Soviet governments were not happy with Reza Shah's pro-German policies, and advised him to expel the Germans. Iran had thousands of miles of borders with the Soviet Union and the Germans saw a way to attack the Soviets through the Caspian Sea, by crossing Iran. The Allies became aware of this new frontier and acted promptly. Warnings to Reza Shah were of no avail and so the British and the Soviet forces invaded Iran from both the north and the south.

The invasion occurred on September 13, 1941. There was little resistance by the army that Reza Shah had built with so much effort. Reza Shah was forced to resign and hand over his power to Mohammed Reza, his elder son. Mohammed Reza was about twenty years of age when he became the second king of the Pahlavi dynasty. Reza Shah was then ordered to leave Iran. First he sent his family, two wives and his ten children and grandchildren, to Isfahan. Later he joined them. On their way out of the country their caravan passed through Kerman, where they stayed for a week. The city's dignitaries, including two of my mother's uncles, visited Reza Shah in his residence. Reza Shah was escorted to a British ship from the port of Bandar Abbas. They set off for the Indian Ocean and their journey ended in the Mauritius. He was later transferred to Johannesburg in South Africa, where he died in 1945.

Life between wilderness and civilisation

Sit down by the side of the stream
And in the rushing of water
Witness the transience of life.
    Hafez, *Collection of Poems*

It was two years into their marriage and my mother had not yet visited my father's homeland. I was six months old when my father suggested this visit. Before then he had travelled back and forth, trading and bringing some money to the family. Although Iran was not directly involved in the war, goods were scarce. In addition, there was an unspoken fear among the people. My mother thought it might be safer to be away from the big city. Everyone was excited and curious to see my father's place. My father was skilful in glorifying everything. He had spoken much about his orchards and boasted about his authority and so my mother was looking forward to seeing everything for herself. It took them some time to prepare for the journey. They bought rolls of fabric, sugar and other necessary goods, made cookies, packed silverware and china in cases and wrapped their mattresses, duvets and blankets in big sheets and set off for the unknown.

Father clarified certain rules before their journey began. My mother was not to take her tar. Villagers had never seen a woman playing a musical instrument and the idea would seem absurd. Instead of my mother being called by her name, father said that he preferred to call her *Khanum* (the lady) because if he did so, everyone else would do the same. Otherwise, my father said, villagers would call her by her first name, showing no sign of respect. This was how my mother lost her name, Afagh, and was known as Khanum for as long as she lived in that area. Apart from my grandmother, my mother's younger uncle, Abdol Karim Khan, and Aunt Iran, by then a young school teacher, accompanied the caravan. They were a close-knit family and wanted to be together on such an adventurous journey.

It was late spring. The road to Dalfard was long and dangerous. They travelled about a hundred miles by truck, the rest on horseback, donkeys and mules. Father had already sent messages to his village for them to bring animals to meet them en route. Everyone found it difficult to ride the animals, as they were not used to it, and it took them a week to get to Dalfard. My mother was so exhausted that she became ill after the journey and had to stay in bed for a whole week.

Father had an orchard adjoining a mountain. As yet there were no buildings, although he had given orders for two cottages to be built in the middle of his orchard near the side of the mountain. The cottages were made out of shoots of wild almond, reeds and palm leaves. Two types of cottages were common. One was a big square (*kavar*), serving as a living-room and bedroom, the other was a smaller, oval-shaped cottage with a low ceiling (*kotook*), serving as stock-room. The kitchen was in the open and the toilet was further away: a low stony wall with no door and a hole in the ground. When it rained, water leaked from the ceiling of the huts, soaking everything.

Streams of visitors, including my father's own relatives, curious to see the urban bride, poured in. There was no privacy and people dropped in as they pleased. In the village everyone was somehow related to everyone else; either by blood or through marriage. Village women who were close to the Shafii clan came to help. Food was cooked over the wood in the open kitchen. Either lambs were slaughtered, or father hunted wild birds. He was the best hunter among his peers. Sometimes his relatives who lived in the highlands hunted wild deer which they would also bring. In the afternoons, when my mother lit the oil lamp, villagers came to see the lamp in amazement. They still used the fire for light.

In rural areas Reza Shah's policy of unveiling had never taken hold. Women had remained in their traditional outfit. People had rarely seen unveiled women from outside their community. My mother used to wear a chador made of textured, flowery light-coloured cotton. She had this chador on her shoulders all the time, revealing her brown hair, softly blowing in the wind. In Dalfard there were no doctors or modern medicine and this frightened my mother in case I became ill. Our family slept under mosquito nets as malaria, along with the eye disease trachoma, worms and other infectious diseases, were rife. There were bandits and outlaws in the region and so at nights my mother would take her valuables, silverware, china and her Singer sewing machine with her under the mosquito net, believing the thin net would protect her from the harsh world outside. She barely used any of her china or silverware.

She hated Dalfard at first sight, but did not mention it to anyone. She kept a brave face and tried to develop friendships with my father's relatives and eventually gained their respect. My father's half-sister, Halimeh, liked her very much and they became very close. Uncle Akbar's wife, Bibi Fatemeh, was the only one rejected by my mother. Although my mother was polite towards her, she decided that she would never be friends with her. This was despite the fact that my mother liked Uncle Akbar very much. 'Wilderness, rivers and wild mountains, no civilisation, nothing,' was how she described Dalfard in her diary.

When the summer ended we returned to Kerman using the same route, leaving my father behind. He did not have much money to give to my mother. She was left on her own to take care of me. For most of the time my father did not feel responsible for our maintenance. He was busy with his addiction and the affairs of his clan. The tiny piece of land in Bardsir was the only source of income for the whole family.

It was 1942 and I was about two when typhus broke out in Kerman. Thousands of people died. My mother caught it and I soon followed. Nobody believed that we would survive. Typhus was accompanied by a high fever. People used a distilled extract of a type of willow tree to bring the fever down. There were no antibiotics then and infectious diseases were cured by herbal medicines. Soon, the only well-known physician in the city, Doctor Irani, who regularly visited the sick in every household, was taken ill. It was typhus. Everyone panicked. People gathered in the mosques at nights to pray, not for their relatives but for Doctor Irani's recovery. Eventually my mother and I got over the disease, so did Doctor Irani. In those days if an epidemic broke out, a large proportion of the population was wiped out. The lack of modern medicine and hygiene left people with no choice but to cure the sick with primitive methods. I remember my grandmother talking of the 'cholera' years and the 'typhus' years, when thousands of people perished.

My mother became pregnant with my sister Simin when I was three years old. Financially, she was almost destitute, so she decided to go to Jiroft and live there for a while, leaving her mother and young sister behind. Jiroft had grown into a big village. Father built a cottage adjoining a room on Uncle Akbar's plot of land in the middle of the village. A few months later we moved to the outskirts of town, about twenty miles up towards the mountains, where nomads lived. My mother stayed with the nomads, who were father's distant relatives, for seven months. I got whooping cough and their herbs helped cure me. My mother had no choice but to learn the name and the use of each herb and eventually kept lots of them in her mafrash. In addition, she had taken with her modern medicine such as Kenin for malaria, and painkillers. She soon became famous as a wise woman and village women and nomads turned to her to treat their children with her medicines or to give them advice on social issues.

People in remote areas such as Jiroft were barely aware of what was happening outside their region, let alone the world war. Apart from being unable to produce sugar and fabrics, they seemed to be self-sufficient. Feudal warlords in the region had their own self-rule and frequently rebelled against government control over their territories. Officials and gendarmes were aliens to both the poor peasants and the landowners alike. They only came around to take something away from people – their sons for military service or their crop – and so people did not trust them. Every year gendarmes and military officials raided the villages unexpectedly, rounding up young male members of the community, sending them away for national service. That meant families were deprived of the helping hand of a son or young husband for as long as two years. Apart from that people were frightened of their sons being sent far away, where they had never travelled themselves. Every place outside their neighbourhood was a mystery. Rumours spread of the maltreatment of young soldiers by their commanders and desertion was a common occurrence in the military service.

Fighting the bandits

My father was famous for his bravery and strongheadedness. Most of the bandits were frightened of him and did not attack the caravans or people associated with him. Sometimes they even sent him presents which had obviously been taken from other caravans. Banditry was rife in most parts of Iran. Bandits were often armed with ammunition they had acquired from outside the southern or eastern borders. During the Qajar Dynasty, province governors, unable to stop banditry, either developed friendships with the bandit chiefs, giving them a free hand in certain areas, or left them on their own to run territories. There was no regular army with a strategy to bring the bandits under control. It was only during Reza Shah's reign that parts of the country were made safe. Still, there were vast areas of the south and west of Iran where warlords and bandits ruled. From the south of Jiroft (Kahnuj, Minab, Bashakard), to the port of Bader Abbas, bandits had absolute rule. They often travelled up to Jiroft and the highlands, raiding the caravans.

One bandit who became very dangerous was Ghanbar Bochagh-chi. He often robbed caravans travelling through Dalfard to Jiroft, killing those who resisted. Father planned to capture him. In the spring of 1943, while my mother was staying with the nomads, my father's informers discovered Ghanbar's whereabouts in a village nearby and also the number of armed men accompanying him. Father organised a group of armed men and surrounded the hills around the village where Ghanbar was staying. A fight broke out and after several hours Ghanbar and most of his men were captured.

Although my mother was not accustomed to fighting and armed conflict, she asked some of the women to accompany her to the area

where the fighting was taking place. They took food and water to
the men and watched the fight from a hill nearby. Ghanbar was tied
up with ropes and taken to the village where we were staying. I must
have been about three and was walking around the tent where he
was kept. Father remembered that Ghanbar pleaded to him on my
life to release him. He then threatened to take revenge once he came
out of prison. The next morning my father and his men took the
bandits to Jiroft and handed them over to the gendarmes who had
been after Ghanbar for a long time but had been unable to capture
him. Ghanbar stayed in prison for sixteen years. When he was
released he was so old and fragile he did not have any strength for
revenge. He knew his time was up and worked as a gardener in Jiroft.
Father gained much respect as a brave chief, and the army chiefs
and other state officers were grateful for his contribution in bringing
security to the area. After the Ghanbar incident nobody attacked
caravans to the north of Jiroft.

By the beginning of summer my mother was getting homesick,
missing my grandmother and Aunt Iran. She missed civilisation and
urban life and, above all, she was seven months pregnant and did
not want to deliver her baby in that wilderness. The nomads whom
she lived with liked her very much and she somewhat enjoyed
being among them. She had shared their secrets of love affairs and
learnt of their mating games and the dating of young girls and boys
which took place away from curious eyes. She sometimes woke up
at dawn to watch the women milking the sheep. She had also learnt
horse-riding and soon became a very skilful rider. It was not the
custom for women to ride horses as a sport but my mother had her
own horse and enjoyed daring young men to compete with her.

Leaving to return to Kerman by horse, accompanied by my father
and a few men, we set off before the heatwave, travelling through
hazardous mountain peaks and desert roads. We arrived in Kerman
a week later and were greeted by my grandmother and Aunt Iran
who were thrilled to see us. I charmed everyone. My mother had
pierced my ears while in Jiroft and had bought me beautiful earrings
from a jewellery shop in the Kerman bazaar. Most women used to
have pierced ears and gold or pearl earrings were a permanent part
of their outfit.

I happen to remember the incident of my ear-piercing, although
I must have been very young at the time. Jiroft was far from
becoming a town. It only had one street where the government offices
were located, along with a few rows of houses. If you stepped

outside this area wheat plantations stretched towards the river Helil. A narrow alleyway separated the wall of my uncle's house from these plantations. On early evenings my mother used to come outside the wooden door and sit on the steps, watching passers by, chatting with them. She liked to watch the green plantations and looked intensely beyond what was there on the horizon, separating her from civilisation. On that evening, when she had me sitting on her lap, she gently started to rub my earlobes until they became very tender. She then plunged a needle into them. I started crying but she whispered something in my ears and kissed me. She mixed turmeric and a type of oil and moistened the thread with it several times until the wound had healed. She used to turn the thread around while putting oil around the pierced lope. I joined girlhood with this incident, which has stayed in my hazy memory for more than half a century.

My mother, the symbol of patience and determination

A few months later my mother had her second child delivered at home. Madame Sheikhi came in time to be with her during the labour. It was a baby girl, which disappointed my father. This time my mother chose the baby's name: Simin. My father expected to have a son like most men of his tribe. Patrilineal traditions were strong in tribal culture. Now he no longer saw the need to hide his opium habit from the family and every morning after breakfast he ordered the maid to prepare the brazier with burning charcoal and smoked for a couple of hours. He did not care about my mother's anger and ignored her comments. Like all opium addicts he was bad-tempered in the morning. Once he became high, he was good-humoured, talkative, told jokes and gave false promises.

After my sister's birth my mother became more frustrated with my father's irresponsible behaviour. She hated him for his addiction and eventually decided to give him an ultimatum: either he stopped smoking or left their house. She wrote in her diary: 'Now I had two children with no future and no financial prospects. Worst of all, I had a husband that did not care about anything except his addiction. He was irresponsible. I decided that I would be better off without him.' And so my father left for Jiroft soon after my sister was born. My mother was in distress. She only had 150 kilos of rice to sell gradually and live off the money. She was too proud to even tell

my grandmother about their finances. Aunt Iran was a teacher at
this time and had a good income.

River Helil, a source of kill or cure

My father returned to Jiroft knowing that he might have lost his
family forever. He could not do much about it. Outside Jiroft he
was a nobody. My mother's uncles were influential in Kerman and
he knew that he could not force my mother to come with him to
Jiroft. He was still the head of his clan and once back he engaged
himself with their affairs, travelled through the region, and smoked
as much as he could afford. Months passed by and he did not hear
any news from my mother. He was living in the outskirts of Jiroft,
near the river Helil, when the following summer arrived.

River Helil is a big river with its source in the mountains of Baft
in the south-west of Kerman. After travelling some two hundred
miles it ends up in the swamps of Jazeh Murian, near the port of
Bandar Abbas in the Persian Gulf. The river becomes wider in
winter. Nowadays, a dam built by Belgian contractors controls it.
In the old days it often flooded in the winter and spring, and its roaring
sound used to scare the villagers at night. There were no bridges
across this river. When it rained the river banks became flooded and
the villages were cut off. Sometimes the villages on either side were
completely swallowed up by flooding. Still, people whose livelihood
depended on the rich mud rebuilt their cottages and cultivated the
same strip of land. When it was vital to cross the flooded river,
professional river swimmers (ab-baz) helped people and their livestock
to get to the other side. On such occasions the whole population
would gather on either side watching the men carrying people on
their shoulders or pulling the livestock through the river.

My father often swam in the Helil on hot days. That summer being
away from his family began to upset his state of mind. Years later,
once we had grown up, he told us the events of those months over
and over again. He was a very intelligent man and could clearly see
where addiction was leading him. One day he thought to himself
enough is enough: 'What type of life was it anyway, to be away from
my family and drowned in that miserable situation?' On a hot
summer day, at noon when the urge to smoke prevailed, he went
for a swim. He jumped into the deepest part of the river and stayed
in the cool waters until his urge had passed. He repeated this self-
treatment for a week, then left for Raman in the highlands, which

was full of springs and cool unspoiled rivers. He stayed with relatives for a month and swam in the cool waters at his smoking time. At the end of this month, to everyone's amazement, he had managed to beat his addiction. He never touched opium again. Looking much younger and full of energy, he yearned to return to my mother but was not sure of her reaction. My mother was a very determined, strong woman, despite her unfortunate fate. Once she had set her mind on something it was very difficult to change it. My father decided to send a mediator to persuade her to make up with him now that he had reformed.

Habib al'lah, a young man who became my mother's confidant in later years, took a letter from my father, along with many presents. Simin was about nine months old and had just started walking. When Habib al'lah told my mother the news, she barely believed it. Nevertheless, because she had suffered a lot raising two children by herself, she decided to give my father another chance. The mediator went back to Jiroft, telling my father that he was allowed to rejoin his family. Upon his arrival at home in Kerman my mother ordered the maid to prepare the brazier with a plate of good opium and to bring it to the room. Father understood and reassured her that his promise was true and his will strong.

My first year at school

Seek knowledge, from the cradle to the grave!
Sa'adi

During my early childhood we lived in Kerman in the winter and went to Dalfard in the summer. I was five years old when I started school in Kerman. Aunt Iran was a teacher at the primary school I was to attend. My mother made my uniform; a special grey fabric (*ormak*) and a white removable collar. In early October I was taken to school by my mother. The school building was located in the middle of the bazaar. It had a big, black door with a brass handle on it. The first day at school was a terrifying experience. I was left alone in the courtyard. Aunt Iran was nowhere to be found; she taught a bigger age group. The bell rang, the principal's deputy (*Nazem*), ordered us to stand in line according to our height. I was the smallest and was placed at the end. The day began with singing the national anthem: 'Oh Iran, the land of treasures; you are full of wisdom and arts ...'

My classroom was located in the basement. It was dark and damp. I hated the school and became more and more frightened of it. The first year was the most miserable in my life. I was left-handed and my mother forced me to write with my right hand. It was a deformity to be left-handed. She pinched me, smacked me and was generally very hard on me until I managed to write with my right hand. Years later it became apparent that my cousin Zarin was also left-handed, but she was allowed to continue using her left hand. I spent three years in that school. Four decades later, a few steps lower than I remembered, I saw that black wooden door with its grand metal handle still standing in the middle of the bazaar. From the dust and dirt which covered the door, it was apparent that the building had been abandoned for many years.

Aunt Iran became engaged to a young man from Bam, a city in the south of Kerman, soon after she began her teaching career. I believe that they must have met at one of the social gatherings which were often held by the education authorities. They were engaged for two years. Her fiancé, also a teacher, often came to visit at my grandmother's house. He was handsome, charming, literate, well-spoken and well-dressed, with a prosperous future and soon became grandmother's favourite. His name was Mr Davud Sadjadi. He was just two years senior to my aunt; while my father was twice my mother's age. Their marriage ceremony was elaborate and afterwards he moved into my grandmother's household. My father and Mr Sadjadi did not become the best of friends.

My mother and my aunt became pregnant almost simultaneously. My brother Manuchehr and my cousin Zarin were born in 1946 within one month of each other. My father was thrilled to have a son. Aunt Iran was busy with her teaching and so my mother nursed both babies. The two cousins were then considered half brother and sister. I was six at the time and my grandmother's favourite. She was the sweetest person I have ever known and used to spoil me as much and often as she could. She would take me with her to the usual visits to her cousins, brothers and one of her sisters. She had one cousin whom she liked very much and visited regularly in summer-time. Upon our arrival at the cousin's house in the early afternoons rugs were put on the veranda and cushions against the walls. The samovar would be lit quickly and the tea made. Different types of cookies, cakes and sweets were brought on silver plates. I loved sitting beside Grandmother, listening to their conversation. Nobody ever came to invite me to play and I do not remember seeing children in that household. After tea, fruits were offered: melon, watermelon and other summer fruits. At the end a bowl filled with all types of nuts was brought in and women sat around, chit-chatting and nibbling nuts. Grandmother would stay until just before dusk and would strongly refuse offers of dinner. By then she had been widowed for a long time and her status as a widow meant she had less respect than women whose husbands were still alive. As a result she was expected to visit relatives but she did not have the means to entertain them in return except, of course, during the New Year. I also used to go to the hamam with her. She always washed me, and gave me goodies on the way back, as hamam used to make me very hungry. Grandmother's skin was smooth and white and I did not miss any opportunity to touch her cheeks and kiss her.

Mourning for Imam Hossein in Kerman

Every year, while we were in Kerman, we mourned the martyrdom of Imam Hossein for two whole months. Imam Hossein was the Prophet Mohammed's grandson. The second son of Hazrat Fatima, the Prophet's daughter, and Imam Ali. In 661 AD the Imam was invited by a group of people of Koufeh, a town in Iraq, to pay a visit to the town and take over the leadership from the then Umayyed Calipha, Yazid. Upon arrival in the outskirts of the town of Karbala he was met by an army who warned him to return, otherwise there would be bloodshed. The Imam, considering himself the legitimate successor to the Prophet, decided to confront Yazid. Yazid's army led by a famous general was well-equipped and after a week it was obvious that the Imam would lose the battle. He gathered all the followers who had accompanied him on the trip and discussed the situation with them. He suggested two options; either they stayed and were martyred or left before it was too late. Most of the men, except his close family of seventy two members in all, left in the darkness of the night. For two days the Imam and his family, who were also cut off from the river Alphorat which supplied them with water, fought the unequal battle. At the end of the second day, which is the tenth day of the month of Moharram (the first month of the Islamic calendar), all men including the Imam himself were brutally killed, their heads cut off and taken to Yazid. The women and children were taken prisoners and sent to Yazid's court.

For centuries, the Shi'at Muslims have mourned Imam Hossein's martyrdom for two months every year. During these months women wear black and attend commemorations held on the first ten days of Moharram. In many cities there are no weddings, celebrations or music. During the two days of Tasua and Ashura, which were the final days of the battle, commemorations are held throughout the Shi'at world. The mosques and *tekyehs* (town squares) become the centre of remembrance rituals. *Tazieh* (street processions) wind their way through the streets of every town and village, made up of groups of men from all walks of life (shopkeepers, bazaaris, labourers), who sing rhymed poetry and engage in the ritual of self-flagellation.

In the city of Kerman, throughout the ten days of commemoration leading to Tasua and Ashura, women would suspend all activity. From early afternoon they would go to the mosques or tekyehs to occupy a place near the *mambars* (staircased pulpits), listening to the mullah's sermons and crying for the innocence of the Imam and cursing the brutality of Yazid and his army. They would carry their young children with their chadors nipped in their teeth and the smell of rosewater and perspiration would be heavy in the air. These ceremonies were an entertainment women never had at other times. They would meet friends and felt free to go from one mosque to another.

My grandmother took me to all these processions. We strolled through the streets, watching groups of men (*dasteh azadaran*) beating their bare chest in rhythms, while someone repeated songs with a powerful voice, sometimes accompanied by drums. Some beat their backs with a bunch of *zangir* (metal chains), rattling harmoniously. Others, wearing white shrouds, inflicted a cut on their foreheads with poniards so the blood dripped from the wound to the white shroud. Each group carried black banners, on which the Imam's name was printed. The more the banners, the more important the group looked. By noon, all the groups reached one point, Sardar Mojalal's house. Sardar was a wealthy and powerful man whose house could accommodate hundreds of people. Each year, the courtyard, as big as a football ground, was covered with a big tent. The house itself was a grand two-storey building which surrounded the courtyard. The first floor had big balconies, circling the courtyard. Hundreds of women went to the house early in the morning of Ashura and got themselves a place to watch the processions. They wailed and screamed when the groups entered the courtyard.

Since my grandmother wanted to watch the street processions, we never were able to reach the balconies. As the groups reached Sardar's house, each competed to enter the courtyard first and sometimes fights broke out. It was believed that Imam Hossein was killed at noon on the tenth of Moharram; that was the time the tazieh reached its peak, then slowly died down. Sardar's household entertained hundreds of people with delicious meals, cooked in the open. Ashura's meals were free for everyone. Even in the mosques one could drop in and have free lunch.

On the third night after Ashura, people were up the whole night (*shameh ghariban*). On that night it was believed the family of the Imam who were in captivity had held a ceremony for the martyred. My grandmother used to buy plenty of candles and when night fell we set off for the mosques and holy spots which were plentiful in Kerman. While going from one place to another, lighting a candle and praying, groups of people could be seen carrying candles and beating their heads, reciting rhymed verses. Thousands of candles flickered in the darkness of the streets giving the processions a mystical, spiritual atmosphere.

While my mother and grandmother were among the flock of women who cried for the Imam in the tazieh or in the sermons performed in the mosques, I was never able to cry. I had no reason to cry. No matter how hard I tried to bring a few drops of tears to my eyes, it was fruitless. I tried to remember a sad event or glare at one point until my eyes became tired and watery but it was no use, I could not cry. Sometimes women cried, remembering their dead relatives or the amount of debt they had or other hardships in life. Sometimes people vowed to commemorate the event in their own house.

There were tens of households which held ceremonies during the ten days of Moharram. The Rowze Khun, or the mullah who came to eulogise, was very familiar with women's psyche and often gave details of how the Imam was brutally martyred in order to unleash sobs. A few moments after he took the crowd to the height of the scene, he would ease them off and stopped their sobbing by adding a 'but' and bringing down his voice which meant an abrupt completion to the whole procession. The mullahs often enjoyed eulogising among the crowd of women, giving them orders to stop their children's noises or talking among themselves, telling them jokes in a serious manner and spotting attractive women by occasional peeps through the side of their eyes. Women talked about the mullahs, their tone of voice and how beautifully they eulogised. Handsome mullahs were the busiest during these days. Women consulted the mullahs on social or religious matters. The role of these men of God was more than mere preaching the word of God; counsellor, confidant, psychologist and sometimes abuser of women's confidence.

The martyrdom of Imam Hossein has a great significance on the psyche of the people. The Imam had gone to Karbala to take power from the Umayyed family. If he hadn't been killed in such a brutal way, he might have been remembered in history books like any other Imam. His martyrdom, however, did not find a socio-cultural dimension until the Safavid Dynasty came to power in Iran. They were the first Shi'at Dynasty, who sought an independent identity from the rest of the Muslim world (the Sunnis), and made themselves the patrons and inventors of Tasua and Ashura, in the way we witness it today. Mourning for the Imam and religio-cultural processions have become a prominent feature of the Shi'ats throughout the centuries. Because the lunar calendar is based on the rotation of the moon around the earth, the month of Moharram changes accordingly. When living in Kerman if Moharram fell in the summer, we would have been in Dalfard. At other times, we would be in the city itself to witness the tradition in full.

The martydom of Imam Hossein in Dalfard

Commemoration of the Imam's martyrdom was different in the villages and rural areas. In Dalfard we often went to the ceremonies which were performed in an open space. My mother wore black for the occasion. On the two days of Tasua and Ashura we children were not allowed to comb our hair or wear flowery dresses, although we did not wear black. I do not remember seeing village women wearing black. It seemed that this custom was observed only in the cities. There were no mosques in Dalfard and no mullahs. Amateurs, such as Kharamat Divdel and other locals, carried out the processions. Preparations were made for days beforehand. Tazieh took the form of street theatre, where one man acted as Imam Hossein, and others posed as women relatives of the Imam and were carried in closed carriages. Karamat always liked to perform the role of Shimir, Yazid's army general who personally killed the Imam. He could be seen wearing a red shawl, riding a horse which was also covered with a red fabric. Red meant that the bloodthirsty Shimir was happy and ready to kill the Imam. Young men carried banners in front of the small group of performers. Yazid's flag and that of the Imam's could be seen in front of the two 'armies'.

Upon reaching the main square from different directions, Shimir's 'troops', a bunch of young peasant boys, would line up at one corner and the Imam's handful of troops of ragged, thirsty and exhausted men, on the other side. The play lasted for a couple of hours, during which the Shimir was the star of the show, galloping his horse from one side to the other, boasting about his might. At the end, he would 'kill' the Imam, take the women and children prisoner and set off for Yazid's court. I presume that Karamat, who played this role for as long as I remember, really enjoyed being in power and manipulating the group of innocent spectators for those few hours. My mother cried for the innocence of the Imam and the brutal way in which he was killed. I do not remember seeing village women crying. To them it was more like entertainment than a commemoration.

Reza Shah tried to curb the rituals and limited street processions which were a strong tool in the hands of the clergy who opposed his ideas of modernisation of Iran. When his son came to power he relaxed the tough measures. Although the world had moved on and radio, television, cinema and modern theatre had expanded in Tehran and other big cities, Tasua and Ashura never lost their importance. Ayatollah Khomeini, in his speeches declared that as long as people kept Tasua and Ashura alive Islam would never die.

Apart from a few events which kept us busy for a few days, summers in Dalfard were a depressing time for my mother. For us children however, they were full of expeditions through the valleys, climbing heaps of blackberry bushes or walnut trees, watching women milking the sheep or making bread, jumping from one low wall to another, chasing butterflies. At night, we were frightened of the tigers' roars in the nearby mountain and in the morning we hiked the same mountain in search of the tiger or collected fossils and colourful stones.

Our maid dies of smallpox

I was six when our maid Fezeh contracted smallpox. She had accompanied us from Kerman to Dalfard. We were living in the old orchard, near the side of the mountain. At first, my mother did not take her infection seriously. Nevertheless, she quarantined her in a hut which was hurriedly built. My mother took over the care of Fezeh and I remember watching her every day, going into the hut with food or clean sheets and then boiling the infected clothes in big pots. She stayed in the hut for a long time, nursing that unfortunate girl. After about a month her condition deteriorated. My mother could sometimes be seen crying. She gave her all the herbs and cool drinks she believed would cure the deadly infection but it was no use, Fezeh died soon after and was buried in a cemetery nearby. My mother cried a great deal for Fezeh's wasted life and her lonely death, away from her family. Fortunately, no one else caught the disease. At the end of the summer, when we returned to Kerman, my mother had the hard task of convincing the girl's family of the circumstances of her unfortunate death. They suspected she might have been murdered. A few years later we were all vaccinated against smallpox.

Life in Dalfard was monotonous. Each small incident attracted interference from the whole village. People talked about the incident afterwards, adding extra descriptions to make it more exciting. Once, early in the afternoon, while my mother was still recovering from Fezeh's death, we heard a crowd arguing in the open space that stretched between our orchard and the orchard nearby. We all rushed out to investigate. A large crowd had gathered in a circle and men were arguing and shouting abuse. Suddenly, one of the women whom we knew rushed home and brought out her baby boy into the middle of the fight. I was surprised and unaware of the intention behind such an act. While shouting abuse, she tried to pass the frightened baby to her husband who was the main party in the fight. Some intervened; the baby was screaming. Finally, people managed to break them apart and the elders, including my father, spoke to both sides, to calm them down.

Later, I found out that bringing children into fights was the final resort in stopping it. Parents were ready to actually throw their children in the middle, killing or injuring them, eventually accusing the other party. Members of the clan would usually testify to this. This cruel tactic worked well in fights between the clans. I heard stories of some children actually being killed by their parents. The disputes were usually over a piece of land, family honour, or water rations.

Curing diarrhoea with a donkey saddle

In the summer of 1948 my father took us to a village two miles away from ours and we settled in an orchard that belonged to a relative. This village was located in a valley with a beautiful landscape. The orchards had surrounding walls and there was a relative degree of privacy, although locals would drop in unexpectedly from time to time for a chat or a meal. A few months into the summer, my brother Manuchehr, who was about two years old, got severe diarrhoea. He became weak and thin and a genuine cause for concern. Herbal remedies did not work. It was suggested that if he was taken to the holy shrine that was on a mountain peak, opposite where we were staying, he might be cured. According to the locals it was very difficult to climb the mountain and very few women had ever done so. Rural women did a lot of other hard work but climbing and riding were considered manly tasks. Due to her different culture, however, my mother did not mind riding horses like men or climbing mountains.

She asked some women to accompany her to the shrine. A few volunteered. The night before they made preparations and at dawn their small caravan set off for the mountain. Although my father did not accompany them, he followed their progress through his binoculars and would sometimes pass them to me. The peak could be seen from where we stood but we could not locate the shrine, which was through a narrow route, normally used by the cattle and shepherds. We could see some green bushes and trees en route, which meant they would be able to rest and take water from the spring. They got to the peak by noon and took Manuchehr to the shrine and asked 'His holiness' to cure him.

However, Manuchehr did not get well and in fact his situation deteriorated. A wise woman who used to come to our house and stay with us once in a while, was there at the time. She used to give advice on every matter; from children's education, to finding husbands or wives, or curing the sick. When a woman died in a family she was prepared to wash the body for burial. There were no funeral services at the time and local people helped the bereaved families. Soghra Beigum suggested that if my mother covered the toddler with a donkey saddle at night, he might sweat and get well. Meanwhile, my father, whose love for my little brother was immense, became desperate and upon hearing that a physician was passing through Jiroft, sent somebody to bring him to Dalfard.

It took the physician two days to arrive and he immediately asked to examine my brother. My mother, in her desperation, had placed him under the donkey saddle, where he was fast asleep, and the physician was so furious at this that he packed his bag and left without examining him, saying 'it is either me or the donkey saddle.' A few days later, someone suggested a herbal root (*myrobalan*) to be boiled and given to the child. My brother was given a few teaspoons of the bitter root each day and was completely cured after a few days.

A feast to be remembered

In the summer of 1949 Manuchehr was three years old when local people suggested a feast for his circumcision. My mother agreed. The feast would be a departure from her monotonous life in Dalfard. In the rural areas of Kerman weddings and feasts lasted as long as three days. Arrangements were put in hand. Extra bags of rice, sugar and flour were bought and cookies baked. Big pots and extra dishes were brought in from other households. A band of local gypsy musicians who lived in Dalfard as a separate community were called in to play during the feast. My mother asked some of the more experienced women to supervise the process. Extra tents were set up for distinguished guests who were invited from other villages. In ceremonies such as this almost everyone was invited. It was an open house party.

The day arrived and the ceremony began early in the morning. The men's tents were located in an open space while the women just gathered around my mother. We children were left on our own to enjoy the feast. One thing that caught my mother's eye was Bibi Fatemeh's (Uncle Akbar's wife), unfriendly act of bringing her own stock of food to cook for herself separately. She arrived on a mule, riding on the top of a fat khorjin. While staying in a tent she gathered a group of women around her, cooked for herself throughout the feast, and ignored my mother. I believe it was after this incident that my mother broke off all relations with her.

Lunch and dinner were served separately; men ate first, women followed. Huge sofrehs were spread on the floor and scores of men sat around, cross-legged, eating with their hands. From early afternoon, the gypsies played dohol and pipes until late at night. Everyone gathered around them and watched. I remember watching a drummer who danced round and round beating on his drum for hours. He was the star of the show. The drums were accompanied by a single sorna. Sometimes men performed a dance which involved hitting two sticks together, while going back and forth, daring each other. Women came to watch and the children enjoyed every moment of it.

Manuchehr was too young to be aware of his importance. Although the feast was originally arranged for his circumcision, he was not circumcised until a few years later. On the third day, after lunch, a high platform was set up with blankets and cushions laid in the middle. My father sat down on it with Manuchehr on his lap. This was the moment everyone gave presents to the little toddler. Presents (*bazl*) were in the form of cash, or transfer of livestock or even pieces of land. An elderly man sat near my father, receiving the presents while somebody else wrote them in a book. Each donor's name was announced loudly with what he had donated. The amount of donation was an indication of the donor's wealth. I remember having seen the same ceremony at weddings where the groom sat on the platform receiving presents. As for my father, I heard from relatives that he had attended many weddings where he had given presents. Since his own wedding was in Kerman, no one had had the opportunity of giving him anything and so my brother's feast compensated for that. These ceremonies were not known in urban areas. There, couples received presents from those relatives and friends who later visited them at their house.

Chapter Three

Mohammed Reza Shah, 1941–79

The moving finger writes; having writ,
Moves on: nor all your piety nor wit
Shall lure it back to cancel half a line,
Nor all your tears wash out a word of it.
  Omar Khayyam, *Rubaiyat of Omar Khayyam*

In 1941 Mohammed Reza became the second king of the Pahlavi Dynasty. His era began in chaos and disorder. He was only twenty years of age, inexperienced and unable to control a country which was virtually occupied by the British and the Russians, and caught up in the war. During the first ten years after he replaced his father, due to his inability to impose an arbitrary rule, Iran experienced relative freedom from dictatorship. Political parties bloomed. Tens of magazines and newspapers were published and trade unions and syndicates formed. Due to the political instability, lack of strong central government and the foreign presence, regional and ethnic demands for self-rule increased and parts of the country such as Kurdistan and Azarbaijan declared autonomy. After the end of World War Two, when Mohammed Reza Shah managed to take control of the army, he sent troops to these regions and brutally suppressed these movements. Nevertheless, he was not in full control until after the 1953 coup.

We settle in Jiroft, 1949

I was nine years old when my parents decided to move to Jiroft permanently. My mother saw no future in Kerman and by then she was familiar with rural life. Besides, my father could not afford to keep us in Kerman. He was not the type of person who was willing to work hard to provide us with a comfortable life in the city. Having three children forced my mother to face the reality of life. I had just finished my third year of primary school in Kerman when we moved. Jiroft was becoming a small town by then; a few streets, offices, schools. Some of the wealthy people had bought plots of land and built houses along the main street.

My parents managed to buy a few acres of land near Uncle Akbar's house. Initially, they built two rooms in the middle of the plot and later expanded it into a proper house. The house consisted of four very large rooms, two on each side of a big hallway. In a large space, outside the house, they built a brick oven in the ground to bake the bread, a hut as the kitchen and a low roof shed for the poultry. The toilet was located at the far end of the plot. Because of plantations nearby foxes were around most nights and frequently attacked the chickens. We were often woken up in the middle of the night by the frightened shrieking of the birds being attacked and in the morning one or two had disappeared, their feathers scattered around the garden. Nevertheless, hens hatched frequently and eggs were plentiful.

Wide verandas were built at both the north and south ends of the building, where we would spend our afternoons and nights. In early spring swallows would suddenly appear and invite themselves to the high, domed-shaped hallway ceiling to build their love nests, painstakingly made out of mud from the river. Once these were made the eggs would hatch and their chicks would grow. Their singing began early morning each day until the chicks grew old enough to fly. They would disappear in the same sudden manner, only to return the following year. In later years, after I had left home, the big hallway became our reception room and one of the rooms was converted into a kitchen, toilet and bathroom. My mother spread a big Persian carpet in this reception room, hung the beige lace curtains my grandmother had given her on the windows and bought a set of high chairs with red flowery velvet covers, a dining table and six dining chairs. Despite this, we continued to eat on the floor.

As Jiroft would become hot by the end of April and there was no modern cooling system, people built special huts over the brooks which ran through each garden. Reeds and cane shoots were the raw materials for these huts. The south and north section of the huts were covered with special thorned bushes. Depending on whether the wind blew from the north or south, water was splashed over the thorns. The wind coming through the wet thorns made the huts cool and soothing. Inside it was dark and hazy and the smell of reeds and wet thorns filled the air. Although the thorns dried out quickly, the smallest breeze cooled the hut. Sometimes the temperature inside was 20–30 degrees lower than outside.

We made such a hut over the brook in our garden. We would spend our days inside this hut from mid-April until we moved away to either Kerman or Dalfard. Local labourers who were accustomed to the hot weather were recruited to splash water over the thorned bushes. Sometimes dust storms came through in their rush towards the Indian Ocean. The Husha wind was a hot current dust storm which stayed for as long as three to seven days. It would almost burn our skin if we came out of the hut in the daytime. We would stay inside until the wind had died down. Inside, we kept watermelon, melon and fresh cucumbers. It was difficult to cook in the hot weather and our meals consisted of dairy products, dates, fruit and vegetables. Sometimes snakes found the bushes a cool place to rest. My father often found and killed them. In the hot climate of Jiroft snakes were very dangerous and the result of their bite was almost certain death.

At the same time that we moved to Jiroft Aunt Iran's husband, Mr Sadjadi, received a promotion at work and upon my mother's insistence transferred himself from Kerman to Jiroft as head of the education department. At the time, government administration in the provinces consisted of a governor-general who appointed state functionaries: a governor for each town, head of finance, education, judiciary and other similar departments. Jiroft's population had increased and officials enjoyed a high status and fringe benefits. Once a man was transferred to another area it was easy, if his wife was also a government employee, for her to be transferred too. That was how my aunt got her teaching job in Jiroft. As Aunt Iran was on the move, my grandmother decided to live with her permanently. She divided her belongings between my mother and aunt, giving my aunt the larger share. My grandmother supervised the household so that Aunt Iran did not have to bother. My mother longed to have grandmother with her but my grandmother did not want to live her. I never knew the reason but I guess my father's bad temper, his irresponsible attitude and the fact that deep in her mind my grandmother knew my father was not an ideal person to live with contributed to her decision to stay with my aunt. Aunt Iran's work made a good excuse for that.

My mother, having now fully realised that my father was not the type of person to provide a promising future, took control of the household. She was very skilful in handling her limited resources and hiding her difficulties from others, even her mother and sister. The town was expanding; rice and cotton plantations had disappeared, giving way to orange gardens. Because of the sub-tropical weather, Jiroft was suitable for cash crops such as oranges. By early 1950 everyone was planting all types of oranges. My mother started to grow orange trees on the land surrounding the building. It was a hard and painstaking task. First she had to grow the small plants and at the end of their second year these had to be grafted to the type of orange she wanted.

My mother designed the garden herself. On the west side she grew eucalyptus trees alongside the brook. On the north side of the building a footpath led through the garden to the gate, along which jasmine bushes, white daffodils and tuberoses grew. At the end of the path two willow trees touched each other. To this day the smell of tuberoses reminds me of the precious memory of my mother's existence. My mother learnt to graft orange trees. Although we had a gardener she woke up very early in the morning and worked in the garden until mid-day. This garden, along with two other gardens which she helped to tend, became our main source of income for years to come. In the meantime my father grew rice and cotton on the plots of land he owned in Jiroft. He also had cattle in the highlands which provided us with extra income. As head of his tribe he received presents, in the form of sheep and other highland products, whenever he settled a dispute or took the people's grievances to the authorities or protected them against injustices.

We had two maids and a gardener at this time. My mother worked alongside the maids, teaching them cooking, sewing and manners. Girls who worked for her found good husbands. It was cheap to have maids in those days. Poverty was rife and people were happy to give their children away to someone who would provide them with shelter and food. My mother was very kind to these servants. She could be heard laughing and joking with them. In later years, when some of these women had their own family, they visited us on New Year's Day, and received presents for their children. Often landlords and male family members abused these young maids, beat them up or even raped them. We heard stories of girls who had become pregnant and as a result were thrown out of the house in contempt. They sometimes gave birth in secret and disposed of the baby. Babies' bodies were found in the streams around the neighbourhood. These poor women, victims of such crimes, did not have anyone to turn to; their parents would probably have killed them and the landlord's wife would have thrown them onto the streets.

Now that we were settled in Jiroft my mother found a place to put her china, silverware and glass work. She had a big *yakhdan* (wooden case) where she kept these valuables. During New Year's preparations this case was temporarily cleared to hold the batches of cookies and sweets baked in our household. The case was always locked. The only person who dared to open it, to steal a handful of cookies, was my little brother Mehdi, who was even prepared to receive a good smack if he was caught red-handed.

Afternoon tea parties

My mother soon found a circle of friends and associates from among the wives of government officials and some locals who had married women from Kerman. Once you were acquainted with a few, the circle snowballed. Each newcomer was introduced to the circle through a member and was invited to the tea parties which were held every two weeks. Tea parties were women's only regular gathering and entertainment. A few days before my mother's turn, she would send one of the maids to each house to invite the ladies in person. Invitations started with the house of the most important person, the governor's wife. If the lady was not available, the maid had to return the next day. Mother made sure that the house was cleaned and all the china plates and silverware washed. It was best if father left the house on the afternoon and we children were warned to behave properly. None of the women took their children to such parties unless they were in their adolescent years. I longed to accompany my mother to such events, although I do not remember that she ever took any of us. On her return, in the evening, the house was filled with her laughter and our excitement at hearing some of the gossip.

At our house women were entertained in the guest room, which was kept locked for most of the time. My mother always wore her best dress for the occasion and the children had to clean themselves and dress properly in case they were met by some of the guests. I was allowed to attend the reception at our house and had to help my mother entertain the guests, put plates in front of them, and take the dirty ones out. An embroidered sofreh would be laid in the middle of the room and silver plates, full of sweets, a big bowl of fruit and

smaller bowls of nuts placed on it. Upon arrival women were led
to their proper places. The governor's wife sat at the top and the
rest had their places according to their husband's rank. This was an
unwritten rule which everyone observed. The wives of landowners
and the town's dignitaries sat where they wished. Mrs Mousavi and
Mrs Ibrahimi, my mother's closest friends, whose husbands were
respected persons, also sat at the top. The tea was brought in by the
maid. Women stayed until dark. Their laughter and chatting filled
the air. After the guests had left, we children rushed into the room
to finish the rest of the cookies and nuts.

None of my father's female relatives had a high enough status to
join these parties. We did not associate with Uncle Akbar's family
because my mother's antipathy to Bibi Fatemeh had abided over the
years. She never let us visit their house, although my uncle would
come round to us most of the time. We only started to build a relation
with our cousins years later when we were adults.

When Aunt Iran's husband came to Jiroft he was housed in the
official residence as a senior civil servant. My aunt and grandmother
joined the tea parties. Now my grandmother would come to stay
with us more often and we were always thrilled to have her around.
Aunt Iran started her teaching job at a local primary school and I
spent the next three years at the same school, completing my six
years of primary education. Aunt Iran and her family would
accompany us to Dalfard when the schools shut for summer holidays.
Huts were made for them near ours. My mother could not have
been happier. Mr Sadjadi and my father were both good hunters
and frequently shot plenty of partridges in the mountains nearby.
They used a fascinating method to shoot these birds. Hundreds of
pieces of colourful fabrics were sown together to make *pardeh* (a
rectangular piece of cloth, to the height of an average person,
strapped upright to big cane sticks at the back with two holes at the
top to allow the hunter to see the birds). When they went hunting,
they carried the pardeh in front of them and moved slowly towards
the birds. The birds became fascinated by the colours and froze and
were shot through the holes. As a result of my father's and Mr Sadjadi's
regular hunting, delicious kebabs and stews were made.

Nowrooz, the New Year

Every year, before winter ended, we prepared for Nowrooz. It is
said that the ancient kings of Persia celebrated the beginning of spring

and the season of fertility. Nowrooz is on March 21 and has been celebrated for many centuries. While grandmother lived in Kerman with her daughters that was taken for granted. Once we had moved to Jiroft my mother longed to spend the occasion with her mother and sister. Now that they were in Jiroft, everything was done together.

Preparations for the occasion would start a month before. Dough, sugar, oil, almond, eggs, coconut, saffron, walnut, spices and the metal moulds which were used to shape the cookies, trays and the baking oven itself, which had been made by the local blacksmiths, were all readied. Two weeks before the day, all other activities were suspended and they would start making the cookies. It took my mother and grandmother a week to bake everything. Before they began they decided which cookies they wanted that year. Each day only one or two types would be made. Apart from the texture, which affected the shape and the taste of the cookies, decorating them with saffron, pistachio and sesame seeds needed much expertise. Trays of baked cookies would be removed from the oven and into a room to be cooled and stored in special containers. My mother and grandmother had to also deal with the children's interference. We were all excited by the occasion and would get in their way. The boys were the biggest problem and smacking and pinching them often occurred. The girls were usually spared because they were meant to learn the relevant skills.

Since I was quiet and well-behaved, I was allowed to be present. At the end of each day everyone got a share of the over-cooked or out-of-shape cookies. The metal moulds had different shapes: star, heart, moon and flowers. Some of the cookies were made just a day before the New Year, so they would not lose their texture. In addition, *samanoo*, or custard, was made from wheat grain. My mother and Aunt Iran divided the cookies between them while they were in Jiroft.

Growing green shoots or grain sprouts took place a couple of weeks before Nowrooz. We examined their growth until they were long enough to be put on the table. Growing greens is a symbol of the fertile season, when everything is revived and nature wakes up from the long winter sleep. Sometimes at our insistence my mother also grew small plates for each of us.

For Nowrooz everyone was meant to have new clothes. Since my mother's resources were limited she altered some of our clothes to fit the younger children and only bought new clothes for the older ones. I was always bought new clothes. Buying shoes in Jiroft was problematic. While we were living in Kerman, the shoemaker measured our feet and made us shoes. In Jiroft there were no shoe shops and no good shoemakers, so my mother had to order our shoes from Kerman. I do not remember my mother buying herself any new clothes. I suppose she could not afford it, although she would never admit to that. Nevertheless, she always looked nice at Nowrooz.

Spring cleaning would take a few days. The curtains would come down and be washed and so would the sheets, and every other item of our clothes. Dishes, silverware and china came out of my mother's wooden case, to be washed and dried. In Jiroft, because of the mild weather in March, white blossoms covered the orange trees and their aroma filled the air around Nowrooz time.

A few days before Nowrooz my mother would send for the local hairdresser. She shaped my mother's, grandmother's and Aunt Iran's eyebrows, took all the unwanted hair from their faces and cut their hair if they wished. Going to hamam before Nowrooz was a must. Everybody, including the servants, had to be cleansed of the dirt of the old year. The hamams were the busiest place in the whole of Iran up to an hour before the year was about to turn.

Nowrooz in Iran, some Middle Asian countries, Afghanistan and among Kurdish nationals is the beginning of the fiscal year. Even Persians (*Parsis*) who emigrated to India after the Arab invasion in the seventh century still celebrate it. It is the beginning of the solar calendar, although Iranians changed it to the lunar calendar after they converted to Islam. Unlike the Western New Year, which is fixed at midnight, our Nowrooz changes time according to the exact moment that the sun reaches the equinox, which might be any time of the day or night. Astrologers often inform the nation of this exact moment.

When we were young and up until a decade ago, Dr Riazi, a university professor, announced the exact timing, months before. Since Nowrooz is the symbol of the earth's fertility and growth, Iranians prepare a *haft-seen* or sofreh on which items which are a symbol of fertility in life and nature are placed. A mirror, a plate full of painted eggs, candlesticks and a goldfish bowl decorate every Iranian's sofreh. Haft-seen can be compared with the Christmas tree and like it does not bear any religious significance. Some religious families also put a Quoran on the sofreh.

Nowrooz day was the happiest day of the whole year. Unless the turning of the year occurred in the middle of the night, everyone would be dressed in new clothes. Like Christmas Day, Nowrooz is reserved for the close family unit. The streets of every town in Iran are almost deserted on the hour. Everyone goes home to be with their family. In rural areas though people do not take this tradition as seriously. Customs such as sofreh, haft-seen and other preparations are only carried out in the strict form in urban areas.

With the arrival of the radio, the announcement of the New Year began with a big bang and special music, consisting of drums and pipes. Then the Shah and the Queen's messages were broadcast. We would all kiss and hug and receive our presents from the elders, usually in the form of cash. The servants were the first to come into the room to kiss my parent's hands and receive 'tips'. We drank sherbet that was made of rosewater or mint extracts. Shortly afterwards relatives and acquaintances would arrive. Since my father was the eldest in his clan and a respected citizen we always received lots of visitors. Visitors were offered sherbet, tea and cookies and some even received tips.

The dalaks, who throughout the year served us in the hamam, all arrived in a group. My mother had to take care of them properly; offering them 'good tips' and plenty of cookies to take home. Nowrooz visitations lasted three days, during which we paid visits to some of those who had come to see us the first day. The children ate plenty of food and cookies and it was a miracle if, as a result they did not suffer from stomach problems.

Special Nowrooz food was rice with vegetables (sabzi-polo) and smoked fish, which depending on the timing was made as lunch or dinner. Fish was not available in Jiroft. Dried, smoked fish was brought in only for the New Year's feast. My mother would soak the fish for a few days, cut it into pieces and fry it. For sabzi-polo, parsley, coriander, chives and fenugreek were the traditional seasonings. Since none grew in Jiroft, my mother replaced them with plants that grew wild in every surrounding garden and plantation and used plenty of saffron to give the food colour and scent.

During the New Year the schools closed for two weeks and government offices for five days. The children collected their own *eidi* (present in the form of cash) which they could spend as they wished, provided their mothers didn't want to 'keep' it. On the thirteenth day of the New Year, nobody stayed indoors. Sizdabedar was a day out for everyone. My mother made preparations the day before. People usually spent the day out in the fields and gardens outside the town. It was believed that if we got angry on this day, ill-fortune would stay with us to the end of the year. My father tried hard to be good tempered; he rarely succeeded. We would take our greens with us to throw in the open fields. Young girls who were hoping to find a husband were advised to tie knots in the green grass and make a wish. For my mother it was the joy of having her mother and sister around to spend the day together. The cookies and sweets which were left over from Nowrooz kept the memory of the New Year alive for a couple of months afterwards.

After we settled in Jiroft our summers changed pattern. Some summers we went up to Dalfard and during others we went to Kerman and stayed there until school was about to start. A big house would be rented and my mother and aunt would send all the children to a local mullah's house to learn the Quoran. This way they could browse in the bazaar for as long as they wanted. I was old enough to be spared. By the early 1950s radio arrived in town. The only brand on sale was Radio Andrea with its tens of batteries that were kept in a shell. Not too many people could afford to have such a radio. We loved to listen to the music and the comedies, father never missed the two o'clock news in the afternoon and my mother knew by heart all the songs that were performed by women singers like Ghamar, Moluk Zarabi, Marzieh, Delkash and Pouran. Later in the decade a cinema opened in Kerman. The first Iranian female movie star was a Kermani woman, who played the role of a tribeswoman. One of my mother's cousins was the cinema operator and once took us to the movie free of charge. It was a summer evening. We sat on the open balcony, flying over the seven clouds as we say, with the thrill of the privilege.

The moon, the stars and the holy shrine

Silver ashes of the moon
At midnight in late June
I have seen
In the absolute valley
In grey clouds of dawn
I have been.
Mehdi Shafii, personal thoughts

We travelled to Dalfard in late May or early June. The entire house contents had to be taken with us. It was too hot to leave the furniture and clothes in the locked rooms in Jiroft for four months. This was one of the reasons my mother hated that region. She felt a sense of

instability, not being settled in one place. It would take her days to
pack everything. Father used to send some men to Dalfard, ahead
of our arrival, to remove the branches from the old huts which were
by then dried and rotten, leaving the basic structure intact. They
would rebuild the huts afresh. Once we had settled in the huts, the
fresh smell of reeds remained for almost a month.

Mules, horses, bulls and donkeys were brought on the day to carry
our packages. We usually departed in the early evening. My father
would become agitated and swore at everyone for no apparent
reason. My mother supervised the loading and preparation of food
and water. My parents had their own horses to ride. We children
rode on the loaded donkeys. The female servants also rode the
donkeys but male servants and labourers walked alongside the
animals. Being heavily laden, the donkeys walked at a very slow pace
and near the end of journey they almost refused to go any further.
When I grew older I was also allowed to ride the horses. I was fairly
skilful at it although I could not compete with my mother. In the
summer of 1955, when I was in Dalfard, I tried to ride a young horse
which was not trained very well. My father warned me of possible
danger but I was too proud to back down. The horse took me forward
a few yards, then stood on her hind legs and dropped me flat on the
ground. I had a backache for some time and never tried to ride again.

After a few hours, when darkness fell, we would camp near a stream
at the outskirts of a village, which was only five miles away from
the town. Alongside the stream green henna bushes grew in
abundance. We children were not allowed to go further into the
village. The aroma of the henna's blossoms filled the air. The animals
would be unloaded and fed by the labourers. The khorjins, full of
our possessions, were arranged in a circle to protect us from the wind.
A carpet would be spread and some of our mattresses and sheets set
out for the night. We would all help gather wood for the fire. My
mother prepared a light dinner. We had already baked lots of bread
and water was carried within *mashks* (sacks made of sheepskin).
Water kept cool for hours in the mashks.

The ghanat (underground water system), which was the source
of the stream and provided water for the village, was a few hundred
yards away. This type of water network existed around most villages.
One could walk through their tunnels for miles. Every few hundred
yards there was an opening to the stream, which from above looked
like a well. We loved to enter the tunnel, play in the water and chase

the small, golden fish that danced in the coolness of the water. My mother always warned us not to go very far into the tunnel.

Soon night would fall and everything became mysterious; hot breeze, our shadows in the moonlight, the silence of the plain and the animals resting further down. Everyone spoke in whispers. We did not want to disturb the night. My father's bad temper always spoilt these little pleasures. We were frightened of provoking him. The nights were lit by the moonlight alone. Soon we would all sleep.

The journey would begin very early the next day. At three in the morning my mother was always the first to wake up and call on the others to get ready. They would hurriedly pack everything and load the animals. The children were the last to wake up. We were barely given the chance to wash. The moon, still in the middle of the sky, lit the road ahead. We would be placed on the donkeys, half asleep. After a few hours my mother would give us something to eat while still riding. We would arrive at our next stop, which was a village called Darb-Mazar, at around noon. Here, sometimes an acquaintance who lived in the village invited us for lunch, which was a real blessing. Again the animals would be unloaded and set free to graze. There was a shrine in this village which we visited every year: a dome-shaped room, located high up a hill, with a low-level door leading into it. Inside it was hazy and filled with aromatic oils. The shelves were full of ornaments, pieces of rugs and handmade kalims.

The building of these shrines has an interesting history. Sometime in the past, the village mullah or the landowner would have dreamt of an imam travelling from Arabia through the region. It was alleged that the imam had stood on the spot of land which was later considered sacred. Villagers would donate money to build the shrine and either the mullah or another person would become its patron, settling near the shrine and receiving donations thereafter.

In all, it took us three days and two nights to reach our orchards. The last resting place was a few miles into the valley. By then we were all exhausted. Fatigue showed on my mother's face but she kept up a brave appearance. Besides, father's temper did not leave any room for her to complain. At the end of the summer we returned to Jiroft with the same ritual. This time we brought back sacks full of bunches of grapes, walnut, quince and other dried fruit. If there was time, my mother made syrup from the grapes to last throughout the winter.

Departure

Aunt Iran's stay in Jiroft did not last long. Although Mr Sadjadi's brother, a teacher, had transferred himself to Jiroft and their mother came to stay, Mr Sadjadi soon asked for a transfer to his home town, Bam. This put an end to my mother's relatively happy years, when she enjoyed the company of her mother and sister. Once more she was left alone to cope with the harsh rural life.

In 1949 my aunt, being nine months pregnant with her second child, set out for Kerman at the end of the fiscal year. She had her baby son delivered on the way to Kerman. A year later, my mother became pregnant once more. She went to Kerman to have the baby delivered. My brother Mehdi, who was given the same name as my cousin, was born before Madame Sheikhi arrived. Before Mehdi, my mother bore a baby boy in Jiroft who died a few days after birth. Aunt Iran, settled in Bam and a few years later had her third child, a lovely blonde baby girl, whom they named Fatemeh.

My mother became pregnant once again in 1952. With four children already it was impossible for her to go to Kerman, so she was attended at home by a local midwife. I remember the day my sister Maryam was born. My father was nervous and walked back and forth on the veranda. We children were not allowed to go into the room where my mother was in labour. Nor did we dare to misbehave. My father was ready to smack anyone he could get hold of. Once I managed to enter the room amid my mother's screams and was told to get out immediately. Maryam was born shortly afterwards. She was a fair-skinned, plump baby whom we later loved to play with. My mother did not want to have a large family but there were no contraceptives available. Women prevented pregnancies by prolonging the lactation period. Other methods were dangerous and often fatal, although women used them if they were determined to get rid of an unwanted pregnancy. In the rural areas large families were appreciated as providing future workers.

In 1951 I finished the six years of elementary school and prepared to go to high school. Although Jiroft had expanded into a small town, it was a long way from having a girl's high school. There were not many girls who wanted to continue their studies and no qualified women teachers. The idea of sending girls onto further education instead of preparing them for marriage was not very popular. Daughters of middle-class families trained to be housewives and mothers. They learnt cooking, embroidery and other skills and waited to be wed to prominent men of their class. Although I learnt embroidery and flower patterns, I was not destined to get married at a young age. My father would have been happy to marry me to a wealthy person, but as far as my mother was concerned it was out of the question. Her own experience was far too painful to let me follow the same path.

In October, when school started, I felt trapped because I had to stay home and I cried for most of the time. Mrs Ibrahimi's second daughter, Mehri, a close friend of mine, was in the same situation. Mr Fatemi, the new head of the education department who visited our house regularly, tried to find a solution. Finally, it was decided that Mehri and I would attend the boy's classes for a few hours during the week on subjects such as maths, chemistry and physics and Mr Fatemi would be our personal tutor for the rest of the subjects. We were then able to sit for the exams. Every day, Mehri and I wrapped our tiny bodies in chadors and set out for school. We sat at the back of the class. Although we knew most of the boys, we did not speak to any of them, or even look in their direction for fear of being stigmatised and banned from the school.

I finished my first year and achieved good grades. The second year started with the same arrangements. A few months into the year, my mother decided to visit my grandmother and Aunt Iran in Bam. She took Maryam with her and the rest of us stayed with my father and the maids. While she was away Mehri and I spent most of our time together. She used to come to our house and we would climb the narrow steps to the rooftop, where we would sit for hours, chatting. We discussed our aspirations and what we wanted to do in the future. Mehri wanted to marry a prince who would take her away, while I had no intention of marrying anyone at all. From among the gardens, which stretched as far as the eye could see, we could not see a soul. Nevertheless, our rooftop expeditions, however innocent, had not been hidden from curious eyes. Women thought that out of sight of the elders we may have been planning something which would tarnish our family name and honour. A month later, when my mother returned, Mr Sadjadi's mother, who lived in a house nearby, was the first to visit and report of our 'sin'. Other women who visited my mother put pressure on her to stop sending me to the boys' school. My mother was frustrated and, in order to stop the gossip, she stopped me from attending school. Mehri faced the same fate.

Staying at home was very hard. I loved studying and was good at many subjects. Mr Fatemi was very busy and could not teach me properly. Besides, I wanted to attend a proper school. My mother and I were both desperate and often cried together. She promised to find a way to make me happy and offered to buy me a new sewing machine, which I refused. In those days, putting gold caps on your front teeth was fashionable. My mother offered to cap my teeth which, again, I refused. I shut myself away from everyone and cried day and night. Being only twelve, I could not understand why I should be banned from school. I cursed Mr Sadjadi's mother and never forgave her for starting the whole episode. Meanwhile my mother wrote a letter to my grandmother and Aunt Iran, explaining the situation. They knew too well how much I yearned to study. In those days we did not keep any secrets from each other and our problems, joys and sorrows were often shared. It was my aunt who came to my rescue. She discussed the matter with her husband and it was decided that I would go to Bam to continue my studies. Although my father did not object to the idea, he did not contribute to it either. In fact, he had already found a few suitors, something that caused severe rows between him and my mother.

Aunt Iran wrote my mother a letter proposing to become my guardian. I could not have been happier. I longed to be with my grandmother and away from Jiroft and its strict feudal-peasant culture. What I did not know at the time was the sacrifice my mother was making by separating me from herself. I was the eldest child and very close to her. Sending me away must have been very hard. I could see her tearful eyes, but the choice was between keeping me at home or sending me away to a better future. She chose the latter. She wrote a letter to Aunt Iran, confirming her decision.

Iran in turmoil, 1941–51

Throughout the 1940s Iran remained free from arbitrary rule, although that did not mean that democratic institutions took root. Some trade unions and syndicates, as well as many other associations, did indeed flourish, but the importance of oil and the consequent foreign interference, made the country unstable. In the internal political scene, a National Front became the centre of small parties and independent nationalists, while at the same time the communist movement backed by the Soviet Union expanded from a small party (the Tudeh Party), into a larger political force. The arbitrary rule of centuries had resulted in a lack of political experience, a shortcoming which the constitutionalists had also faced at the beginning of the century. The politicians, left, right and centre, began to fight amongst themselves to achieve power. Within a period of ten years, from the time that Reza Shah left, Iran witnessed numerous governments.

After the war ended in 1945 Iran remained under foreign occupation. Mr Ghavam, a notable statesman, negotiated with Britain and the Soviet Union to withdraw their troops from Iran. This did not begin until 1946, when Stalin agreed to pull his troops out. Meanwhile, politicians, including Dr Mohammed Mosadeq, an MP and the leader of the National Front, approached America, in the hope of reducing British interference. Dr Mosadeq, an aristocrat and educated nationalist, aimed to free Iran from foreign rule. He played a major role in the country's politics in years to come.

As with the oil, Iran did not benefit much from her rich resources. The Anglo–Iranian Oil Company (AIOC) paid more in British taxes than were paid as Iranian royalties. Besides, Iran did not have any control over the company's accounts and inflation had actually reduced her revenues from oil. The US companies, which by then operated in Saudi Arabia, offered more favourable terms.

In the early 1950s Dr Mosadeq, in collaboration with some members of the parliament, put a motion to the parliament to nationalise oil. People overwhelmingly favoured this motion. After the motion passed through the parliament, Mosadeq became a national hero and the Shah was forced to appoint him as prime minister. The British and some other Western countries, angry at the nationalisation of the oil, waged a world-wide campaign against Iran. An embargo, led by the British, was imposed and warships were sent to the Persian Gulf. In addition, the British took the case to the United Nations. Dr Mosadeq attended the UN session in October 1951, and his eloquent speech and reasoning convinced the members to vote in his favour. Although the British lost their case in the UN, in anger and frustration they took it to The Hague International Tribunal. The team of Iranian lawyers managed to win the case once more. During this period the Americans gave Dr Mosadeq the impression that they had sided with Iran. In reality, fearful that Iran might fall into the hands of the communists, they secretly supported the British. Together, they waged a campaign to undermine Dr Mosadeq's plans and discredit him. At the time, Iran provided 10 per cent of the world's oil consumption and Britain and the US were fearful that this might fall into the hands of the 'reds' after the death of Stalin in 1952.

Simultaneously, Mohammed Reza Shah, who for almost a decade had remained on the sidelines, entered the political arena by giving the peasants the deeds his father had taken from the landowners by force. By then, he had divorced his first wife, Princess Fouzieh, an Egyptian princess, and married a woman (Queen Soraya), whose mother was German and father an influential Bakhtiari tribal chief of southern Iran. Although in the course of the nationalisation of the oil industry Dr Mosadeq developed differences with the Shah, he did not want the monarchy removed. He wanted the Shah to remain a constitutional monarch, and not to interfere in the country's affairs; something the Shah had indeed aimed to do. The pro-British members of the parliament, on the other hand, were opposed to Dr Mosadeq's policies on oil and in collaboration with other opponents hampered the bills he put to the parliament in order to take over the oil installations from the AIOC. So, in the end, Dr Mosadeq was forced to put the dissolution of the seventeenth session of the parliament to a referendum. Although the opponents declared the referendum illegal, people supported Dr Mosadeq's proposal overwhelmingly and showed their support in street demonstrations and public gatherings. At this time, the communist Tudeh Party was the only major political group outside the parliament which opposed Dr Mosadeq's policies and played a crucial role in undermining his attempts in the process of oil nationalisation. The Tudeh Party called the nationalisation an 'imperialist plot' and only in the last stages of Dr Mosadeq's premiership, when it sensed the dangers of a coup, stopped its attacks and opportunistically showed him some support.

In the US, at the same time, during the presidential elections, the outgoing Truman administration had hoped that a British–American joint venture would take over the oil distribution. This was rejected by Dr Mosadeq. Eventually, the Americans, who at the beginning answered Dr Mosadeq's calls positively and supported him, could not tolerate his independent stand. Their hostilities intensified when the Republicans won office in 1952 and General Eisenhower became president. Meanwhile, in Iran, the embargo imposed by the British began to have its effects and the increasing differences between the royal court and Dr Mosadeq created a political as well as an economic crisis. Unemployment escalated, prices soared and the case of the political murder of General Afshartous, Dr Mosadeq's chief of police, threw the country into chaos. Now the Americans, along with the

British, planned to topple Dr Mosadeq and reinstate the Shah's power, who had promised to cooperate with them in full. In line with this, the CIA and MI6 drew up the plan for a *coup d'état*. General Zahedi, a top-ranking officer and the Shah's confidant, was selected to replace Dr Mosadeq. This was in August 1953.

I witness the coup, 1953

The bridge of familiar voices is broken
And in the distance
The massive chains of despair
Have stopped the movement of all bright planets.
Shadab Vajdi, 'Distance'

In the summer of 1953 I was in Kerman with my grandmother. I was thirteen years old. I had recently discovered a bookshop in the bazaar which sold story books. There were no bookshops in Jiroft. I loved to get money from my grandmother to buy books. The first book I bought was a translation of *Les Miserables*. I sat at home for hours and finished it. There were books on the French Revolution and stories by Alexander Dumas and some other European writers. Persians writers were far behind their Europeans counterparts in writing novels, fiction and stories.

In the afternoon of August 18, my grandmother and I, unaware of the outside world, set out for Shahpoor Street for a stroll. This was Kerman's high street. Before we reached it, we heard the sound of shouting and saw a crowd running towards the street. Curious, we followed and saw thousands of people gathered on both pavements of the street. Army personnel were marching and soldiers were patrolling in their jeeps. The shops had their shutters down and a sombre mood dominated. Everyone seemed agitated somehow. That was the *coup d'état* day, one of the darkest days in our history. For the first time in centuries we had an independent state, run by Dr Mosadeq, whom people trusted; now it was all being destroyed before our eyes.

Throughout the country groups of thugs and hooligans, who were paid cash by the CIA and MI6, had attacked every office and establishment that belonged to the National Front and the communist Tudeh Party. In Tehran, members of Dr Mosadeq's cabinet had been arrested. A group of thugs, led by a man called Shaban Jafari, had taken control of Tehran's streets. The part of the army loyal to the Shah had destroyed Dr Mosadeq's house, in an effort to capture him. He escaped from danger via the back garden; his bodyguards were all killed. The army took control of important establishments and thousands were arrested on the spot. Many fled the country in haste.

The communist Tudeh Party, the biggest mass organisation with thousands of members, trade unions, syndicates and offices throughout the country, withdrew its partial backing of Dr Mosadeq at the last minute. Although the party was in a position to mobilise the people, it left them with no specific directives as to what they might do on the morning of the coup. The primary aim of the party's leadership was to get themselves out of the country, while the grass root organisations had to face the blows from those supporting the Shah. Dr Mosadeq's foreign minister, Dr Fatemi, was among those arrested and later, along with many others, executed. Later, Dr Mosadeq surrendered himself to the military generals who took power. He was put on trial for the dissolution of the parliament and not obeying the Shah's orders. The military court found him guilty of the charges and sentenced him to three years' imprisonment and thereafter permanent house arrest. The Shah was too frightened to have him executed. He was an old statesman, much loved by the people, and the Shah did not want to make a martyr out of him.

On the day of coup in Kerman, many figures of authority were arrested and some killed on the spot. The shrieks of 'Down with Mosadeq', 'Viva the King' could be heard. We were in the street, watching the crowd, when I noticed a jeep driving slowly and people watching in amazement. When it reached where we were standing, I noticed a corpse being dragged behind the jeep. We were very frightened. My grandmother, holding my hand, tried to find a way out of the crowd. She lost one of her shoes while we ran towards home. The corpse belonged to Colonel Sakhai, head of the police force and one of Dr Mosadeq's supporters. Nobody knows how many were killed on that day. Iran went under another dictatorship.

Chapter Four

Bam, a town south-west of Kerman

Bam is located on the borders of the salt desert Lut, a hundred and fifty miles to the south-west of Kerman. A few miles outside the town the desert stretches for hundreds of miles. Bam's weather is dry and rain scarce. At night, close above your head, the desert sky is full of glittering stars.

Bam was once a prosperous town and the centre of the textile industry of southern Persia. However, after centuries of invasions by different tribes, the infrastructure of this industry was destroyed and from the seventeenth century onwards people cultivated plantations, growing oranges, palm trees, henna and pomegranate. Irrigation of the gardens and farmlands was mainly by the subterranean water system which had been developed in the pre-Islamic era. To this day, the best Iranian dates, pomegranate and henna come from Bam. Outside the town, mountain ranges appear on one side and the desert on the other. If you travel for about an hour into the mountains, valleys covered with orchards and villages come into sight. Here, the weather is cool and summer fruits plentiful. Many of the rich own lands and orchards in the valleys where they spend their summers.

Agha Mohammed Khan, the founder of the Qajar Dynasty, was the last person to invade Kerman and Bam in the nineteenth century. The pyramid he made from the people's heads remained in Bam for fifteen years. His policy was to support the feudal landowners who had confiscated most of the rich lands from the farmers. For this reason Bam remains a town with a highly structured class system. It has a minority of rich aristocrats, with artisans, small businesses and peasants making up the rest of the population. In 1953 there were 500 large landowners. Those who were related to them, either by blood or marriage, controlled the town's economy and commerce. At the beginning of this century, Reza Shah, en route from Zahedan, passed through Bam and ordered further development of the town. Two main streets were built, cutting through the orchards of the wealthiest landowner Sardar Mojalal. The old bazaar was renovated and government offices built in the town centre.

According to the official census, in 1956 the population of Bam was 78,076. Most houses in Bam were located in the middle of orange gardens and parts of each garden were allocated for growing pomegranate. Around the garden walls red roses were planted for extracting rose water. Streams and brooks, their source the underground water system outside the town, passed through every garden. Streets were mainly narrow, with high walls on either side. At the end of winter and beginning of spring, roses bloomed, oranges blossomed and their mixed aromas filled the streets. Sometimes a stream stretched alongside the streets for some distance, suddenly disappearing into a garden through a narrow opening. In the 1950s Bam was a mixture of ancient gardens and ancient traditions with people who lived in between the old and the new times.

Farewell home, sweet home

It was September 1954 and the schools were about to start. My mother packed my suitcase and we set off for Bam. I was unsure of what was to follow and had mixed feelings about leaving home. I was glad that I was getting away from the peasant society of Jiroft. I was sad because I was leaving my brothers and sisters and my childhood behind. Aunt Iran, her husband, and above all my grandmother, had assured my mother that I would be fine and that she should not worry. Mr Sadjadi, who by then had been appointed as a school inspector, registered my name at Parvin High School, the only one in town. The school was located in the middle of the bazaar, far away from my aunt's house. It was an hour's walking distance. My mother had already made the uniform and a cotton chador for me. As in Jiroft, no one went to school unveiled. Once inside the compound, we took off the chador.

The school building was old and gloomy. Several classrooms circled the courtyard. A pond with stale, green water stood in the middle. There was no playground or any recreation facility. It reminded me of my first school in Kerman. We had both male and female teachers. Men taught science subjects, women Persian literature, English, drawing and so on. I could hardly understand the sciences. I had not properly studied them in Jiroft. It was then suggested that it would be better for my future if I started afresh in a lower grade. I agreed reluctantly. It meant that I would be a year behind. This, though hard to accept, helped me to catch up with the lessons. I was very good in subjects such as literature, English language and essay writing.

Mr Sadjadi's father had divided his property amongst his four children, giving the two girls half of their brothers' share, only keeping a house and a garden for himself. Bam had this unique custom. When children grew old enough to marry, if parents had properties and wealth in excess of their own needs, they would divide them among the children. This way young adults had enough assets to start independent life comfortably. In other towns parents kept everything for themselves until they died. Fights broke out and disappointments were experienced among the children after the parents were gone. According to Islamic law, which was the state law, boys inherited twice as much as girls.

Mr Sadjadi's house was a big compound. Its entrance was through a barn where they kept cows and chickens. A gardener with his family lived near this barn. The actual house's wooden gate opened onto a dark corridor. This led to a central courtyard around which several rooms were located. On the right hand side of this corridor there was a big guest room. A howzkhouneh, with a pond in the middle and a high chimney with huge openings, was located at the far end of the courtyard. A second corridor opened onto a back garden. The garden was full of orange, palm and pomegranate trees and a stream passed through it. Underneath this wing a door opened down to a basement. The basement was dark and cool in the summer and had a tunnel at the end which opened to the garden. In the summer the wind from the garden came through the tunnel, cooling the basement. Here grandmother used to keep tens of bottles of distilled herbs and vegetables, pickles, jams and other fruit.

Aunt Iran was the head of a primary school in the neighbourhood and my grandmother, who by then had lost her own household, lived with them permanently. She did not have her own independent life or any friends or relatives in Bam. All her associates were Mr Sadjadi's relatives and occasional guests of Aunt Iran from the school. Mr Sadjadi respectfully treated her as part of 'his' household. She did not have much income; only some money from the land she, my mother and aunt had bought in Jiroft, after selling what they owned in Bardsir. She had the role of housekeeper, although there were plenty of maids and servants around. She had a room to herself on the east side of the house. The room was simple with a few pieces of furniture. Her situation was typical of widows and unmarried daughters, who joined part of the family and helped with the household and children. When I arrived I was not given a separate room; instead, I joined my grandmother. Unlike our house in Jiroft, which had little furniture, Aunt Iran's house was full of embroidery, Persian rugs, crystals, china and plenty of copper pots and pans.

Unlike my father, who was irresponsible and left all the burdens of life on my mother's shoulders, Mr Sadjadi was very authoritative and strong. He had full control over everything, the household, children and money. As a result there were constant arguments over money. He wanted to control Aunt Iran's salary, which she often refused. Although he was addicted to opium, this did not affect his ability to control his household. For years, even before I went to Bam, he and my aunt had quarrelled over his addiction and had at some stage come close to divorce. He had never bowed to my aunt's wish and made no effort to wean himself off opium. It was only when his health deteriorated years later that he eventually stopped.

In Kerman addiction to opium was as common as modern-day cigarette smoking. Nevertheless, most women hated their husband's opium smoking habit. Very few were as determined as my mother in forcing their husbands to break it forever. On the whole, Aunt Iran and Mr Sadjadi were very fond of each other and had a lot in common. Apart from the occasions when they were cross with each other, they chatted constantly and played backgammon throughout the long winter nights. Their boasting, cheating and laughter could be heard late into the night. They had a large circle of friends from the education department and town's dignitaries. Every once in a while they entertained people who stayed for lunch or dinner. On such occasions grandmother was busy preparing for days beforehand.

Mr Sadjadi was a very literate man. He had read and kept lots of books and subscribed to almost every magazine and newspaper published in Tehran. Once I had settled in Bam, I discovered a room near my grandmother's full of magazines and books. I was thrilled. Nothing gave me more pleasure than drowning myself in reading. Every afternoon after I returned from school I went to this room, which had a musty smell of old papers, and read until someone finally came to fetch me. In Jiroft, apart from a few books which I had bought, there was no real literature available. The only books which could be found were the Quoran and the collections of Hafiz and

Sa'adi's poetry books. My mother was too busy with her daily life and reading was not my father's concern. In years to come I read almost all there was in that secret hideaway. I memorised poems and read hundreds of stories which appeared in monthly magazines. Most of the literature was poetry or about poets. There is barely a literate Iranian who has not written a few lines of poetry, at some point, out of love, depression or just to praise nature and life. We read Hafiz, Sa'adi, Ferdowsi and other great Persian poets and cherished them. Novels and stories became popular from the 1960s onwards. Ironically, out of thousands of poets, there are only a handful of women. The only female poet I knew of in my adolescence was Parvin Etesami, who wrote about general issues and sometimes advised women to be virtuous and to accept their miserable fate.

Adolescent years

A few months into the year I was busy with my studies and the new environment. I felt distanced, not belonging in the way I did at home. Although everyone was very kind and considerate, I was homesick. Being only thirteen, I had to grow up quickly to understand the customs and culture of the people around me. I had to watch out for myself and to behave properly and observe all the unwritten rules of the new society. I found out that Bam's society was much stricter than Jiroft's. I remembered now that it was Mr Sadjadi's mother who had first alarmed my mother about my rooftop 'secret', which had finally forced me to emigrate from Jiroft. These people were more urbanised and therefore more rules, customs and traditions prevailed. In those days it was unusual for parents to send their daughters away just for the sake of studying. My aunt had to do a great deal of explaining and in return I was not allowed to misbehave. I was expected to be a 'perfect' girl in order to stay with my aunt to continue school. Difficult as it was, I bowed to all these restrictions and confined myself to studying.

My grandmother, who was by then in her fifties, was a world of love and compassion. Even before I went to Bam, I was her favourite grandchild. She made sure I had everything I needed. She would keep extra food and fruits for me to eat at bedtime. She always thought that I did not eat enough when sitting with the others at the sofreh. She prepared my lunch box and made sure she cooked the food I liked. Although my father had agreed to send money or goods for my expenses, he rarely did. Aunt Iran and her husband, however, never mentioned or showed any sign of dissatisfaction regarding my expenses. It was I who felt a burden. The first year, my mother, who often wrote to me and my grandmother, invited the whole family to Jiroft for Nowrooz. When we arrived, it seemed like I had been away for a long time. My mother did everything to compensate for the months I had not been there. Although I was glad to be home, I felt no desire to live in Jiroft again. In my mind that was decided forever.

And so life went on and three years passed. By 1957 I was grown up and was more mature than my peers. I was more independent and made my own decisions. I chose my dresses for Nowrooz and ordered shoes to be made from the patterns I saw in magazines. I cut my grandmother's and Aunt Iran's hair and above all I was a very good student at school. Teachers, who came to visit us at home, took a personal interest in me and praised my courage and determination in getting ahead of many girls who had a more comfortable life.

Some of the girls who belonged to wealthy families looked down on those who were not of their rank. One such girl was Sahba, the only daughter of a famous landowner. She was two years my senior. She had her dresses made in Tehran and came to school with a driver. Before she finished high school rumours spread that she was to be married to one of her father's foremen, who was years older than her. Nobody knew why; had she fallen in love with the man, or was she seduced by him? We heard all sorts of gossip. He brought her lots of presents from Tehran, including a case of Pepsi Cola. No one else at the time knew how it tasted. Eventually they married and Sahba left school to become a wealthy housewife.

Later our school moved to a new building outside the bazaar. The purpose-built building was two storeys high, with a big yard containing a volleyball and tennis court, and table-tennis located on the ground floor. I started playing tennis with some of the male teachers. For almost a year I woke up at five in the morning and arrived at school at seven to play until the bell rang. Two of the young teachers who were graduates of Tehran University were my tennis partners. I became very good at tennis and in a competition I won the trophy.

After the 1953 coup Americans had poured into the country. A programme under the title of Point Four had been introduced. Under the plan Iran received about $23.4 million worth of aid. Point

Four's programmes concentrated on the development of rural areas, reforming irrigation systems and establishing healthcare centres and educational establishments. Those Iranians who spoke good English were recruited by Point Four and my mother's cousin, Hassan Khan, was one of them. The Americans, by injecting money into Iran's economy, became serious rivals to the British who had been there for 150 years.

In 1957, in mid-term, the headmistress announced that a group of distinguished figures of authority were due to visit Bam and she wanted us to welcome them when they arrived. One of my classmates, Zahra Assad Pur, who was the daughter of a wealthy landowner, was assigned to read a welcome message. On the day they arrived we had our best uniforms on and went to the street in front of the governor's office to greet them. The girls stood in line, unveiled, the boys alongside them. The head of the delegation was Dr Eqbal, the new prime minister, accompanied by a few Americans. After they left, the school received boxes of presents. We were told that the American youth had sent the presents as a gesture of friendship. My share was some pencils and colourful writing pads which I kept for years as a souvenir.

In the middle of our fourth year, in 1958, a girl whose brother was an army officer assigned to Bam, joined our class. Soheila, a tall, attractive and very outspoken girl, came from Tehran. Her arrival changed the ethos of our closed community. She had already had boyfriends in Tehran and after she settled in Bam rumours spread that she was having affairs with one of the wealthy gigolos. Up until then speaking about boys had been taboo and those who expressed such interests were branded as 'bad', which was enough to make them the talk of the town. We were constantly being advised to wait until our parents found us a suitable husband but, in secret, everyone fancied someone. Male teachers were always the first targets that girls fell for. Their feelings did not go further than a confession to a confidante, or writing poetry in the margin of books the teacher taught. Teachers were very vulnerable to accusations and tried hard not to pay attention to any girl who might want to get close to them. Girls were supposed to marry the man their parents chose for them. It must be said that the custom had lapsed since my mother's time, with my aunt being the best example of such change, but there were still rules to observe.

Soon after Soheila arrived we saw boys wondering across the road near the school gate. Soheila came to school unveiled, had faint

make-up on and looked at the boys in eager anticipation. First we
were frightened to befriend her. After a few months she was one of
the best friends we had. She was a happy, normal girl who had been
brought up in the more liberated atmosphere of Tehran. After her
arrival some of the boys found the courage to pass a love message
to the girls they fancied.

In April and May, Bam was full of red roses and fresh red apples.
Boys spent time in writing a word or two on a rose petal to put on
a girls' hands as they passed through a narrow street. God knows
how many petals were ruined before a correct word came through.
Fresh May apples were much better for the purpose. One could carve
a poem or short message and drop the apple in front of the sweetheart.
The boys knew only too well that the possibility of a closer encounter
was very remote. Nevertheless, they tried their luck. Soheila
encouraged many of us to talk to some of the boys, but we were
too frightened of the possible scandal.

Life in Bam was not as dull as I had imagined. Gradually, I found
a large circle of friends. I went to their houses or spoke to them on
the phone for hours. The telephone system was connected via an
operator who was able to connect three houses at the same time.
We went on picnics at the weekends or visited relatives. By 1958
Mr Sadjadi had bought a jeep, which was started by turning a handle
in front of the engine, while he sat at the wheel. He took the whole
family to the villages nearby. Sometimes his cousins and their families
came along as well and on these occasions we made a group of about
forty people. The gardens outside Bam covered enormous areas. Rows
of oranges, palm trees and henna bushes could be seen for miles.
Mr Sadjadi also went deer hunting on the outskirts of Bam, near
the mountains, where deer were plentiful. When he shot more than
one my aunt would divide the meat among all the relatives. They
could also keep the meat for a week in the refrigerator. Unlike my
mother, who did not have one, my aunt had purchased a refrigerator
when they moved to Bam. It worked with oil.

In general, I was doing well at school, although maths and physics
were difficult to understand. By the time I finished high school my
English was far better than my teacher, Mrs Gerami's. Among the
teachers, our Persian literature teacher was keen to instil his knowledge
in us, to teach us to the best of his ability. Sa'idi Sirjani was a young,
romantic poet who had already published two volumes of his work.
While studying at Tehran University, in the early 1950s, he had fallen
in love with a girl and most of his poetry was related to that period.

His love had created a scandal which almost cost him his degree. In years to come, he became one of the prominent masters of Persian literature. In 1994, imprisoned for being critical of the Islamic regime, he died in what some would describe as suspicious circumstances. His wife and two daughters never found out what really happened to him. When I heard of his death, and the international outcry that followed, I remembered the young, outspoken man, who expressed his first love in his passionate poetry.

From 1957 onwards my grandmother complained of constant stomach aches. She could not eat properly and sometimes vomited during the day. I loved her so much that any sign of her discomfort made me very anxious. The doctor came round and prescribed medicines but the pain would return after a while. Despite this problem, grandmother fasted during the month of Ramadan, which was the month of fasting and mortification. During the long hours from dawn to dusk she would not eat or drink anything. Grandmother was the only one in our family who took her religious duties seriously and could not be persuaded to stop observing them. I used to wake up to keep her company and would fast two or three days just to please her. Our family did not observe religious rituals in a strict way and hence we were not brought up to perform such duties properly.

During the six years that I spent in Bam, Nowrooz was the happiest time of the year. My mother and Aunt Iran had agreed on a rota for the two-week holiday. When it was my aunt's turn in Bam, grandmother would mobilise everyone for the preparations. All through the day, the scent of the newly blossomed orange buds and the distilled herbs which came out of the cellar would fill the courtyard. At night, when my grandmother came to bed, exhausted after the long day's work, she would smell of the sweet scent of saffron, which decorated the cookies with a bright orange colour.

My mother would usually send some money, prior to the New Year, for my extra expenses. I always went to the shoemaker and ordered new shoes. Nylon stockings had just arrived in Bam and I had purchased a pair. I loved to wear them on Nowrooz visits, with my new-style shoes. By the late 1950s a bus service operated between the two towns of Jiroft and Bam. Still, it took a whole day to travel the hundred mile distance. While all together, we would go picnicking, or visit the *Imamzadeh* (the holy shrine). Mr Sadjadi's relatives came around. From early in the morning until late at night, my grandmother, mother and Aunt Iran spent their time together, talking and laughing. On departure, they decided on where to spend the summer holidays.

It was 1959 and I was about to finish high school. I was determined to enter the university to get a degree. By then, most of my classmates knew what they wanted to do. Families in Bam were reluctant to send their daughters away to Tehran to continue their studies, although boys were sent immediately they finished school. Even before we finished school a few girls got married and left, before getting their diploma. Our biology teacher married one of our classmates. They held a grand ceremony although none of us were invited. The teacher, being in his mid-thirties and feeling embarrassed about marrying such a young girl, would not look us in the eyes for a long time after he returned from his honeymoon.

In the summer of 1959, while I was with my family in Kerman, my mother found out that she was pregnant once more. She was 38 by then and another child was the last thing she wanted. Being distressed, she did everything to abort it. Most days she would be seen carrying the heavy stone mortar, running around the courtyard. We thought she was losing her sanity. She cried a lot but in the end she could not abort the child and had to accept the pregnancy. It was my final year and I had to work hard to get a good grade for the university. There were not many universities in Iran then. Tehran and some big cities, such as Mashed, Isfahan, Shiraz and Tabriz, were among the few. To enter the university or higher education colleges, one had to take the lengthy and difficult entrance exams, since the number of applicants were far more than the places available and competition was stiff.

Unfortunately, in mid-February, I became ill with a high fever. The doctor was unable to diagnose my illness. There were no laboratories then and the medicines available could not cure me. I stayed in bed for almost three months. By then, I was so weak and thin that I could not get out of bed. My grandmother and Aunt Iran did everything they could, but at the end of the second month they thought it would be wise to inform my mother. She had just given birth to a baby boy, whom she named Massoud. When she heard of my illness she came to Bam immediately, with the baby who was only twenty-five days old. Eventually my fever abated and I was able to get out of bed. By then I had missed a lot of schooling and was not sure if I would be able to catch up. Some of the teachers and my friends who regularly visited me helped with the lessons. Although it was very hard, I raced against time and passed the final year with relatively good grades.

In mid-May, I went to Kerman to attend an entrance exam for the Tehran Teacher's Training College. There were many candidates including most of my schoolmates. I was due to travel to Tehran for the university exams shortly after school finished. My grandmother had volunteered to accompany me. Although she was ill for most of the time, she would not send me on my own. In the early 1950s some of my mother's cousins on her mother's side, including Nahid, who was married to an army colonel, had settled in Tehran. Nahid was very close to us all. My grandmother wrote her a letter, explaining my situation. She agreed we could stay with them until I knew what I wanted to do.

Chapter Five

Iran in the aftermath of the coup, 1953–60

After the Shah reinstated himself, the country's policies and priorities changed direction. Two things happened simultaneously. At an international level, a few months after the coup, several American and British delegates visited the oil refinery in Abadan in the south of Iran and fresh negotiations over the terms of a new contract after the nationalisation of the oil industry began. Although the British had lost their demands both at the United Nations and at The Hague, they put pressure on Iran to negate Dr Mosadeq's proposal of an equal share for Iran. Apart from that, they were seeking compensation for lost revenues. In addition, the Americans had entered the scene and demanded a share as well. After negotiations, a new Consortium comprising Americans, British and Iranians was established and a contract was drawn up, in which Iran's share was reduced to a quarter of what Mosadeq had proposed. The 'Contract of the Sale of Oil and Gas' was even more discriminatory than the old one.

At the domestic level, a wave of arrests and executions followed immediately after the coup. There were about 600 arrests, mainly of members of the National Front and the communist Tudeh Party. Well-known opponents were sent into exile to the remote Khark island and other places. A famous journalist, Karimpour Shirazi, who had openly criticised Princess Ashraf's private life, was allegedly set alight and burnt to death.

As for the Tudeh Party, many of its leaders and top-ranking army officers, who were unable to escape in time, were arrested. They were put on military trial and either received the death penalty or long prison sentences. Some of those who were captured 'confessed' to their crimes and signed letters of condemnation of their former comrades. Newspapers and magazines which had flourished during the earlier decade were banned and their offices were closed. The free expression of thought and speech became once more a thing of the past. People started to whisper their thoughts.

Richard Nixon visited Iran a few months after the coup and announced that he was glad that 'In all Asian countries, the destructive forces have withdrawn and the forces of development were gaining momentum.' Mosadeq, at his concluding speech in his trial said, 'My only crime was that I nationalised the Iranian oil and put an end to the colonial influence of the biggest empire.'

Further to the increased presence of the British, who had left during the oil nationalisation but now returned to claim their offices, Americans and other foreign investors poured into Iran. Thousands were employed by the new Consortium. The policy of open doors attracted more than 500 big companies to Iran. Now America, by granting the biggest aid package and credits to Iran, was able to dictate its policies.

Among the programmes put forward by the Americans were the abolition of the traditional system of agriculture, the expansion of a consumer economy, the development of the urban middle class and the establishment of an assembly-line industry. Although by then the British had recruited more Iranian politicians to their freemasonry ranks, nevertheless they were not able to compete with the level of American financial investment and the influence which that bestowed.

The generation of Iranians who had studied in America in the 1940s and 1950s returned to run the country. They replaced those older and more experienced statesmen who were mainly trained in Europe. By the mid-1950s the Shah, now in his late thirties, gradually took control of the country. His secret police (SAVAC), along with parts of army intelligence, were trained by MOSSAD of Israel and the CIA of America. Under a US initiative, the Shah entered a new security treaty with Turkey, Pakistan and Iraq and signed many contracts with the US to expand Iran's military capacity.

Social change

In the mid-1950s, the Shah divorced his second wife, Queen Soraya, because she could not bear children. He needed an heir to the throne. Farah Diba, a student at an art college at Sorbonne University in Paris, was chosen as the Shah's third wife and mother to the crown prince. They married in a lavish ceremony. In years to come Queen Farah portrayed herself as an intellectual, liberal woman, in support of the development of art, music and cinema. She bore four children and in the later stages of the Pahlavis' rule became involved in politics, a rival to Princess Ashraf, the Shah's twin sister.

In 1959 a Women's Association, headed by Princess Ashraf, was established. Princess Ashraf was the only woman from the Pahlavi Dynasty who got involved in politics, from the running of the country, the economy, and international affairs to women's issues. Rumours around her life-style, the number of lovers she had and her involvement in the running of the golden triangle of drug trafficking in Asia were spreading all the time. Whether she was as powerful and corrupt as was claimed, or she was being tarnished for interfering in the men's world, needs further examination. What the public understood was her determination to support her brother and her ability to influence his politics.

In the period after the coup, a programme of land reform was put forward by the Americans. However, distribution of land did not go ahead until much later. Pursuing the open door policy, by the beginning of the 1960s more than one thousand foreign companies operated in Iran and big merchants, who until then had supported a national economy, became official representatives of these companies.

The social policy of Americanisation replaced the radical Left policies of the previous decade. This put its mark on everything: radio, film, theatre, cinema and the press. In 1956 the first TV station was established by an entrepreneur, Mr Sabet Pasal. Two years later the state-owned television station opened as part of a public broadcasting company. In 1959 the Iranian National Airline was established and General Khademi, a faithful officer to the Shah, be-came its president.

In art and music new faces appeared on the scene. In literature, especially novels and poetry, Iran witnessed the emergence of new styles, some borrowed from the West. Poets such as Nima, Akhavan and writers such as Hedayat, Jamalzadeh and Simin Daneshvar had already revolutionised Persian literature. This decade witnessed the emergence of feminist poets and writers such as Simin Behbehani and Forough Farokhzad. Forough's direct approach to the female expression of sexuality was a new phenomenon which brought controversial debates into Iranian literature. Her work didn't rely on the stereotypical shy, submissive and virtuous female who was constantly in search of love and protection. She spoke of her deep feelings and experiences. No woman had previously had the courage to break the taboos and speak about her sexuality openly. Forough soon became the symbol of courage and independence, a woman who represented our generation and our aspirations, a woman who we all yearned to be. Her sudden death in 1963 deprived us of one of our most radical feminists.

While in the 1940s the pro-Soviet Tudeh Party imported Russian films, translated socialist literature and opened theatres and cinemas which showed heroic, radical revolutionary art, after the coup American junk movies and lumpen populist shows expanded rapidly. Cabarets, casinos and nightclubs mushroomed. Needless to say other sectors of the economy developed in line with government policies. The building of roads, factories, new banks and commercial businesses expanded rapidly. Several universities and colleges opened in the big cities and foreign tutors poured in. As a result of economic prosperity, due to the sale of more crude oil and American aid, foreign goods became plentiful, while at the same time, the rural areas, which made up about 70 per cent of the population, declined rapidly.

In search of a better future

No one can fish a pearl
In a humble stream
That ends into a marsh.
   Forough Farokhzad, *Rebirth*

Soon after I finished my final exams my grandmother and I set off for Tehran, which was about a thousand miles away. A regular bus service ran between Kerman and Tehran. I took off my chador and travelled unveiled; although Grandmother wished me to take my chador with me until we reached Tehran I convinced her to leave it behind. The veil and such tight restrictions belonged to smaller societies.

The journey took three days. First we stopped for lunch and then stayed overnight in the city of Yazd in the heart of the desert. Yazd was a large, ancient city where buildings and houses seemed to be suited to the environment; dome-shaped roofs with high wind turrets, the colour of the surrounding plateau; dusty-beige. There were many farms in the distance stretching into the barren land. Irrigation was provided by the subterranean water system. People of Yazd were famous for their hard work on these farms which produced many products, including the best Iranian melons. Yazd was also well-known for its quality gold, silver and special sweets, cookies and halva. After we arrived at the bus station and got a room at a guest house, my grandmother suggested that we go to the bazaar for shopping and sightseeing. Women were not allowed to walk on the streets of Yazd unveiled, so I had to borrow a chador. Yazd was a strict, religious city and did not tolerate new ideas. People were as tough as the desert around them and had kept to their traditional way of life no matter what changes had occurred in other parts of the country.

The next morning we set off early, and reached Isfahan in the evening. Because of its beauty and historic sights, Isfahan has been called 'half the world'. During the Safavid dynasty Isfahan was the capital of Iran. They had built tens of castles, mosques, hamams and towers, not to mention the bazaar with its many passages and hundreds of shops.

The next day we drove the whole day, only stopping for lunch at Quom, the holy town and centre of the religious schools and madrases. We then drove the whole night and arrived in Tehran at dawn. I was astonished and thrilled at the sight of so many streets and buildings in one place. Compared to where I came from the capital seemed huge. We took a taxi and went to my mother's cousin, Nahid. Jiroft, Bam and my family seemed far away. That was in June 1960.

Tehran, the city of opportunity

We arrived in Tehran amid new developments. Back home we had not been aware of these. All we knew was what we heard on the radio and read in the state-controlled media. The intense publicity to portray the Shah as 'the shadow of God' and the 'saviour of the people' could well be digested in the remote areas of a vast country like Iran. We grew up respecting the Shah and even sometimes praying for his health. We were happy he divorced his wife Queen Soraya, who could not bear children. Magazines and newspapers were decorated with the royal family's pictures and the grand wedding of the Shah to his third wife. Soon they had a son which thrilled us. She even delivered the baby in one of the hospitals in the south of Tehran, where the poor lived in shanty towns. How considerate and sweet of them to do such a thing, we thought.

Compared to Bam or Jiroft, Tehran was a giant city. It already had a population of about a million. Tehran had been built about two hundred years ago on the slopes of the Alborz mountains, close to the ancient city of Rey. The Alborz mountain range stretches from the north-west to the north-east of the country in a straight line. At the eastern end the Damavand peak can be seen on sunny, clear days. These mountain ranges shield Tehran from the north of the country. The rest of the city is an open plateau stretching as far as the desert of central Iran. There were hundreds of villages and small towns on all sides of the city, some of which were swallowed up by urban expansion in later years. During the last two centuries Tehran has expanded from a small village to a city of 700 square kilometres with a population of fifteen million (unofficial reports of 1995). Tehran is divided into different areas. The densely populated south, with small houses along narrow alleyways, and the north, which has traditionally accommodated the rich and middle classes. From the 1950s onwards shanty towns mushroomed around the south and east of the city and luxurious apartment blocks and mini castles expanded in the north.

Reza Shah contributed to the architecture of Tehran by building the longest avenue, Pahlavi Avenue, which starts from the farthest part of the north, near the mountains in the district of Shemiran, and continues across the city to the main railway station in the south of the city. Thousands of plane trees were planted along both sides of Pahlavi Avenue. Over the years, thousands of roads, streets and alleyways, lined with houses, were built parallel to, or crossing, Pahlavi Avenue in straight lines. Reza Shah built his castles and government administration buildings near the city centre. He also built other castles in the north of the city in Shemiran. By the 1950s Tehran was a prosperous city with many bazaars, shopping areas, cinemas, theatres, restaurants, cafés, museums and libraries. There were tens of roundabouts with the statues of famous kings, poets and writers. At the centre of Shah Reza Avenue, which cut Pahlavi Avenue, in front of Tehran University, stood Reza Shah's giant statue, showing him riding a horse, conveying the might of his power.

Since Tehran was built on the slopes of the Alborz mountains, the difference in altitude in the north and the south of the city is significant. Streams of underground water which surface in almost every big street, rush downwards towards the south, taking all the rubbish and dirt with them. Tehran is not a green city, although trees were planted alongside all the streets and in the courtyards. Being close to the desert of central Iran, the climate is dry; hot in the summer and cold in the winter.

My cousin Nahid's rented house was located in the south-east of the city, a two-storey terraced building which had a courtyard in the front. Upstairs, there was a big room used as a stock room. We were offered half of that room. Grandmother hung a curtain to divide the room and we settled in temporarily.

Nahid had five children. She was a very attractive and kind woman who had travelled throughout Iran with her husband. Army officers were assigned to posts in the small towns for periods of two to three years. While on such assignments they received lots of allowances and benefits; a junior soldier as their servant and free accommodation. Once they were transferred to the city permanently, all fringe benefits were cut and they were left with a meagre salary which was not enough to run a household. Most officers accepted bribes and commissions which helped them to have a comfortable life. Colonel Naderi, Nahid's husband, was not among them.

Upon arrival I was not sure if I would ever be able to travel through Tehran on my own with all the crowds, cars and noise. On the streets of the central and north parts of the city women and young girls were seen in fashionable clothes, without stockings; their legs clean shaven, their eyebrows well groomed. I had hairy legs and thick eyebrows. I was ashamed of that but I did not dare to ask my grandmother or cousin Nahid for advice. Grandmother would have killed me if she had known that I was thinking of such things before anything else.

Nahid's brother, Hassan Khan, often visited us. He was very helpful and supervised me like a big brother. If I wanted to pass the entrance exams, I had to attend extra evening classes which were plentiful in town. I registered my name for the exam which was held in August at the main university campus. Tehran University was located on the west side of Shah Reza Street; a big campus of faculties, surrounded by gardens full of tall trees and flower borders. I wanted to either enter the medical school or the school of sciences. Unfortunately, this was not possible. My knowledge, in comparison to the thousands who were well prepared, was not enough. Some of my classmates were accepted at a few faculties. However, I was accepted at the Teachers' Training College. Most of the girls from Kerman passed as well. I had to settle for this college, although I had not planned to become a teacher.

Teachers' Training College, 1960–3

The Teachers' Training College was a part of the Ministry of Education and independent of the university. Students received an allowance from the college in exchange for a five-year contract with the ministry after they finished training. Being located in the north of Tehran, on the Old Shemiran Road, the college was far from where I lived. It was a five-storey building with a library and laboratories set in a huge garden. I had to take three buses to get there. I did not know what I was meant to study, nor did my other friends, for our subjects were given to us according to our grades. Those with higher grades were assigned to sciences, the rest, literature and humanities. I was offered a newly established subject: Scientific Geography! I was the only girl in the class.

Most of the students had come from other parts of Iran and their home region could be identified through their languages, behaviour and manners. Almost all girls except a few were well-dressed, without the hejab. Boys, who had not been in mixed-sex environments before, did not know how to take the girls' presence. They fell in love easily and expected to restrict their girlfriends. One of the boys in my class, who came from Tabriz, fancied me. He was tall and handsome although very backward. I did not know what to do. Starting a relationship was out of the question. I was very naive and besides I was not prepared for any romantic encounters, so I ignored my feelings and was soon busy with the excitement of life in Tehran.

A few months into college I befriended a couple of girls from the English Department and I was sometimes allowed to attend the English classes. Lecturers gradually took an interest in me and eventually, one of them, a young Englishman, John Green, suggested that I transfer to the English Department. Of course I preferred to study English instead of geography, and he managed to obtain the Dean's approval. So, I joined the English Department after the first term and soon became one of the best students. We studied literature; Shakespeare and other classics. Iranian lecturers taught us Persian literature and teaching methods. The first year passed amidst much excitement. We were often taken by our methodology lecturer, Dr Pasargadi, on picnics, hiking in the Alborz mountains and visiting places of interest. Apart from my friends from Bam who were at the college, I found new friends and began the happiest time of my life.

In June, after the end of the year, grandmother and I went to Kerman. My grandmother was not feeling well. Her stomach aches had intensified. I was very worried for her. Although Nahid was kind and hospitable, she made it clear that it would not be possible to lodge me the following year. This was fine with me, since I preferred to share a flat with the girls near the college. Many of the students who left home to study in Tehran lived on their own or in shared accommodation. My grandmother could not stay with me any more as she was too ill and life in Tehran was very hard for her. I was out for most of the day and she felt very lonely. I assured her that I would be able to manage on my own. After leaving her with Aunt Iran, I joined my family for the summer holidays in Dalfard. They were thrilled to see me after a year. My mother's worries as to what might have happened to me abated, although she knew that she had lost her elder daughter forever.

My sister Simin, who was three years my junior, had the same difficulties with high school as I did. After I had left Jiroft a middle school for girls had opened. That meant girls could study for nine years, although they still had to study three more years to obtain a high school diploma. During my last years in Bam Simin had come to stay with us, but Mr Sadjadi refused to have her the second year. She was disobedient and would not listen to what Aunt Iran or Mr Sadjadi said. The year after she was sent to Kerman to stay with one of my mother's uncles. She still had two more years to get her diploma. I made the bold decision of asking my mother to let her join me in Tehran. At first, she refused. It was hard enough for her that I was going to live on my own and now I wanted to take my young sister as well. I reasoned passionately and assured my parents that it would be best if she stayed with me. At the end of the summer they accepted the fact that their second child was departing as well as the first one.

We set off for Tehran at the end of September and arrived at the bus station at night. It was too late to wake up my cousin, so I took a room at the small guest house above the bus terminal. Early in the morning we got a taxi to my cousin's house where I left Simin for the day and went to the college to find my friends and get lodgings. I found a room in a house which belonged to a gendarme, who was a big, stocky man with a Turkish accent. I paid the month's rent and hurried back to get my sister.

We did not have much furniture: a rug, a few blankets and mattresses. I bought some pots and pans, an oil stove and a few other utensils. The landlord agreed to give us a shelf in his refrigerator. I had never cooked before and the first omelette I made was unforgettable. I burnt the food and the pan. Soon I started looking for a high school to register Simin at. Well-known schools were all located in the centre of the city, far from my college. Finally, I registered her at Shahdokht High School. There were others but their standards were high and they would not accept pupils from other cities. I showed my sister the bus route and accompanied her a few times to show her the way. I also warned her of the dangers and advised her to be vigilant.

Budgeting our money was my biggest worry. The monthly allowance my father sent us, plus the grant I received from the college, made a total of £30 a month, half of which I paid out in rent. The rest had to cater for all our expenses: food, books, travel and entertainment. I had learnt from my mother to economise and although it was difficult, we lived fairly comfortably. Later, I bought two chairs and curtains and gradually decorated the room.

By mid-term I had befriended a young woman, about my age, who worked in the college library. She always wore black and had a beautiful but sad face. We became close very quickly. Fereshteh had been about fifteen when she had fallen in love with Fereidoon, a young engineer from the Iranian Oil Company. He was handsome with a prosperous future and they married against his parent's wishes. A few years later a baby son added to their happiness. When the baby was only twenty days old, Fereidoon went on a mission to the north of the country. His car was involved in an accident and he died a few days later. That was how Fereshteh became a widow at the age of twenty. Her husband's family confiscated everything she had, even her personal belongings. Now they were the child's legal guardians.

Under Iranian law the husband's male relatives have the right to the custody of the child in the case of his death. They also have the right to control their son's property, and all the couple's assets, until the child is eighteen. Fereshteh was not the sort of person to give in. Together, we looked for an apartment for her and with the help of her mother and friends she furnished it. Fereshteh was a very talented painter. She had painted the agony of her husband's death in paintings which she kept in her living-room. Her apartment, although it had little furniture, was covered with her beautiful paintings. We often took the baby to the park or, when she found a babysitter, we went to the cinema. She was the one who took me to a beauty parlour to remove the unwanted hair on my legs and eyebrows. I became fashion conscious, had my hair cut and bought out-of-fashion shoes and clothes at the downtown market at a cheap price.

By the middle of the term in my second year the college became involved in sporadic demonstrations and strikes. At first I did not know what was happening. Although I knew of the Shah's coup in 1953 and his systematic repression, I was not politically mature enough to understand the situation. In November the whole college was disrupted by a wave of strikes. One day we were asked to go to Tehran University to attend the commemoration of three students who had been killed by the Shah's guards a few years earlier. Much later the same year we attended a rally which was held by the teachers in front of the parliament. I was accompanied by Akhtar, my best friend. We held hands the whole time, for fear of being lost in the crowd. The rally was disrupted by shots. Later, we were informed that one of the teachers, Dr Khan Ali, who was an outspoken person, had been shot by the police. A wave of demonstrations and strikes followed and the prime minister was forced to resign.

It was in college that we mostly heard about the world outside. I knew about colonialism and how Western powers dominated other parts of the world but my knowledge was not deep enough to analyse everything. Once the students were asked to sign a telegram which was sent to the United Nations to protest against the killing of Patrice Lumumba, the national liberation leader of the Congo, by the Belgian colonialists. I did not know where the Congo was actually located or why Lumumba had been killed, except that he was a national hero like Dr Mosadeq. Another telegram was sent to his widow on behalf of the Iranian students.

There were always a few students who acted as leaders and told the others what to do. My humanist feelings were strong enough to make me participate in mass protests. Nevertheless, I hated class disruptions and wanted to continue with my studies, but our classes were frequently suspended when students walked out. The remnants of the National Front and the Youth Organisation of the Tudeh Party who had escaped the Shah's persecution after the coup were behind these activities and secretly worked among the students. The secret police prevented any overt political activity and if they were suspicious, students were immediately detained.

In the summer my sister and I left for Kerman. I sent Simin straight to my parents and went myself to Bam to see my grandmother, who was by then very ill. She was glad to see me. She kept my picture under her pillow and whenever she missed me she held it to her chest, calling my name, crying loudly. I was very sad to see her in that state but there was not much I could do.

I left my grandmother after a month and joined my parents in Dalfard for the rest of the holidays. While spending the holidays with my family I proposed to my parents that they let my brother Manuchehr continue his studies in Tehran. Manuchehr was a very talented boy. Now that I was settled, I thought that he would have a better future if he studied in the capital. After much discussion, they reluctantly agreed.

Manuchehr was the apple of my parents' eyes. They both adored him and I suppose having him gone was an emotional blow to both of them. I remember my father smacking my brother Mehdi or my sister Simin whenever Manuchehr complained about them. He was given everything he wanted. He was quiet, polite and thoughtful, unlike Mehdi, who was naughty and rebellious. Although Mehdi was the sweetest child in our family, my parents never treated them equally.

The three of us went to Tehran in September, while my mother loaded us with all she thought we might need. Now she was left behind with three young children and a husband whose bad temper was getting worse every day. Back in Tehran, the first thing I did was to register Manuchehr at a high school. It was Mera'at High in the east of the city. Manuchehr soon proved to be a very good student and I did not have to worry about him.

I used to write to my mother and grandmother regularly. There were no direct telephone lines then. I sent telegrams whenever it was necessary. In the middle of the third year I found out that my grandmother had cancer and might not live very long. I do not remember how many days I cried. I did not know what to do. I loved her more than anyone and I was very sad that I was not even with her in her last days.

Having my teenage brother and sister with me, however, kept me busy for most of the time. I had changed our lodgings and moved to a bigger apartment which was close to the main road. We had two rooms and a kitchen with a terrace in front of the rooms, though we had to pass through the landlady's courtyard and face her curious eyes. Although in Tehran some houses had hamams built in them, the old ones did not. We had to go to the outside hamam. Our landlady, Mrs Shad Aram, was a very traditional Tehrani lady. Nevertheless, the need for extra income had forced her to rent out part of her old-style home. She was vigilant though in not allowing her children to mix with us strangers.

In the 1950s and 1960s thousands of young people had migrated from their homes in small towns to continue their studies in the big cities, where higher education establishments were located. Although Tehran University had built a big campus, where its halls of residence accommodated thousands of students, there were still students who could not get a place. People who lived near these establishments rented their spare rooms to the students and gradually a culture of tolerating strangers developed within the closed, traditional families.

A year later, in October, when we returned from holiday, I changed Manuchehr's school. The new school, Hadaf, had a reputation for maintaining high standards. Considering myself their guardian, I was keen to monitor both my brother's and sister's schooling.

Manuchehr and Simin were both very good at chess and poetry. At the time the national radio station had a regular programme of poetry contests. Two contestants would compete for half an hour every week. One contestant would read a poem while the other had to respond by reading another poem which would start with the last letter of the former. Sometimes it would take the contestants several sessions to win these competitions. Manuchehr attended these competitions several times and each time won a good prize. At the final session he won an eight-piece suite as the grand prize. Upon receiving the suite, he hired a van and brought it home with much excitement. He rushed upstairs to inform me of his prize and asked for the money to pay the driver. Being at the time very short of money, I became angry and, instead of praising him, I shouted at him and told him that I did not need any suites. Finally, I had to borrow from Mrs Shad Aram to pay the driver. I believe Manuchehr never forgave me.

I was due to graduate from college in June 1963. We had been trained to become high school teachers, specialising in the subject we had studied. I planned to stay in Tehran and teach. Fereshteh, who by then had quit her job as librarian and had been recruited at the National Oil Company, decided to marry one of her dead husband's former colleagues. Although she did not love him, being a beautiful, young widow she found it almost impossible to work in an office without being constantly harassed by men who expected sexual favours.

The loss of my beloved grandmother

During the New Year holidays in March 1963 I rushed to Bam to see my grandmother, who was in her final days. The cancer had developed so much that she was not the sweet, kind person I had known. The pain did not let her show much affection to me. I felt terrible. I would have given anything to see her well again. I wanted to stay for her last days but my aunt convinced me that there was nothing I could do. Besides, I had my final year to finish and a brother and sister to take care of. I said goodbye with a broken heart. I will never forget her last look when I left the room. I had such sweet memories of her tender touch and her gentle voice and the unconditional love and affection she used to give me. Now I was losing her forever. While sitting in the bus for the three-day journey back to Tehran, I did not even cry. I just held on to those precious memories. A month later I received a letter from one of my mother's cousins, telling me of my grandmother's death on April 25. She was only 60. My mother and aunt were too distressed to inform me. I did not attend college for a week and mourned my grandmother's death until I had no tears left.

In the middle of the second term of our second year a young American, who had been assigned to Iran as part of the Peace Corps, had become our new lecturer. He was a charming, shy person, and being lonely, he tried to develop personal friendships with some of us. He would usually accompany us on our picnics and mountain hikes and tried to learn Persian. I was still in mourning when John informed me of a scholarship for a trip to America. He knew of my grandmother's death and to change my mood, he encouraged me to register. Two other students from our class were nominated as well. We attended an initial exam with hundreds of other students. After I came out of the examination hall I forgot about the whole thing. A week later, John called me to his office and told me with a broad smile that I had passed the exam and was entitled to a scholarship in a programme called 'Experiment in International Living'. I couldn't believe my luck and still in confusion and disbelief I told him that I had to first inform my family.

Iran, early 1960s

The policy of the 1960s was further development based on the open door policy and foreign investment. The Shah, who by then had become an autocratic figure, had introduced a Six Point Plan to bring Iran into line with other capitalist states. These plans were part of what was called 'The White Revolution'. Under the plans illiteracy was to be eradicated by the formation of a Literacy Corps and health improved by the creation of a Health Corps.

As part of these plans women had to enter the social arena in large numbers and possibly gain suffrage. Already women's associations and those who were influential in high society were pressing for women's rights. In the early 1960s they had lobbied ministers, deputies and politicians and, as a result, the law granting women suffrage was drafted in 1962, but due to the opposition from the establishment clergy, its implementation was postponed. Women's associations intensified their campaign to implement the law, signed petitions and sent letters of protests to the media and even had a one-day strike, on January 24, 1963, when teachers and civil servants joined protest rallies and demonstrations. Finally, on February 27, women achieved the universal right to vote.

The Six Point Plan itself was put to a referendum and gained the overwhelming support of the people. After this so-called 'White Revolution' the Shah, confident of the people's support, abolished the system of group decision-making, which had existed at the top level of government, and began an arbitrary rule. He also came to the belief that he was inspired by some unknown powers which led him along the right path. He was, as a matter of fact, becoming more fanatical, despite the image portrayed of him to the general public.

Meanwhile, during 1962–3, while the state was occupied with the 'White Revolution', new opposition to the Shah's policies was being formed. At the international level John Kennedy had been elected as the US Democratic president in November 1960. Unlike his conservative predecessors, his relations with Iran were conditional. President Kennedy limited the sale of arms to Iran and expected the Shah to observe human rights and initiate more reforms. The implementation of reforms was not as easy as the Shah had thought it would be. Although the communists and the national front had been crushed, the ulama, who traditionally supported the monarchy, emerged as a new force, opposed to the Western-style reforms, especially land reform and the vote for women.

above My parent's wedding photo, 1938.

below My mother's grandparent's house in Kerman.
My grandmother Bibi Attieh is in the centre (with the
white collar dress). Aunt Iran (second on the right),
my mother (third on the right) and my father
(standing beside my mother). The rest are my
mother's uncles, their wives and children and some
cousins. The picture was taken shortly after my
mother's marriage to my father in 1938.

At our house in Jiroft. My mother with me (eight), Simin (four) and Manuchehr (two) in 1948. The eucalyptus tree, which my mother planted alongside the brook and is partly shown behind us, has now grown into a giant 60 foot tall tree.

Nowrooz in Bam. This picture was taken on New Year's Day in my grandmother's room. From left, me, Fati, my mother, Simin, Maryam, Aunt Iran, Zarin and my brother Mehdi, 1959.

above The countryside outside Jiroft in the spring of 1955. My mother is on the right with the hunting rifle with Aunt Iran and me. My mother has just permed her hair.

below At my aunt's sister-in law's house, Showkat Khanum in Bam, 1956. Standing: from the left my grandmother, me, Aunt Iran and Showkat Khanum (after the revolution she converted into a religious fanatic and devoted all her wealth to the religious foundations). Sitting: from the left my cousins Mehdi, Fati and Zarin.

With my friend Ismat at the Teacher's Training
College in Tehran in 1960. I had just cut my hair
very short.

A group of us at the Teacher's Training
College in 1961. We were keen to keep up
with the latest fashions.

Iraj's family at a wedding in the early 1950s.
From the left: Gilan Khanum, the groom (Mr
Omidvari), Jahangir, the bride (Rejin
Khanum) Mehri, Iraj and Iraj's father.

My engagement party. Iraj, me and Manuchehr (right), in the courtyard of our house, Yusef Abad, Tehran, April 1965.

At a function in the Army Officer's club in Tehran in 1967. A group of Iran Air flight crew in full uniform. Centre is General Khademi and his wife. I am standing beside them in the flowery, mini-dress. Iraj can be seen behind the General.

Women demonstrating against the Shah's
regime, 1978.

Ayatollah Khomeini is welcomed back to Iran in early February 1979.

below Mullahs and revolutionary guards fight together during the Iran-Iraq war, 1980–1988.

Among the most prominent dissident figures was Ayatollah Khomeini, who taught at Quom, the religious city and centre of all schools of Islam. In a letter to the Shah Mr Khomeini objected to the capitulation of the country to America and ferociously attacked women's right to vote. He pointed to the dangers of Americanisation and corruption and encouraged Muslims to stop these developments. In 1963, as a result of these campaigns, a series of demonstrations spread throughout the major cities, including Tehran, forcing the Shah to resort to force. The Shah's commando squad and the secret police attacked the religious madrases in Quom, beating up the clerical students and arresting a number of them. This attack was condemned by the high-ranking leaders of the Shi'at clergy who resided in Iraq. Meanwhile, Ayatollah Khomeini declared an all-out war against the Shah's regime. On June 5, however, the Ayatollah and some of his followers were arrested and sent to Tehran. He was later sent into exile, first to Turkey and later to Iraq, where he stayed for fifteen years, encouraging the seeds of revolution.

My scholarship; a gloss over the political unrests

There were seventeen of us chosen for the scholarship programme from different faculties; eight girls and nine boys. Some had to pay part of their expenses because their grades were not high enough to win them a full scholarship. Others like me were fully sponsored. According to the briefing we were expected to stay with families and visit a few universities and some big cities on the east coast of the US. Mrs Rad, an Iranian lady who had lived in America for years and was working at an American institute in Tehran, was appointed as our tour leader. We filled in forms and questionnaires, indicating our hobbies and interests. Based on these, we were matched with the families who had volunteered to foster us. I sent a cable to my parents, telling them of the trip. To my surprise I did not receive a reply. Instead, my father asked my mother's cousin, Hassan Khan, to give me the money I needed. Hassan Khan gave me 15,000 Rials, which made $200 on the exchange market. Some of the students in my group had as much as $5,000. Since the death of my grandmother I had rarely had any news from my family. I put it down to the grief and distress my mother must have suffered. Besides, I was busy with my final exams and the new opportunity to travel so I didn't suspect anything.

After the introductory session, everything was out of our control and we were swept by a tide of unexpected events. We were informed that we were going as members of an Iranian Youth Organisation, though we had not heard of this organisation before. A Mr Khodayar, whom I already knew as a radio broadcaster, was the head of the 'youth organisation' and invited us to be briefed about the organisation which we were expected to represent. Our departure was scheduled for June 5, and then we were informed that we were to be introduced to His Majesty the Shah a day before our departure. We all considered this occasion a big honour, unaware of the fact that we would be an attractive topic for the Shah's publicity machine and a means to divert attention from what was simultaneously happening in the country. We were aware of the disturbances in Tehran, and actually on the way to the passport office in the south of Tehran we had seen the streets under military siege and had heard gun shots, but since the college was almost closed at the beginning of June, I did not have any sources to find out what was going on.

His Majesty received us at Sadabad Palace in Shemiran, north of Tehran. On the afternoon of June 4 we went to the palace, accompanied by Mr Khodayar and Mrs Rad. At four-thirty we were taken to a big reception room where we waited for a while. Suddenly, His Majesty entered from a door at the far end of the room. Everybody was nervous. He looked smaller than I imagined but was very well dressed. He passed along the line, shaking hands with everyone, asking a few questions. When he shook my hand, I did not bow to him, like other girls. Instead, I gave him a broad smile which made him pause and ask me which college I had attended and what I wanted to do. He then gave us a brief speech, talking about the 'dark' reactionary forces who wanted to take Iran back into the dark ages. I did not know what he really meant.

The next morning my picture, with the broad smile and the warm handshake, was all over the front pages. We were now being treated like celebrities. Reporters poured to the airport to take our pictures for publicity. I do not think anyone in our group knew what was really going on. We were just a group of young enthusiasts who could not wait to see America.

Chapter Six

Unexpected events

Beloved
Whenever it is, come to me
And bring me a torch
With a little window
To look through the crowded road
To look at the contended code.
  Forough Farokhzad, *Rebirth*

We were flown to the east coast of America as scheduled and were placed with families for a couple of months. Later, we visited some universities as well as the cities of New York and Washington. To me, America of the early 1960s seemed like a dreamland. My first view of the country was one of admiration and fascination. However, once I was staying with the family and had socialised more with the people, I was amazed at their general ignorance, their racist and patronising attitudes towards us and their perception of themselves as the best in every respect. Although I was offered a scholarship to study for an MA by two universities, I was put off by these attitudes and rejected the offers. Apart from this, we all had a nice time and returned home on a late-night flight, full of excitement and stories to tell. My family were at the airport, anxious to see me after so many months.

I was so excited, talking about my trip, giving everyone their presents and showing them the photos, that I did not notice my mother's unusual silence. The only thing which attracted my attention at the airport was the scarf she was wearing. The next morning my sister told me what had happened in my absence. During my grandmother's last stage of illness my mother, taking the two younger children Massoud and Maryam with her, had gone to Bam. Aunt Iran could not cope on her own, so my mother had stayed there for almost two months, caring for Grandmother until she passed away. She then attended the lengthy rituals of forty days' mourning. On her return to Jiroft, after such a stressful time, she had developed headaches coupled with vomiting. My father did not know what to do. My mother was the one who ran the household and made decisions. Now she was too ill to do anything. Finally, my father decided to take her to Kerman to see a specialist, who found a brain tumour. He recommended an immediate operation.

Back in June, when I had sent my telegram informing them of my trip to America, my mother had been in that serious condition. Nevertheless, she had advised my father not to mention her illness to me. That was the reason I hardly heard from them before my departure. They arrived in Tehran shortly after I left, taking the three young children. Not being familiar with Tehran, plus my mother's illness, left my father in a state of helplessness and Simin had taken on all the responsibility. My mother was immediately taken to Dr Sami'i, the best brain surgeon in Tehran. He advised an operation, which took place a few days later in the Bazarganan Hospital, miles away from where we lived. Bazarganan Hospital had recently opened and was well equipped with operating theatres and good nursing staff. Simin had to take care of the kids, take father to the hospital every day and nurse my mother, as much as her time allowed. After the operation, Dr Sami'i informed them of a cyst which had developed in the cerebellum area of mother's brain. He said that he had tried to remove as much of the cyst as possible and hoped it would not return.

My father's financial situation had added to the family's distress. He never had any savings or extra money and in this emergency he was forced to sell a piece of land to Uncle Akbar to finance my mother's operation and their expenses in Tehran. When I arrived back from the trip my mother had been out of hospital for almost two months. She seemed healthy, although her hair, which had been shaved for the operation, had not re-grown properly, which was the reason for her wearing the scarf. Looking at her in the morning I could see that she was not herself any more, although at the time she was only 41.

Devestated by the news I tried to give them as much love and attention as I could, but I also had to get on with my own life. By the end of September I was due to report for my teaching post. I had to fulfil the contract with the Ministry of Education, which bound me to work for them for the next five years. In those days Tehran was the ideal place to work and there were tens of graduates who pushed for posts in Tehran with very few graduates volunteering to go to other cities. Out of the group of almost twenty students who had originally come from Kerman, only a handful wanted to return. Finally, I was given an assignment in Tehran at the Nowbavegan High School in the south of the city, on Sepah Avenue. It meant that I had to move to the town centre.

After the operation my mother was reluctant to return to Jiroft. She wanted to be with us and close to the doctor. Unfortunately, it was not possible. Financially, we were not in the position to accommodate such a large family. My father was not capable of earning enough money and besides, he was desperate to have my mother back in Jiroft. My mother returned, fearful for her health and uncertain of what fate lay ahead of her. At the time, Mehdi was 13, Maryam ten and Massoud three.

Shortly afterwards I rented a two-bed apartment in Kakh Avenue, a few miles away from the high school. Aunt Iran sent my cousin Zarin to stay with us for her final year at high school. My salary as a teacher was £90 per month, barely enough to cover our higher rent and other expenses. Aunt Iran sent some money for Zarin and my father managed to send the same amount he used to send us during my college years. Now I had a family of three teenagers, which meant that I had to be tough for most of the time. Plus, we all had friends and our little apartment was filled with young people who enjoyed an easy student life.

My teaching career

I reported to the headmistress of the Nowbavegan High School. Mrs Sadughi was a serious, middle-aged woman who received me very formally. Her deputy, a fat, round-faced, authoritative woman, whom everyone was frightened of, took me at first for a new student. Looking much younger than my age, I was sometimes mistaken for one of the students in their last year of high school. I was assigned to teach English to the first and fourth years.

In Iran, English was part of the curriculum, replacing French which had been taught in the pre-war period. Knowing a foreign language was instrumental in gaining access to good jobs in a country which was developing quickly. I started my career with little confidence. The classes were crowded; thirty to forty girls, packed into small rooms. Their noisy chatter and perspiration was unbearable. The first thing I noticed was that my Kermani accent was a problem. Before this I was mainly in an environment where people came from different parts of the country with ethnic languages and dialects. At school, everyone was from Tehran, whose accent was considered to be superior and the best among Persian speakers. I had to change my accent quickly so as not to be ridiculed by my students. Bringing the class into order was a hard task. I did not want to punish the girls. I wanted to be their friend and their teacher at the same time, something which was almost impossible. Teachers often found it easier to control the students by being strict and punishment was rife. That was against all I had been taught at college and I wanted to practise what I had learnt. Sometimes I stayed after school hours and tutored the girls who confided in me and asked for advice on their personal problems. In addition, young teachers were required to help organise special occasions such as His Majesty's birthday celebrations and to accompany the girls on parades at the Amjadieh Gymnasium. While I was at the college we had campaigned against such extravagant celebrations. Now I was being asked to contribute to them. I was frightened of refusing. Nevertheless, I always left the parades once we were out of the school premises and on our way to the gymnasium.

In the summer of 1964, after a year of teaching, I decided to register for an MA course at Tehran University. Since I did not want to continue teaching English I registered in the Social Sciences Department. In those days every stage of higher education was accompanied by an entry exam. I had to study a great deal to pass the exams: economics, sociology, psychology, history and philosophy. I was not sure if I would be accepted. To my surprise and joy, out of many applicants, I was among the few who had passed. I registered for the evening classes with much enthusiasm.

By the end of my second year of teaching, while everyone, including the ever-frowning headmistress, had acknowledged that I was a good teacher, I decided I was not meant for the job. Teaching was a low-paid job with no social status. I was young and ambitious and did not want to tie myself to the Ministry of Education for the next thirty years. Iran's economy was prospering and there were lots of opportunities for people like me. Newspapers were full of recruitment adverts. I applied for a few.

In mid-summer I was invited for an interview at Iran Air for the post of flight service instructor. The advert promised a good salary, training in Iran and America and other fringe benefits. Iran Air was modernising and expanding rapidly. It required young, dynamic people with knowledge of English at all levels. Iran Air was headed by an air force general, who had been appointed by the Shah himself. General Khademi, a tiny, short man, with scrutinising eyes and a keen interest in updating the establishment, had signed agreements with the Pan American Airlines to use their expertise to promote Iran Air at the international level. In 1965 there were tens of Americans and other foreign nationals working in the technical, operation, dispatch, training and passenger service departments. It had been agreed that Iran Air would recruit young Iranians who would replace the Americans after comprehensive training.

I got through the first interview and a few days later I was invited for the second, when I was briefed on the job. I was to train the passenger service staff, mainly cabin crew, prepare manuals, and carry out the in-flight checking after each training course. My initial training to qualify for the job was six months in Iran, after which I would be sent to the Pan American Training School in Florida for further training. In the meantime, I would be flying on all Iran Air routes to become familiar with the actual job. My initial salary was twice that of a teacher. In addition, I was paid travel allowances and given discount tickets.

After the second interview I was waiting for the bus to take me home, outside the airport building, under a tree which hid me from the summer heat. I was approached by a young, blond man, with a soft, gentle voice who inquired about my interview. His name was Iraj and he was the second appointee for the job. We chatted for a while. He had already been working for the airline for almost three years, and, having seen the opportunity to move from his boring job in the accounts department, he had applied as an internal applicant. He had been offered the post on the same day.

A week later I was officially informed that I had been given the job and, if I agreed, I would start the training at the beginning of October. I gave my approval and immediately sent my resignation to the Ministry of Education. In return, I received a fat bill which was the balance of what was owed on my grant for the remaining three years of my five-year contract with them.

The return of my mother's illness

Although my mother wrote to us regularly she did not make any references to her illness and we took it as a sign of her full recovery.

In September, when I was occupied with the job search, I received a letter from her indicating her wish to come to Tehran for a check up. When she was picked up from the airport, we found to our horror that she was seriously ill. She had lost her balance, her speech was impaired and her headaches were back. She was taken immediately to Dr Sami'i, who informed us of the return of the tumour.

It was a difficult time for all of us. I was about to start my new job, Simin and Manuchehr were busy with their second year in college and we also had the three young children to take care of. I was very depressed and cried a lot for my mother and for our bad luck. Simin was on the verge of a breakdown.

On October 1, my mother was taken into hospital for a second operation. Unfortunately, this was also my first day at the airline and I did not know what to do. When she was taken to the operating theatre, I left for the airport in haste. I stayed there for a few hours but was unable to concentrate. Finally, I told my boss of my mother's operation and my worries and left for the hospital. When I reached it she was still in the operating room and the whole family was waiting in the hallway. It took the surgeons eight hours to remove parts of the cyst which had spread in the cerebellum. Dr Sami'i did not know what the outcome would be and did not give us hope of a full recovery.

For the next three months, while my mother stayed in hospital, half in a coma and later partially paralysed, we stayed with her day and night, nursing her until she was allowed home. Finally, after initial complications, she recovered to some extent. She now spoke with difficulty and her balance never returned to normal, although she could walk without help. Being only 42 years old at the time we hoped that the tumour would not return and she would recover completely. By then, through our long observations at the hospital, my sister and I had learnt how to nurse her. We were able to give her injections and change the pads on her wound.

My mother was not in a situation to return to Jiroft now and so she and the rest of my siblings stayed in Tehran. My father preferred to return to Jiroft to take care of his properties and send us some money. Since my mother's illness the family's financial situation had deteriorated, as my father was not able to manage money as well as my mother. Now I had to change our accommodation and get a bigger house. Although I had a further salary increase and was earning £150 per month, a good amount for an Iranian income, I was spending almost all of it on rent and other expenses.

Iranian airlines

Apart from my training on the ground at the airline I had to observe the flight service crew in operation, to gain experience and detect shortcomings. Iran Air had a number of DC3, Viscount and DC6 aircraft and had planned to purchase Boeing jets at the end of the 1960s. I frequently travelled as an additional crew member on local flights, as well as on international routes to the Gulf States, Germany, Britain, France, Italy, India and Pakistan.

My training at Iran Air took almost six months, during which time I and my colleague Iraj worked closely together. Sometimes we flew together, or on separate schedules. We also shared an office in the training department. In between my mother's illness and my job, I sometimes attended my MA course in the evenings. It was difficult to keep up with other students and at the end of the year I passed only a few subjects. On some occasions, in the evenings, Iraj used to come to the college and accompany me home. We went to the cinema, or a restaurant or just walked along the streets, talking about everything: film, poetry, and our job. Iraj had a good memory and often recited poems artistically. The only thing I did not like about him was his drinking, as he became cheerful and talkative once he drank a few beers. The two of us came from different backgrounds. In his household women did not have much control over their life. He found it hard to understand my sense of independence and how I coped with all the problems surrounding me.

Iraj originally came from Rasht, a northern city near the Caspian Sea. His family had moved to Tehran in the 1940s when he was about five. Iraj's mother, Gilan Khanum, was the only daughter of an educated doctor. Both her parents had died when she was seven years old. She had been fostered by relatives who had later moved to Baku in the Soviet Azarbaijan in the early 1930s. She had stayed there for some years, where she had attended a stage school. When she returned to Rasht in the late 1930s women's associations, active in Rasht, involved her in some of their activities. Eventually, she was employed as a nursery teacher and also acted at a local women's theatre.

Gilan Khanum married a man some years her junior. They had three children. Iraj was the second. Iraj's father, a clerk at the Notary Office in downtown Tehran, was a real dictator who controlled both his wife and their daughter, Mehri. When they moved to Tehran he had forbidden Gilan Khanum to take up any employment and she became a housewife. Iraj's sister Mehri was married at the age of seventeen to a man much older than herself. She did not continue her studies and when I came to know the family, Mehri still lived in her father's household with her three daughters and a demanding husband. Her father never allowed them to move out and have an independent life of their own. Their household was the centre of tensions and arguments for most of the time and the row over Mehri's unhappy marriage, and who was to be blamed, never ended.

After several months, however, my friendship with Iraj deepened. He started to think more seriously about us. To me, he was just a good friend and confidant, while he talked about us getting married. I had already experienced a lot in life and had taken lots of responsibilities, but I had not had any serious relations with men and wasn't thinking of marriage. Although Iraj was a year older than me, he seemed young and immature. Nevertheless, after six months of friendship and constant discussions, he convinced me to think seriously about his proposal. In general, I liked older men because they were mature and contributed to my intellectual thought. Although Iraj was very charming, he did not look like the husband I had imagined for myself. I knew I had to marry one day and longed to fall in love, but so far life had been very hard on me, leaving no time for close relationships.

Marriage against all the odds

Marriage in those days was still the expected thing for a woman to do. Although I was able to stand on my own two feet, sometimes I thought it might be better to share life with someone, even if the relationship was based on friendship rather than a passionate love affair. Having the responsibility of younger siblings had drawn me into a state of keeping up appearances and being a role model. I had not allowed myself any pre-marital relationships. Besides, I thought marriage would relieve me from the mental stress of trying to take care of my mother and siblings while doing my job. I was not aware of the complications marriage would bring, especially when the husband is a young, inexperienced man.

Finally, upon his insistence, I accepted Iraj's offer on two conditions: we would both hold on to our personal independence, and share decisions, leaving no room for him to ever order me around. He accepted my conditions, not knowing what the consequences might be. I told my mother about my decision. She had already met Iraj on several occasions and was fond of him. By then the generation of educated, career women like me had distanced themselves from the practice of arranged marriages and had the liberty to choose their own husbands. Arranged marriages were now confined to traditional families and the rural areas.

When Iraj informed his mother she was furious and threatened to commit suicide. His father also opposed the idea and Iraj had a hard time trying to get their approval. They believed he was too young to get married. They had seen me on one occasion and did not approve of me. From their point of view I was too skinny. Besides, Iraj's father wished him to marry one of his nieces or someone from their home town. They didn't agree with the unconventional way we had chosen each other and tried to persuade him to change his mind. He only told me of these objections years after we were married. Had I known at the time, I would have refused to go ahead with it altogether.

Once Iraj's parents were convinced that they couldn't change his mind, they calmed down and visited us on several occasions, before the engagement, as was customary. At our household, on the other hand, everyone was happy I was to become engaged. In those days it was the custom that a few women from both sides of the families would accompany the couple on their shopping for jewellery and the wedding dress. The bride's family would normally want to choose expensive items, while the groom's would want to spend as little money as possible. This was of course an unwritten rule which was to be performed delicately and with much tactfulness. With us I did not expect Iraj to buy me anything or spend any money. I arranged everything the way I wanted and did not listen to anyone's comments. I ordered a turquoise silk mini dress from the tailor for the engagement party. We went shopping on our own, and chose our wedding rings. We arranged two receptions; one night for family and relatives and one for our friends. In June 1966, a couple of months after our engagement, we went to Miami to attend the Pan American training school. We stayed there for three months on a comprehensive training course. At school Iraj was one of the few males among the many females. Being witty and charming, girls approached him, unaware of our relationship. I thought he regretted being engaged to me and I assured him that he was free to enjoy himself if he wished to do so. In the meantime, I made friends with some girls and we went out at nights and on some weekends. I never asked Iraj whether he took advantage of my liberalism or restained himself. It was his personal space and I didn't want to invade it. In late September we returned home and immediately started our work as cabin crew instructors. For the next two years we were busy writing manuals, establishing training courses and building the foundations of a new training centre, which became one of the best in the Middle East.

Fortunately, my family's situation had improved. My mother's good health returned to a large extent and she had taken charge of the household. Simin and Manuchehr were in their final college years and performed their share of the household responsibilities. Aunt Iran had moved to Tehran permanently because her children needed further education which she could not give them in Bam. Mr Sadjadi transferred himself to Tehran, while Aunt Iran requested early retirement.

Iraj and I got married in March 1967. At our house in Yousef Abad we held a simple ceremony, with little extravagance. I hated the lengthy and complicated traditions which were observed in Iranian weddings. A few weeks before the wedding I travelled to Hamburg in Germany to buy myself a white mini-skirt dress with long gloves and a crystal necklace to match. When the mullah came to register our marriage we thought that he would object to my mini skirt. Instead, he sat beside me, reciting the wedding rituals. Iraj's father had hired a cook to prepare the dinner for some fifty guests. The man got drunk after he served the dinner and his yelling and drunkenness left us with an unforgettable memory.

I did not move out of the family home until much later. Iraj stayed in his parent's house as well. We both had financial obligations. Iraj's father believed that we should take a room in their household until our finances improved. To me, the idea seemed absurd. I had lived independently since a young age and intended to do so thereafter. We began to have arguments as to where to settle. Iraj wanted to be near his family because his mother wanted to see him regularly and I wanted to be near my mother because of her condition. In the end, we decided to move away from both our families. We rented a two-bed apartment in Amir Abad in the northern centre of the city. Although, according to tradition, my parents were expected to provide me with basic necessities I was against this old-fashioned idea and didn't want to even discuss the matter. The only items I accepted were a handmade quilt and a few pieces of antique embroidery, which my mother herself had inherited from her mother. We also received lots of presents from friends and relatives who came to visit us in our new home. I bought our furniture, all on credit, and paid for it over the next four years.

When General Khademi, the director of Iran Air, found out about our marriage he congratulated us personally and sent us a nice dinner set as a present. Nevertheless, the company's policy was against couples working in the same department, so he planned to transfer me to another department. I was a hard-working, disciplined person, something the general appreciated and as a result, by late 1967, I was promoted to the post of flight service manager and moved to the airport buildings. Flight service was one of the biggest departments and needed a complete shake up. The general gave me a free hand to reorganise the old set up and bring it up to modern, international standards.

In the first few years of our marriage, apart from occasional rows on family matters, I felt fairly happy. Our main differences stemmed from our different cultural backgrounds and being almost the same age. I did not pay much attention to what Iraj wanted because I did not take him seriously. To me, he was too young and inexperienced. Besides, he did not have firm views on many things, from choosing our furniture to other more major decisions, which left me to decide on my own most of the time. Our family traditions and worldviews were totally different. Iraj was good to have fun with but he was not for serious conversation. Gatherings, partying and travelling made him happy; when it became serious, he became bored. This small but important difference in our relationship tore our world apart in years to come. We had differences about friends. At the time, I had many male and female friends whom Iraj did not approve of. We had occasional rows over whom we would socialise with. Gradually, he either developed friendships with some of my friends and pulled them away from me, or drove them out of my life by deliberately irritating them. After a few years we developed our separate circles and did not socialise with the same people for most of the time.

At my workplace, after I was given the new assignment, I moved to the newly built passenger service building, where a big wing was allocated to the flight service. My office was a big, sunny room with an adjoining secretarial office. I was supervising over one hundred employees and all cabin crew operations.

Flight service was under Tom Temple's supervision. Tom and I spent the next three years establishing a modern organisation. Young and educated applicants were recruited to replace the old ones, although a few had to remain in their posts despite their poor performance. These were the ones who had connections to the higher authorities and I was warned not to touch them. Between 1967 and 1969 my job took priority in my life. I frequently travelled abroad, attending international conferences, training courses and seminars in the Middle East, Europe and America.

Iraj also travelled a lot, either on training courses, or to recruit foreign personnel. Iraj and I had occasional rows over my career. He did not like my tough management style because it had created hostility towards me. He befriended many of my employees who tried to use him and take advantage of his friendship to ask favours from me. Rumours circulated that he had affairs with a few. I knew of some instances for a fact, but did not care about his interludes, as long as they were not at my expense. To me, he was still too young and had a long way to go to mature. Sometimes I regretted I had married him but didn't think of dissolving it.

In those days Iran Air female flight crews were among the most sexually liberated women in the country. Because they travelled most of the time and were admired and sometimes seduced by men, they often took advantage of their situation by finding wealthy boyfriends or husbands. Male flight crew, especially the pilots, on the other hand, sometimes mistreated them. If a female crew rejected their advances she got herself into trouble. I tried to eradicate this practice and supported those who put a complaint forward. In addition, I taught the women to respect their profession and report the incidents of sexual harassment. On my frequent trips on Iran Air flights I tried to explain this to some of the male flight crew, who often ridiculed and ignored me. Nevertheless, by 1969 things had changed to a great extent.

In general, sex discrimination was widely practised in the airline. For example, women in the flight service department were not allowed to have children while flying. Once they got pregnant, they were not even transferred to other sections. They were dismissed from the airline altogether. No one was even to talk about such discriminatory practices. It was only in the late 1960s that those women who had connections to higher authorities were transferred to other departments once they got pregnant. This practice was abolished in later years. I happened to be one of the few successful women who won promotion and managed a big department on my own initiative. Despite this, I was still discriminated against. I was warned not to get pregnant because of my frequent trips. My annual increment often went to my husband because the personnel manager believed I should not be paid more than my husband as he was the head of the family!

Another issue which put me under pressure was the expectations of the Security Department who wanted me to cooperate with them in reporting any suspicious, anti-royal and anti-regime activities among the flight crew. Colonel Dadvar, General Khademi's brother-in-law and the head of security, frequently harassed and threatened me. In fact, I had instances where some of my employees, who travelled on international flights, were suddenly dismissed, without my knowledge. Whether they had connections with the opposition outside the country, or were active in the anti-Shah's campaigns, I never knew. Since the royal family travelled by Iran Air security was tight in the flight service and the Operations Department as a whole. Suspicion of an individual was not tolerated and resulted in immediate dismissal. Pretending that I knew nothing about such politics, I never involved myself in cooperating with security, or working against it.

After four years of intense work I was facing mounting pressures and began to think of quitting my job. Intellectually, I was dissatisfied. I did not even have time to read a book properly or to meet the type of people I liked, and I felt drained. The opportunity arose when in early 1969 a woman, a general's daughter, joined the airline as deputy to General Khademi. She was keen to get herself involved in my department, which had an excellent reputation. At the time, the general's office was preparing for a big ceremony in honour of Princess Fatima, the Shah's sister, and women from my department were expected to act as hostesses. The new deputy began interfering and I had a row over the scope of her authority. Finally, her interference infuriated me and I took the opportunity to resign from the airline altogether. The general received my letter of resignation two days before the ceremony and was enraged, believing that I had challenged his authority and let him down. The general's administration concluded that I intended to sabotage the royal event by my sudden resignation and started an investigation. It did not get them very far. There was nothing behind my resignation. I did not want to sabotage anything. I went home, pulled the telephone out and locked myself in for a couple of months. I started writing the thesis for the MA I had abandoned for three years. It was about the

'Social Attributes in Teenage Delinquency'. I submitted it in the autumn and received the MA shortly afterwards.

The Ministry of Labour

In the autumn I applied for a position at the Ministry of Labour and Social Affairs, and was recruited on a contract basis without any difficulty. I was assigned to work at the International Department under the title of 'Expert in International Affairs'. At the beginning I did not know what was expected of me. The head of the department, Mr Kari, who had held the post for twenty years, put me in a room, three metres by three, and piled my desk with conventions, agreements, labour legislation and international labour codes. I felt like a trapped mouse. At the airline my job had been accompanied by lots of physical activity, constantly moving between buildings and the aircraft at Mehrabad Airport, which was very different from being in this tiny room with the smell of rotten papers.

For almost three months I did nothing except read documents and have occasional briefing sessions with Mr Kari. Correspondence in Persian was my biggest problem. At Iran Air almost all our correspondence had been in English. Manuals, letters and circulars were written in English because all the heads of the departments were American. I had to take the time to learn how to write reports in the eloquent Persian style customary at the top ministerial level. By the end of six months I was confident in the job and Mr Kari was pleased with my progress.

The Ministry of Labour was an establishment which traditionally attracted politically minded people. During the early 1940s and 1950s communist elements had infiltrated its rank and file, in the hope of changing labour legislation in favour of the working class. The ministry had the responsibility for drafting the labour legislation, supervising labour regulations and inspecting the factories. I understood through my colleagues that the ex-party members who worked at the ministry were constantly under scrutiny and control. If there was political unrest some of the employees would disappear for a few days. They were taken to secret places, and interrogated by SAVAC. Although the Tudeh Party had disintegrated and most of its members were cooperating with the regime, some were still used as scapegoats every once in a while.

The ministry had a big security department which was headed by a woman who wore the hejab. Mrs Ghaem-Maghami was a religious woman, who took her religious duties seriously and who did not hesitate to report anyone to SAVAC for interrogation and detention. Almost all the employees at the security department were women. Since their office was across from my room, they tried to befriend me, which I cautiously rejected. Interestingly enough there was a large number of women working at the ministry at all levels, including a woman deputy to the minister and a few deputy directors.

Children of yesterday, the youth of today

By the end of the 1960s my sister, Simin, who had finished a degree in business studies and an MA in International Relations, was employed at the Central Bank. She was now a long way from the girl who had come to Tehran in search of a better future. Now she was an ambitious, independent woman who knew how to stand up for herself. Manuchehr had finished two degrees simultaneously, one in business administration, the other in political sciences. Later, he got an MA in International Relations, all of them with honours. In the late 1960s Manuchehr was drafted into the compulsory military service, where he spent two years outside Tehran. Mehdi had also finished his high school and was in the military as well. Maryam was in her last years of high school. Although my mother's health was relatively stable, we were constantly worried the tumour might spread again. Apart from Mehdi, who had spent most of his time with my father, because my mother could not tolerate his rebellious nature, the rest of us had not gone to Jiroft for years. None of us were close to my father and we didn't really miss him.

Mothering, a sweet and sour experience

After I left the airline I planned to have children. I got pregnant in the summer of 1970. Dr Nafisi, my gynaecologist who had trained in the US, advised me to have a complete rest because he believed I might have a miscarriage. I got sick leave from the ministry for nine months. Since Iraj was busy at work, I moved to my mother's household. I stayed in bed for three months. After the initial danger was gone, Dr Nafisi permitted me to get up, and so I moved back to our apartment and began decorating a room for the baby I had long wanted to have.

At the time, it was a trend among some Iranians to travel to a Western country to have their children delivered. Some advised me to do the same. This way, they argued, the baby would have a Western nationality as well as an Iranian one. I rejected the idea ferociously. Who needed a Western nationality? I often repeated. Nevertheless, Iraj made a trip to London to buy necessary items which we had chosen from the Mothercare catalogue. He also brought a few books on childcare and child psychology which I read with much interest. Since Massoud's birth eleven years earlier we had not had a baby in the family and everyone was looking forward to the newcomer.

I expected to have the baby in mid-April but there were no signs of it then. On April 24 I was taken to Asia Hospital to have a caesarean section and ten minutes later a baby boy, weighing eight pounds, was carried outside the room into Iraj's hands. I stayed in hospital for ten days, while friends and relatives came to visit. Iraj's family were glad to have a male grandchild. Their daughter Mehri had four daughters by then.

Naming the baby was a custom. Unlike most Western names which do not have a specific meaning, Persian names bear meanings which reflect the culture, class, beliefs, ethnicity and education of the parents. If parents come from a religious background children's names are usually religious names, Ali, Reza, Fatima and so on. When you are an educated couple names are taken from the old Persian legends or heroes or ancient kings. Names from nature are also popular: flowers, birds, aromas, herbs and concepts which form around the sea or dreams, with poetic, soothing pronunciations. During historical periods, revolts and upheavals, specific names get preference. For example, during the 1979 Iranian Revolution religious names traditionally chosen by religious circles and names relating to the national heroes and those who fought against the tyrants, invaders and dictatorships became fashionable: Hossein, Abuzar, Yaser, Arash, Babak, Mazdak and so on.

As for our son, we preferred a name which was derived from the ancient Persian era and at the same time was easy to pronounce both in Persian and English. Finally, on the third day, Manuchehr, aware of our indecisiveness, carved the name 'Parham' on a gold coin and brought it to the hospital as a present. The name Parham can be found in ancient Persian mythology and had been on our final list.

Parham was taken home with much excitement and joy but it took me some time to get used to him because he cried for most of the time. Being a mother was a new and unique experience. Although I loved him dearly he made me angry with his demanding nature and his manipulation of my body and soul. I had to arrange everything around his needs. He deprived me of sleep, leisure, pleasure and what I really wanted to do. He demanded my full-time attention. I wondered how clever he was; when I held him in my arms he would be quiet, but as soon as I put him on his bed or gave him to someone else, he would begin screaming. Sometimes I was angry at having had him at all, knowing that from now on I would never be as free as I had been and that this creature which had been created out of my body and who drew sustenance from me would manipulate me from now on. Nevertheless, the irony was that my love for him was unconditional, something which he must have known right from the beginning.

Motherhood in the Iran of the 1970s was different from previous decades. While my mother and grandmother had brought up their children in an environment where experience and common sense prevailed, my generation was obsessed with educational and philosophical dilemmas and bringing up children according to the latest theories developed by Western psychologists. Physically, I learnt how to lay him on his stomach, how to bathe, feed and change him. I was not very keen to give him my milk, because it was considered unnecessary. Needless to say the milk dried up after a month. I made a lot of fuss about his hygiene and would not let anyone go into his room, unless I was sure they had washed their hands. I would not let anyone hold him for long in case he became spoilt. My obsession often irritated Iraj's family who wanted to come around and treat their grandchild the way they wanted.

Despite all this, I did not plan to stay at home and be a full-time mother/housewife. I was not the type. No matter how passionately I loved the baby, I still wanted to go back to work as soon as possible. What was the use of me staying at home, regressing socially and intellectually? I believed it was possible to employ a trained nanny to do my job and I would spend quality time with the baby whenever I was available. Many women did the same. After three months of staying at home, I found a suitable nanny and returned to the ministry. The problem was that I had now become a government civil servant on a permanent basis. Government civil servants were not well paid in comparison to those in the private sector. My salary did not even cover the nanny's wages. I resigned from the ministry and applied for a better paid job.

I got a temporary part-time job at the Iranian Air Force Language School. The school was the biggest in the Middle East and catered for those who were initially employed by the air force as pilots, cadets and engineers. The school had about four hundred part-time and full-time English-language lecturers, mainly foreign nationals.

During the 1960s and 1970s the army, the navy and the air force were expanding at a phenomenal speed. Academies, schools and colleges had been established all over the country. Apart from these establishments, thousands were being sent to the West, especially America, to be trained with the sophisticated arms the Shah was constantly ordering. To become an English lecturer you had to pass a proficiency exam, then they would put you on a six-week training course to learn how to teach English as a second language. When I applied to the air force Iraj decided to apply as well. He had lots of free time in the afternoon after he came home from his job at the airline and together we earned good money.

I befriended a couple who had recently come from America. Massoud and Mary Ann both worked as full-time lecturers. Massoud had been in America for nine years, where he married Mary Ann and brought her to Tehran with their one-year-old son, Michael. We began to socialise on a regular basis. Mary Ann was witty, sensitive and at the same time very antagonistic towards the traditional way Massoud's family lived. Massoud's mother, having a big house in the north of Tehran, had allocated her upstairs flat for them to live in. Mary Ann rejected her mother-in-law's interference in their personal affairs. While Massoud had not practised his religion in America, now he performed all the religious ceremonies, to 'please his mother'. His mother did not like this foreign bride and often called her *najis* (unclean) because she was not a Muslim. Mary Ann did not comprehend the micro politics of some Iranian mothers.

During the New Year celebrations, after constant rows, Mary Ann decided to leave Iran. Our consultations and advice did not help. While she was packing to leave she was informed that she would not be allowed to take her son, Michael, with her. That devastated her. She was not aware that under the Iranian law the father had the right to custody of the child. The law also gave him the right to keep her in the country as his wife if he wished to. Mary Ann had passed the stage of making compromises, especially when her mother-in-law was determined to get rid of her. She left Iran while her son was ill with a fever. In a letter which she wrote to me from New York she explained the agony of leaving her sick child behind. She had been heartbroken and on the verge of a nervous breakdown for quite some time. She asked me to keep her informed about her son because Massoud would not communicate with her. I visited Massoud and Michael for a couple of years. He had changed Michael's name to Ali and had made him forget he had ever had an American mother. Later, Massoud married an Iranian girl his mother had chosen for him and the son forgot about his real mother altogether. I met Mary Ann a year later in New York, when she talked of nothing but her baby. Sadly, I lost contact with them both in years to come.

The love of my life in a bundle of joy

I had my second child a year later in 1972. This time I did not have to rest and therefore I continued working for the whole nine months. I drove to the hospital myself to have the caesarean section. Our baby girl weighed seven pounds. She was a beautiful baby, very quiet and slept for most of the time. We did not have much problem naming her. We were looking for a name to correspond with Parham. We agreed on Parastou (Swallow), which reminded me of the wild, immigrant swallows that appeared every spring at our orange garden in Jiroft.

Parastou was a bundle of love from the beginning. She was a quiet and sweet baby and I did not feel any pressure raising her. Unlike Parham, who was demanding and particularly attached to me, Parastou showed her independent character right from the beginning. Iraj and I tried hard not to discriminate between them and gave both of them as much love and affection as was possible.

Raising two children and working at the same time was horrendous. We had a nanny and a young girl from Jiroft, whom father had sent to help me with the household chores. While we were home we were both busy around the clock taking care of the kids. Iraj proved to be a very responsible father, although he was not such a responsible husband.

By the early 1970s my brother Manuchehr had finished his military service and had begun work for a year to save money for his eventual trip to America to get a PhD. At the time Mehdi was our biggest problem. Although he was very intelligent and could easily have been accepted at university, he was rebellious and frequently got into fights. He had no plans for continuing his education. Instead, still in his teens, he wanted to marry a girl he had fallen in love with. Once he finished his military service we decided it was best that he was sent abroad to study. Convincing my father to pay for his expenses, he left Tehran for London in 1972. By then, the orange gardens my mother had helped to grow in Jiroft made enough money to provide for Mehdi's expenses abroad. By this time my youngest sister Maryam had finished her high school and was working at the National Shoe Company as a clerk. Massoud was attending the middle school.

Iran on a slippery road, 1970–5

The taller you get, the harder you fall.
                    A Persian proverb

After the turmoil of the early 1960s the Shah had established his arbitrary rule by introducing ambitious plans of development in all areas. The increase in oil prices had money pouring into the country. In 1973 Iran's revenue from oil was $5.6 billion, while three years later it went up to $20.5 billion. From the late 1960s and early 1970s the country began a phase of rapid development. The Plan Organisation had drawn up a five-year plan to modernise Iran, bringing it into line with the developed states. During this period thousands of Iranian companies, headed by the royal family and entrepreneurs, formed partnerships with foreign companies to invest in Iran. The building of dams, hospitals, ports, shipyards, customs departments, transit roads and warehouses began to take shape. As a result, by the middle of the 1970s, there were about seventeen foreign banks, apart from tens of Iranian banks, financial corporations and insurance companies, hotels, casinos, multinational corporations, and agricultural cooperatives, all of which had mushroomed within a short period.

Now the Shah had established himself as the leading politician in the Middle East and took Iran on to the international scene by investing in other countries such as Krupp in Germany and large American corporations. In 1972 the Iranian Oil Company and the British Oil Company signed contracts to drill for oil in the North Sea. In 1974 Iran agreed to give Britain a loan of $1.2 billion. In 1973, in an interview with a Belgian reporter, the Shah said that apart from a Belgian–Iranian oil refinery in Belgium, Iran had entered into partnerships with 300 such schemes in other countries.

More ambitious than the rapid industrialisation was Iran's defence expansion, which made up a third of the country's expenditure. In 1974 Iran's arms' purchases were more than the whole of the rest of the world had spent the year before. The US lifted all restrictions on arms' deals with Iran (except atomic power) and directors of big arms factories competed forcefully for Iran's purchases. The Shah's ambition to become a super power in the region, plus the US strategy of making him the 'gendarme' of the Persian Gulf, protecting 'their' interests, increased Iran's military expenditures proportionally to oil revenues. As a result productive resources were diverted from the public sector to the military build up.

By the early 1970s the Shah, who ideologically opposed liberation movements and communist upheavals, volunteered to dispatch troops and military aid to the 'friendly' regimes which were fighting such movements within their territories. As a result of this policy the Iranian army was fighting in Zophar in the Yemen, in South Vietnam alongside the Americans, in the Congo in Africa and the Polisario in the Sahara. By then the Shah promised, 'Within twenty years, Iran will be one of the powerful industrial states.'

Politically, in the three decades after the coup of 1953, no real political party formed. Two of the Shah's self-made parties, the Iran Novin (New Iran) and the Mardom (People's) Party were headed by his close confidants, Mr Alam and Dr Eqbal. In the middle of the 1970s the Shah ordered the dissolution of these parties and the establishment of a new party, the Rastakhiz (Resurrection) Party. This meant a one-party state. Every Iranian was required to register as a member of Rastakhiz, otherwise the Shah advised, 'Those who do not approve, get their passports and leave the country.'

The Shah now believed that he had established an everlasting empire and was immune from any real threat. He therefore initiated the revival of the ancient Persian Empire with himself as the emperor. In 1970, based upon this notion, Iran hosted thousands of foreign guests who gathered in Persepolis, in the southern province of Shiraz, to mark the celebration of 2,500 years of monarchy. According to some critics the world had not seen such extravagance for centuries. For ten days kings, presidents and heads of state, along with thousands of dignitaries and reporters, were entertained in Persepolis to mark the occasion. Millions of dollars were spent on this single event. In 1974 celebrations to mark the fiftieth anniversary of the Pahlavi Dynasty coupled with the change from the Islamic lunar calendar to that of the beginning of King Cyrus's kingdom (who established the ancient Achaemenid Dynasty) were held. On the one hand, these extravagant celebrations brought the Pahlavis respect and friends among the world politicians, and on the other hand, they dug their grave.

Women of the royal family, a force behind the social change

Two women were influential within the royal family – Queen Farah, the Shah's third wife, who had liberal views and advocated Western style practices, and Princess Ashraf, the Shah's twin sister. The queen had established her own administration, where a circle of intellectuals introduced progressive social and cultural programmes. She encouraged social events, seminars and conferences which promoted her ideas of liberalisation. In 1967, for example, she inaugurated an international women's lawyers conference in Tehran. Farah's Charity Foundation implemented programmes of development throughout the country. She became the patron of the Shiraz International Art Festival, and many other art and cultural institutions. In addition, she was in close contact with the American Aspen Foundation and regularly lectured in the US on Iran.

Princess Ashraf, on the other hand, was interested in politics and the running of the country. It was known that she acted as adviser to her brother. In 1941, when Reza Shah was ousted from power and Mohammed Reza replaced him, Princess Ashraf stayed with her young brother to help him with the running of the country. As part of her involvement in politics, in 1968 she chaired the UN Human Rights Conference which convened in Tehran. For almost 15 years Princess Ashraf stayed at the UN as head of the Iranian delegation and deputy to the UN Human Rights Commission. This was ironic, because at the same time Iran was at the top of the human rights organisations' list of human rights abusers. Princess Ashraf aimed to be appointed the first woman UN Secretary General. In 1975 she headed the Iranian delegation to the first International Women's Conference in Mexico. Her influence and the huge amount of money paid by Iran towards the conference, secured Iran as the host of the next women's conference of 1979. Before the Mexico conference a gathering convened in Tehran, where hundreds of women celebrated the fortieth anniversary of the unveiling. In the 1970s, with the support of Princess Ashraf and Queen Farah, the Iranian Women's Organisation which had been established in the late 1960s, expanded throughout the major cities. Mrs Homa Afzal, a lawyer who headed the IWO for many years, along with other women activists, put forward radical plans to the legislature to change the situation of women within the family. Family Protection Law, ratified in 1967 and re-written in 1975, changed the Shari'at law, bringing it into line with secular law. Under the family law, men's unilateral right to divorce was abolished and divorce had to be granted by secular courts. Polygamy became more difficult and children's custody went under the courts' rule. These changes were opposed by the ulama and those who advocated the Shari'at as the law of land. In the late 1960s a ministerial post on women's affairs was created and an American-educated woman, Mrs Afkhami, was appointed as the first minister. In line with modernisation, more women entered the job market and a few held positions of power. Dr Farokhru Parsai, the headmistress of a well-known girls' high school in Tehran (Nour Bakhsh), was appointed the Education Minister. Women were elected as members of parliament and to the senate, and employed at the foreign office as ambassadors and consuls. By the end of the 1970s there were a considerable number of women judges and lawyers (estimated at 500), and hundreds of thousands of women in other non-conventional jobs. Needless to say the situation of women in general was far from being equal to that of men. Nevertheless, in a country like Iran, where change had always been slow and brought about from above, the existence of powerful women within the royal family and at higher levels of Iranian society brought a degree of advancement to women which otherwise would not have been possible.

After being granted suffrage in 1963, women were expected to do military service like men. However, instead of being trained for front line battle, women were assigned to the literacy and health corps which had been created as part of the White Revolution. During the early 1970s an estimated 6,000 women were engaged in these corps. A few years later a number of them were promoted to the military ranks by the Shah's decree. Nevertheless, not every sphere of women's lives became equal to that of men. Women had no freedom of movement and travel. Written permission from their husbands was needed for them to travel abroad. The gap between boys and girls still existed in matters related to inheritance, job attribution and socialisation for future roles. Despite all this, Iran was well ahead of some other Islamic countries such as Egypt, Algeria and Morocco.

An examination of the developments

Healing must be sought in the blood of the wound itself
It is another of the old achemical truths that
No solution should be made
Except in its own blood.
                    Nor Hall, *Mothers and Daughters*

The Shah's ambitious pace towards modernisation in Iran did not involve the majority of the people, 35 per cent of whom were illiterate. Millions still lived on an income of around $100 per annum. This figure was general and there were regional variations and hierarchical structures in the rural areas. The labourers who worked for the peasants, cattle raisers, and migrant workers who got seasonal jobs were paid much less. The land reforms of the 1960s did not bring prosperity to the agricultural and rural areas. Instead, they ruined the old structure of peasant–feudal relations without replacing it with a workable system. It has been estimated that only four thousand villages benefited from the land reforms of the 1960s. Of 55,000 villages, only 5 per cent had piped water and electricity. The way the oil revenue was being spent magnified the weaknesses of the Iranian economy. As a result, rural migrants poured into the cities and swamped the outskirts, creating shanty towns. These were the ones who witnessed the gap and stratification between the rich and the poor and were where the seeds of revenge grew for years to come.

With the introduction of reforms and the haste towards bringing Iran into line with modern states, old cultural values began to crack, while the new cultural mores, such as women's liberation and Western-style development, were not accepted by the masses. The grandiose plans of development, massive importation of food and consumer goods, the rapidly rising rate of inflation, spread of corruption and above all the decline of agricultural productivity contributed to the demise of the regime. The unequal distribution of wealth meant that 10 per cent of the population held more than 32.5 per cent of all the revenue. The Shah's empire was being built on loose foundations. Modernisation, especially its cultural manifestations, was a gloss over an old, decayed society, where the majority of the population, culturally and intellectually, had not come further than the Middle Ages. Cracks began to appear as soon as the gloss dried out.

The emergence of new opposition groups, 1965–75

He who plants wind, harvests storm.
          A Persian proverb

From the early 1950s, after the initial phase of the coup, opposition to the Shah began to form. Merchants, shopkeepers and retailers were traditionally opposed to modernisation and foreign capital because they ruined their livelihood. Modernisation not only conflicted with their business interests but it was also a danger to the old cultural mores which ruled their domestic lives. Maintaining the veil, Islamic marriage, polygamy, temporary marriage and laws concerning inheritance, were the backbone of their opposition to reforms and change. In the early 1960s, when the late Ayatollah Khomeini opposed the Shah's reforms, especially women's suffrage, these classes supported the Ayatollah, mobilised the masses, financed the opposition and were in the forefront of the upheavals of 1962–3.

The ulama and the mujtahids, leaders of the Shi'at branch of Islam, who had traditionally resided in Iraq since the eighteenth century and were out of the king's jurisdiction, frequently defied the kings, unless they themselves were part of the ruling circles. Since people paid them Islamic taxes (*Khoms* and *Zakat*), the ulama were financially well off and able to mobilise the opposition. They put themselves above the secular law and defied the Shah's decrees. Reza Shah was the first to limit the ulama's power by sending them into exile and discrediting them. Mohammed Reza was more lenient towards them. He had developed religious beliefs and superstitious notions himself and alleged that he was being guided by 'unknown powers'.

In the 1950s a few Islamic elements who opposed the Pahlavi regime formed a militant group and, as their first political act, assassinated Prime Minister Mansour. They were the first organised Islamic militants who openly resorted to violence in their opposition to secular government. They called themselves Fedaian Islam.

Ayatollah Khomeini was among the group of ulamas who made no compromise in matters relating to modernisation and Western investment in Iran. From the very beginning the Ayatollah had aimed for an Islamic state where Islamic laws prevailed. This Islamic utopia had no specific aim except for the overthrow of the monarchy and the establishment of an Islamic state whose structure and nature were not clarified. After Ayatollah Khomeini went into exile in 1963 his sermons, teachings and directives never failed to reach his followers inside the country. He, and a group of followers, established a network of communication which grew stronger as other religious and non-religious opposition groups formed.

In 1965 three young Islamists formed a militant group, Mujahidin Khalgh, which included elements of socialism in its doctrine and presented a reformed version of Islam. Three years later this group increased in number and formed its first executive committee of thirteen. Supporters of the Mujahidin emerged from among the young and educated Muslims who were in search of solutions within Islam. The group's activities included underground guerrilla warfare against the Shah's regime. They took responsibility for a number of assassinations and acts of sabotage and bombings.

By the early 1970s, as the Mujahidin grew stronger, the Shah's secret police stepped up its effort to eliminate them. A number of their leaders were killed in battles with SAVAC, or later executed in prisons. Nevertheless, it was the era of Che Guevara-style warfare and the Third World liberation movements which appealed to the youth and contributed to the emergence of such groups. The Mujahidin grew in number as part of the popular movement, especially among the young Muslims who rejected the old, traditional clergy establishment.

In the 1960s and 1970s a few individuals emerged whose doctrines had a great impact on Iranian society. The most prominent were Jala Al Ahmed and Dr Ali Shariati. Al Ahmed, originally a secular writer, began his campaign against modernisation and open door policies by an attack on the 'Westernisation' and 'Westoxication' of Iranian society. In a famous essay Al Ahmed attacked all manifestations of modern Iran and called for the re-instatement of Islamic society and Islamic values. Being originally secular, Al Ahmed's ideas appealed to many intellectuals whose limited world-view and hostility to Western culture corresponded to this doctrine.

However, the emergence of the word 'Westernisation' in Persian literature had destructive consequences beyond the literary. Since then, any attempt to modernise Iran, to bring it into line with other modern states has been rejected. Modernisation corresponded with Westernisation and was interpreted as dependency on the West, infiltration by Western culture and the disintegration of traditional Iranian society, and hence rejected by the bulk of lay religious thinkers, as well as some of the intellectuals. To this day, very few writers have tried to deconceptualise 'Westernisation', replacing it with other concepts which have more relevancy to the modern world; a world which Iran was part of and should have remained so.

The second individual whose ideas found strong ground among the Muslim intellectuals was Dr Ali Shariati, who aimed for a reformed Islamic society, based on his interpretation of Islam. Shariati's ideas appealed to thousands of young Muslims who wanted an Islamic state. These reformist views became popular and were adopted by some reformist mosques and religious schools. Dr Shariati was an excellent agitator and propagandist. The mosque he lectured in (Hosseinieh Ershad in Tehran) was eventually closed down by the authorities in the late 1960s and Shariati himself fled the country in 1976. A year later he died in London in suspicious circumstances.

Apart from religious opposition to the Shah, in the late 1960s and early 1970s elements of the communist Tudeh Party's youth began regrouping in an underground Marxist organisation. These people, like the Mujahidin, resorted to arms in order to put their message across. This guerrilla movement (Fedaian-Khalgh) declared its existence by attacking an army post in Siahkal, in the north of the country, where they were captured and sent to prison. Their leader, Bijan Jazani, wrote about his political theories and analysis while in prison and sent them out in secret to be published as guidance to his followers. Later, nine of the captured Marxist guerrillas and two of the Mujahidin were executed while in the Evin prison.

Those communist guerrillas who escaped the Shah's persecution at the time, along with their ever-increasing numbers of supporters, established an organisation which became the backbone of the biggest Left movement in Iran, after the Tudeh Party. The Fedaian took Marxist-Leninist ideology and the Che Guevara guerrilla warfare style as strategy, to combat the Shah's arbitrary rule. Although with few arms and poor training the guerrillas of the 1970s, both the Islamists and the communists, were successful in some of their armed attacks and became a thorn in the Shah's side, who saw himself unable to eliminate them, despite his secret police and having the biggest army of the Middle East. Interestingly, among the ranks of both the Mujahidin and the Fedaians, the number of women guerrillas was considerable. In the early 1970s, for example, a woman guerrilla, Ashraf Dehghani, escaped from Evin prison in a dramatic scenario and fled Iran. Her memoirs which were translated into many languages, created an international outcry against Iran's abuse of human rights. During the 1970s prisons were full of anti-Shah groups and the knowledge of their heroism and resistance under the most barbaric tortures spread among the people, inspiring thousands to join their ranks and fight the Shah's tyranny.

Outside Iran, both in America and Europe, Iranian students formed the biggest opposition group. The Iranian Students' Confederation campaigned at the international level, exposing the Shah's pro-US stand, arms' purchases, the country's lack of democracy and poor human rights record and her dependency on the West. The Confederation had branches in most European and American cities, with many Western politicians, writers and intellectuals supporting its struggles for a free Iran. Later, when the revolution neared, most of the Confederation's activists took sides with one of the opposition groups, either Fedaian, Mujahidin or the pro-Khomeini groups, and returned to Iran to help the revolution materialise.

A picture of the Shah himself and his personal views on social and political issues is best shown in an interview he had with an Italian journalist. In October 1973 Oriana Fallaci had an interview with him, during which he revealed some of his ambitions. Fallaci wondered whether, 'This cold-eyed, slim man who has reigned the hottest spot on earth, belonged to the era of Soloman's flying carpet, or the computer era.' She later wrote: 'He was a sad dictator who reminded me of the moment the dead are carried to the cemetery.' In the interview the Shah confessed that he was a lonely, sad person, very religious and often inspired and protected by the unknown powers. He said that he did not believe women were equal to men, although he had given them equal rights. 'Women are admired for their beauty and their womanhood,' he said. 'What do these women's movements want? Women are not capable of being equal, if you excuse my words. When women rule, they are crueller and bloodthirstier than men.'

As far as democracy was concerned, the Shah believed that in a country with 35 per cent illiteracy, democracy was meaningless. He said that he did not want a 'Western-style democracy, where everyone is allowed to go on strike and march on the streets'. He did not need to consult anyone, especially women, who were not important enough to be consulted. His best friends were the Americans and as long as he had the oil, he would sell it and spend the money the way he wanted. This was the man who ruled Iran for thirty-seven years.

Chapter Seven

The Iranian Bank, 1973

Once my children were old enough to be left alone with the nanny for longer periods, I decided to leave the part-time teaching job at the air force and get a permanent job. In Iran, like many other countries, it was easier to find a job through personal connections and so I asked some of my friends and relatives to inform me if a proper opportunity arose. Before long a relative informed me of a vacancy as head of administration at the Iranian Bank. I applied for the job.

The Iranian Bank was a private establishment, run by Mr Abolhassa Ebtehaj, the chairman and the main shareholder, and his wife, Azar Ebtehaj, in cooperation with the National City Bank of New York. At the time, Mr Cyrus Sami'i, an American-educated banker, was the bank's president. The Iranian Bank had established a tradition of promoting women into management ranks. Because Mrs Ebtehaj, a wealthy, powerful woman in Iranian high society, was on the board of directors, it gave women the opportunity to be promoted to higher positions along with men. In 1973, out of fifteen departments, eight were headed by women. Women were also given positions as deputy assistants at the bank's branches, the foreign exchange, and credit and loans.

The bank's purpose-built 12-storey building, located on the prestigious Persepolis Avenue, had tinted windows and a huge, gold lion emblem at the top which could be seen from a far distance. The bank's offices had been designed by a top firm of architects and decorated in orange, royal blue and deep green, Mr Ebtehaj's personal choice. Each floor had open plan offices, where the managers sat in the front rows, the secretaries and the staff at the back. The whole building was connected through loudspeakers, which often played light Iranian or classical music, according to Mr Ebtehaj's personal taste. Both the chairman and the president had their offices on the top floor, with an internal telephone system connected to the managers and the branches.

Although I had knowledge of general management and administration I knew nothing about banking. So, first of all I familiarised myself with the organisation by spending some time in each department. I took over the administrative department in October 1973. It was a big department, consisting of procurements, insurance, public relations, bank records and administration of the building. I had eight employees working for me. Of the twelve storeys, five were occupied by the bank, the rest were leased out to big companies who in their contract were obliged to maintain the building's high standards. As part of my job I was expected to deal with these companies; renewing their leases, seeing to their needs, collecting rents and dealing with their insurance policies. Working directly with the president and the chairman was very stressful. I had to be in the office early in the morning, stay for meetings until late and get involved in the politics of the establishment. Nevertheless, the salary was good and through the bank I came to know most of Iranian high society.

Mr Ebtehaj was one of Iran's top managers. He had helped to establish the National Bank of Iran (Bank Meli Iran) and had run it for some years. He had been appointed as head of the Plan Organisation which drew up the five-year development plan for the country. In the latter stages of his pubic service, during Reza Shah's reign, he had developed differences with the American financial consultant Dr Melipso and as a result had resigned from public office and entered the private sector and established the Iranian Bank. Nevertheless, he kept his personal friendship with Princess Ashraf, whom he invited for lunch at the bank every once in a while. When I joined the bank Mr Ebtehaj was about eighty years of age. Being a sportsman, he did not look his age at all. He played tennis regularly and walked from his home in the north of Tehran a few miles down to his office every day. Once he reached the bank's building he used to climb the stairs to the eleventh floor, without even stopping on the way.

Azar Ebtehaj was an interesting, outspoken woman. She had once been married to a wealthy man by whom she had two grown-up children. Eventually she had fallen in love with Mr Ebtehaj, divorced her husband and married Mr Ebtehaj. Being influential at the highest level, she did not hesitate to visit the prime minister and other cabinet members if she had any grievances. She enjoyed a certain degree of power and was able to influence some politicians. The Ebtehajs had apartments in Nice and London as well as in the north of the country at the seaside, where they often spent their holidays. Mr Ebtehaj was also an antique and art collector. His house, where every once in a while he entertained the bank's senior personnel, was full of precious items. It was equipped with a swimming pool, a tennis court and had a huge garden. After the revolution the house was confiscated by the revolutionary guards, who made it their headquarters. I often wondered what happened to the many antiques which had been collected over the years by the Ebtehajs.

Mr Sami'i, on the other hand, was a US-educated banker, who brought with him a group of technocrats and had control of most departments in the bank. Mr Ebtehaj and Mr Sami'i's managerial styles were sometimes contradictory and clashed with each other, making it difficult to keep a balance between them. Factionalism was evident on such occasions. Senior managers were pressed to side with one faction. Since I had come from the outside, not being originally related to any of the factions, I was confused as to which side to take. Personally, I preferred Mr Ebtehaj. Having seen the American environment firsthand, I did not find it to my taste.

Another person who was influential at the bank was Robert Shot, who had lived in Iran for almost twenty years and spoke good Persian. His title was 'adviser' to the bank but it was alleged that he was one of the official CIA agents in Iran. There may have been some truth to this because Shot never engaged himself in the bank's affairs; he was more interested in collecting information on influential individuals and kept a directory of all the public and private managers in Tehran. Personally I did not like him for his meddling in other people's affairs. The last time I saw him was at the height of the revolution. I was on a march, soaked by the intense rain, when I noticed Shot, walking on the opposite side. Our eyes locked for a moment. He knew I disapproved of him, as I had indicated with my remarks, and he ran away from the scene before I could talk to him. He probably thought I would let the crowd know who he really was. Actually the thought did not come to mind until much later, after I had left the march for home.

Both Mr Sami'i and Mr Ebtehaj liked to hold receptions every once in a while as part of the publicity to attract customers. My department was responsible for the organisation of such parties, usually attended by more than 900 people. A few weeks before the occasion I was expected to prepare the guest list, menu, and the budget for Mr Sami'i's approval. Bank managers were also present at these parties where dealing, money transfer, and customer hunting took place. Although stressful, I had to be present to oversee everything and play the hostess. Sometimes groups of foreign investors, who visited Iran, were entertained as well.

Initially, I enjoyed these receptions and meeting so many 'important' people. Gradually, my eyes opened to what was behind this high society and I began to realise where Iran was heading. The bulk of the top managers were nothing but people who were plagued by greed, corruption and hypocrisy. Some had returned from abroad with the notion of developing and improving the state apparatus. Others returned with bad habits of boozing, clubbing and gambling, instead of importing the high culture of Western societies, and became involved in behind-the-scene politics at micro and macro levels. Conspiracies against each other, holding onto their positions at any price and walking over others, bribing and receiving commissions were rife within Iranian high society. Some of the top managers spent money on apartments for their mistresses, trips either abroad or to the Caspian Sea resorts. The extremes between a sophisticated, privileged minority and the traditional backward majority clashed with each other, creating a storm which swept away everything in its way.

Life in the early 1970s

I climbed the ladder of doubt
I saw through the certainty of sorrow
And love was born of me.
    Mina Dastgheib, *In the Brightness of Dawn*

From the time I left Iran Air in 1969 Iraj's position in the organisation had improved dramatically. The training department had expanded and Iraj had become deputy director. He had a big office, a secretary and a number of instructors working for him. When I left there were 150 flight crew. In the mid-1970s there were 1,200 cabin personnel, including 400 foreigners, mainly British nationals. Working at Iran Air was very fashionable among young people both in Iran and abroad. The recruiting panel interviewed thousands of applicants in week-long sessions, only to select a few hundred.

Due to our work situation, our life-style became very unconventional. Iraj and I did not spend much spare time together, the way other couples did. The positive aspect of our union was the independence we kept. Although to some people it looked 'unnatural', I never doubted that our arrangement was the best. We had few common interests and our friends and associates were not necessarily the same, though we had a number of mutual friends. Although I was sometimes suspicious of what he did or who he associated with, I was too busy myself to worry overmuch about these matters. Although Iraj's complained that I did not love him enough to feel jealous, I believe I trusted him a lot, more than I should have done. As for him, he was jealous of all my friends and irritated me with his sarcastic remarks. Our hectic life-style gradually separated my world from Iraj's. We developed lots of differences but it always ended in maintaining the status quo. I sometimes thought of separation but legally that was very difficult. He threatened he would take the children away from me and create a scandal so that I would lose my job. I was afraid of this and the lengthy court procedures which were on his side anyway. Besides, we were both very emotional, sensitive people. Although we knew that as we grew older, we had less in common, we were not able to go our separate ways. But one thing we had agreed on was to never raise our voices in front of the children. That would be harmful to them and we avoided it at any price.

Keeping in line with men at work needed an enormous effort. I had to gain their respect and prove that I could be even better than them, be more disciplined and hardworking. Almost all the successful women I knew were tough and hardworking. It was impossible to use female strategies to advance yourself at work. If you did, you were branded as having affairs and bribing your way by means of your sexuality – leaving you in danger of losing your reputation in a society which was harsh on women and not used to their presence as independent people.

Sometimes it was hard to keep up with everything, bringing up two kids and having a full-time job at managerial level. I tried to spend as much time with the children as possible and supervised every detail of their growing up. Between 1975 and 1977 my responsibilities increased when my sister Simin got a scholarship from the Central Bank to study in the US. My brother Manuchehr was already in Chicago. I had to see my mother more often once my sister went away. Simin stayed in Washington, where she married a man she had met in Iran. They had their first daughter, Saviz, before they returned home in 1977.

Along with our busy life, Parham and Parastou were growing up quickly. Both were happy kids, dearly loved and cared for. I never missed waking them up in the morning myself, having breakfast with them and bathing them in the evening, and putting them to sleep. They had different personalities. Parham was very attached to me and found it hard to socialise with strangers. Parastou, on the other hand, was a warm and friendly child. In 1974, when they were three and two respectively, I decided to send them to a kindergarten. Full-time nannies were expensive and hard to keep. Besides, I believed that it was healthier if they socialised with other kids. After some search I came across a French kindergarten (Petite Poucet). Mrs Mohtashemi, a Frenchwoman who had married an Iranian, ran the establishment. Although it had a long waiting list I managed to register both children. Iraj and I had an arrangement for our income. He usually paid for the rent and the bills, I paid for food, the children's expenses and other necessities. Because the kindergarten fees were very high I had to economise on other things in order to pay the fees. We barely had any savings. Since the kindergarten closed at one in the afternoon, I had to recruit a part-time nanny as well.

In 1974 just a year after I was employed at the Iranian bank, we decided to buy a plot of land to build a house. Since our marriage in 1965 we had been living in the two-bedroom apartment we had rented in Amir Abad. Iraj was cautious about undertaking such a heavy financial commitment. I, on the other hand, was determined to build us a house. I started looking for the land and finally found a plot in Shemiran, the suburb north of Tehran. It was located in a cul de sac, off the famous Niavaran Avenue, and there were three other houses in the street. Since we had no savings I asked the bank's president to give me a loan to buy the land, which he agreed to do. Shemiran was traditionally a summer resort for wealthy Iranians. The whole area, some ten square miles, was located on the slopes of the Alborz mountains. At the time we were looking for land, there were hundreds of unspoilt orchards, full of jasmine and rose bushes which hung from the walls, filling the streets with their aromas. Shemiran's market place, with its old bazaar and a holy shrine, its fruit and vegetables shops was a famous place for exclusive products. We planned to begin the construction as soon as we obtained a loan from another bank.

In 1975 my young sister Maryam, who worked at the Meli Shoe company, met a young accountant and decided to marry him although I believed she was too young. Being only twenty, she had not experienced life the way Simin and I had. Nevertheless, we did not object to her decision. Because of my mother's illness, those children who lived at home could not enjoy family life, the way others did. My father had washed his hands of all responsibilities by staying in Jiroft and we were busy with our own lives. Maryam's husband came from Tabriz, the centre of the Azarbaijan province. Persian was their second language and they spoke Turkish for most of the time and kept to their strict customs and traditions. After her marriage Maryam had to move to her in-laws' household and, being young and inexperienced, she had to accept her mother-in-law's superiority for many years, learning their language and following their customs. When finally she had two daughters and matured enough to stand up for herself, she separated her house from theirs.

My workplace in turmoil

By 1975 dramatic changes happened at the Iranian Bank. Suddenly, out of the blue, a super wealthy man, Hojabr Yazdani, appeared in Iranian high society. Yazdani, a cattle raiser by profession, came from Semnan, a city located alongside the eastern deserts. He moved to Tehran, transferred his money into business and began investing in many areas, including banking. One day we heard that Mr Yazdani had bought all the 29 per cent of shares which belonged to the City Bank. As a result, all foreigners who worked at the bank, apart from Robert Shot, left.

Yazdani was an uneducated man, from a peasant-feudal culture, who came to the bank with two bodyguards. To show off his wealth he had bought himself big diamond rings, many carats in weight, and employed the guards to protect these rings. He bought himself a mini-castle in Shemiran, which later became the centre of extravagant parties for high society. Yazdani was a macho patriarch who did not have any respect for women. He liked to make sexual jokes with female staff. His arrival coincided with rows and mounting differences between the chairman and the president, and we, as managers, were the first victims. Being caught between the politics at the top, I lost my position and a man who was the head of the foreign currency department took over my job.

I was not offered another post. Although my salary was being paid regularly, I stayed side-lined for almost a year. Some other managers had the same fate. Meanwhile, the president himself was replaced by someone from the Central Bank. The Ebtehajs lost their authority and Yazdani became the big boss.

A new airline

At the end of 1975 I ran across an acquaintance from Iran Air who had recently been appointed director of a small airline, Vigeh Airways. The airline was a joint venture between Iran Air and the Ministry of Agriculture. The ministry had a few spraying aircraft and aimed to expand its operations into a bigger money-making business, spraying farming cooperatives in the north of the country. Abbas Mir-Rashidi was looking for a team to get the project off the ground. He invited me to join and after some negotiations about the position and the salary, I accepted the offer. I resigned from the bank to become the personnel and administrative manager of this new establishment. Apart from me, there were just five other managers, all male.

Mir-Rashidi was an ambitious man who came from a middle-class family in Quom, the holy city. His wife belonged to a religious family and often wore the chador. Nevertheless, Abbas himself was not a religious person. We got on very well. His position at Iran Air was not much higher than mine and knowing the same circle of people, I felt very much at home. I had a free hand to plan and reorganise the establishment. Vigeh had its base in Qazvin and its head office in Tehran. I travelled to Qazvin, either by small Cessna aircraft or by car, interviewing the staff and listening to their grievances and adjusting their salaries. Within one year, I had doubled everyone's salary and given them many fringe benefits which they had not had before. As part of my job I also travelled abroad to recruit personnel to fill our technical and flight staff shortages. Once I travelled to Pakistan to recruit mechanics. I was accompanied by the technical manager. In a week-long session we interviewed almost a thousand people, to employ only seven mechanics. Foreigners, especially Third World nationals, competed for employment with Iranian companies as the pay and fringe benefits were good. Among our personnel at Vigeh we had all nationalities: American, French, Filipino and people from the sub-continent.

My children's schooling

Parham and Parastou attended the French Petite Pucet for three years, after which I registered Parham at a French primary school, Saint Luis, and Parastou at the Lycée Razi. The Saint Luis principal was a Frenchman who had made Iran his home. His school was famous for its high standards and discipline. Lycée Razi was the oldest, mixed, French school in Tehran. Both schools taught lessons in Persian and French. Since we frequently travelled abroad, particularly to England to see my brother Mehdi who was now studying for a degree in Industrial Design at Ealing College, the children had learnt some English. I wanted them to learn another language. In addition, I believed in the French educational system more than the British or the American. The memory we had of the French presence in Iran was of their high culture, gracious social manners and their love of literature, art and the Eastern people. The French had never had any direct colonial involvement in Iran and that contributed to my perception of the advantages of a French education for my children. Both Parham and Parastou continued their education in French schools until a year after the revolution, when these schools were ordered to close down. The day I took Parham's file from Saint Luis the principal, in tears, told me in his perfect Persian that he had been ordered to leave the country and go home. 'Where shall I go after 33 years?' he asked me. 'This is my home.'

Building our dream house

By the beginning of 1977 we had drawn sketches for our house. I gave the architect details of what I wanted and, after we signed the contract with a builder, the work began in early spring. We had to oversee the construction and buy building materials ourselves. Iraj was often out shopping and I was at the building site in the afternoons and also whenever I could leave my workplace during the day.

It was a four-storey building and took us two years to finish and decorate. Before the construction finished, I travelled to London to buy locks, bolts, door handles, mirrors and other small decorative items. Since our old furniture was not suitable for such a big house, I spent time and money in ordering beds, suites, curtains, bookshelves, garden and kitchen furniture, kitchen shelves and other necessities. I used a lot of expertise from the Iranian Bank to do the woodwork, painting and the finishing touches and thoroughly enjoyed the whole process. We moved to the new house in mid-summer 1978 before the decoration was finished. The children could not have been happier. They were excited to have their own spacious rooms. In the neighbourhood there were many children of their age and since the street was quiet and safe, they were allowed to play outside or go to their friends' homes. The only thing we didn't have was a telephone line which took years to get. Tehran, with its shining surface, and a population of five million, was a long way from being fully equipped with modern technology.

The neighbourhood's social background was different from those of Amir Abad, who came from mainly lower middle-class civil servants. In Shemiran our neighbours were either top managers in the private sector or government establishments. There were big gardens on all sides, where tall trees circled the swimming pools. Apart from us, all the neighbours had swimming pools. We did not build one because our money ran out. Alongside our street a brook of underground water surfaced, giving the alley a natural beauty. I planted poplar and plane trees alongside this brook. A few years later they had grown tall, producing a cool shade against the heat of the summer.

In years to come, I grew poplar trees alongside our rear garden walls. I grew fruit trees, cherries, pears, figs, in this garden and decorated the borders with different roses. On the side of the street I grew flower beds and a type of grape which soon began to harvest. I was proud of my garden which now competed with the other gardens around. Although we built the house from almost empty purses, the sale of the upstairs flat helped us to pay off most of our debts. We had worked hard to reach that point and I wanted us to enjoy every moment of it.

Chapter Eight

Political unrest: the beginning or the end?

Through a confusion of splendour
Through a night made of stone let me plunge my hand
And move to beat in me a bird
Held for a thousand years.
   Pablo Neruda, 'The Heights of Macchu Picchu'

From 1977 cracks began to appear in the Iranian state apparatus. There were strikes and sporadic demonstrations. In intellectual circles we talked about where things were heading and in my trips abroad I read about Iran's ambitious plans and how the oil money was being spent on arms. In the West the Shah had become a famous figure. He had distanced himself from the puppet regime whose power had been consolidated by the US administration in 1953. This was against the fact that Americans had heavily invested in Iran, both directly and indirectly.

Because of Iran's international prestige and the Shah's generous donations to some of the foreign countries, we were respected abroad. Most countries had lifted visas for Iranian subjects. Britain was one of them. Our money seemed strong and the exchange rate good. I remember I was in a taxi in central London once when the driver asked me where I came from. I told him that I came from Iran. He looked at me in the mirror and said, 'Lucky you, so much sunshine and so much oil.'

However, this prosperity did not last long. During 1973–4 a crisis began in the Iranian economy, because military spending consumed most of the revenue and prices soared, so the opposition to the Shah increased. The first time I heard of a sabotage was in 1974, when a bomb exploded on the pavement, opposite the Iranian Bank, where the Lufthansa offices were located. We were told that a woman had been carrying it, aiming to destroy the airline building but it exploded on the pavement, killing her. I only saw the big hole in the ground. On TV we watched a show trial of two figures of an opposition group in a military court. Golesorkhi and Daneshian were accused of planning to assassinate Queen Farah. Both were executed by order of the military court, while other members repented and were later set free. To us, these developments, however serious, did not mean the downfall of a powerful regime such as the Shah's.

In October 1977 the Shah was invited to the US by President Carter. Thousands of Iranian students demonstrated in front of the White House when the Shah and the President appeared to deliver their speeches. Simultaneously, Ardeshir Zahedi, the Shah's son-in-law who was the Iranian Ambassador to the US, had paid hundreds of pro-Shahs to wage a counter-demonstration. To stop the confrontation between the two groups the police threw tear gas into the crowd. The wind blew the gas towards where the Shah and Carter stood, filling their eyes with tears and newspapers printed pictures of them, both trying to keep a poker face.

In January 1978, on the way back from a trip to Moscow, President Carter and his wife Rosalind arrived in Tehran to spend the New Year with the Shah and his family. In his annual New Year speech, which was broadcast on Iranian Television and the American Channel in Tehran, Carter called Iran 'The Island of Stability', among the disturbances of the region! How ironic, we thought. Iran was in the middle of a crisis itself and President Carter had just not noticed it. At the same time, outside Iran, the Students' Confederation was active at the international level, exposing the Shah's human rights' record, his use of the secret police, SAVAC, and his policies of arms purchases and militarisation. Inside the country opposition groups covertly built up their struggle. The Islamic groups, mainly Ayatollah Khomeini's supporters, used mosques and religious events. The two other main underground guerrilla movements, the Fedaian and the Mujahidin, resorted to arms and acts of sabotage to overthrow the regime. Writers and poets formed an association and held cultural nights, reading poems and articles against the arbitrary rule and tyranny of the Shah and for the establishment of a democratic state.

I was among those who advocated reforms at every level. When my brother Manuchehr returned to Iran after seven years, we had heated debates about revolution or reform. I argued for reforms. I believed that if the intellectuals who entered the state apparatus had not got engaged in money-making businesses and become corrupt, and had put their expertise into the development plans, Iran would have gradually improved. Manuchehr, on the other hand, believed that the state was far beyond any reforms and only the overthrow of the Shah would bring real change. Later, I realised that my brother was an active member of the Confederation in America.

However, for most of us who were not seriously involved in any political activity, life went on as usual. In 1975 we decided to send my youngest brother, Massoud, to London. By then Mehdi had almost finished his degree and promised to take care of Massoud. Although my mother had agreed to send Massoud abroad, she became heartbroken once he left and would write him passionate letters.

In the summer we arranged a trip for my parents to London to visit both sons and they stayed there for a month. My mother did not like Mehdi's girlfriend, Alex. She did not approve of Mehdi marrying a foreign girl. Although Alex tried hard to seek their affection, my mother was sceptical of her and reminded Mehdi of her disapproval, comparing her to all the potential candidates in Iran. Alex was a cheerful, young Scottish girl who had fallen for Mehdi the first time she saw him in a restaurant. At the time I met Alex, in the mid-1970s, she was working in Boots. She used to help me buy cosmetics and informed me of the latest fashions. I liked her very much as Mehdi's girlfriend but did not think their relationship would go any further. To us, Mehdi was a handsome young man, with a prosperous future, who would return home after he finished his studies.

By 1976 my mother's condition had once again deteriorated. She had almost lost her balance and could not walk properly. Her speech was quite impaired and she was confused for most of the time. When we took her to the doctor he informed us that the tumour was expanding rapidly. By then my father had sold an orchard in Jiroft, enabling us to buy my mother an apartment near where I then lived in Amir Abad. Although not well, she was happy to have her own place. Because of her deteriorating condition we all visited her frequently. In between my job, the kids and the construction of our house, I visited her almost every day.

A snowball down the hill

In October 1977 we heard the news that Ayatollah Khomeini's son had died in suspicious circumstances. We only remembered the Ayatollah for his part in the 1963 upheavals, his disapproval of women's suffrage, and his opposition to the Pahlavi regime. The death of the Ayatollah's son, like that of Dr Shariati in 1976, was never proved for certain to have been the work of SAVAC. Among religious circles, mourning sessions of forty days were held in major cities, along with sporadic protests against the government.

By the end of 1977, and the beginning of 1978, the economic crisis was coupled with political crisis. Prime Minister Hoveyda, who had run the country for almost thirteen years, was removed from his post and replaced by Jamshid Amuzgar, an American-educated finance minister who had served the government for many years. This was the beginning of the shake-up of an administration which had lost its credibility long ago. Other famous people, such as the notorious General Nassiri, head of SAVAC, were also removed from their posts. At this time, radio, television and newspapers took up the momentum and became engaged in criticising the government and espousing the need for reforms.

In December 1977 an article with a bogus signature was published in the daily newspaper *Etel'at*, attacking Ayatollah Khomeini and his followers. The *Etel'at* paper was owned by Mr Massoudi, a senator and an influential journalist. The article accused the Ayatollah of being reactionary and resulted in strikes, demonstrations and chaos in major cities. The offices of the Rastakhiz Party were burnt down and the government of Mr Amuzgar was forced to declare martial law in a number of cities, including Isfahan, Tabriz and Mashad. No one took responsibility for the article, though later it was revealed that the Shah had personally ordered the article to be published. The purpose of such an article, which had a serious backlash on the Shah's administration, was never revealed.

At this time thousands of the Shah's opponents were serving prison sentences. Over the years hundreds had been executed, many of them women. Those who were inside were said to have been maimed under torture. Ayatollah Taleghani, an intellectual religious figure, was kept in prison for 23 years. Other religious figures such as Mr Rafsangani, Khamenei, Montazeri and some of the National Front and the Tudeh Party members were also among the many prisoners. Nevertheless, the bulk of the prisoners comprised the Mujahidin and the Fedaian underground guerrillas. International campaigns for human rights forced President Carter to take a stand against the Shah's social policies, demanding the observation of human rights in Iran. The Shah was forced to approve visits from Amnesty International and the Red Cross to Iranian prisons.

By the beginning of the summer of 1978, when schools shut and unaware of the events to come, we took the children for a short holiday to Andorra, between France and Spain. While we were away for two weeks, dramatic events took place back home. French television showed demonstrations on the streets and tyre burning. We returned in haste, to find the political mood unstable. General Khademi, Iran Air's director, had been removed from his long-standing position. The media had become free of tight censorship and newspapers were full of reports, exposing corruption, sleaze and mismanagement.

To see the world through a different lens

From the mid-summer of 1978 the Iranian administration was heading towards more chaos. Army generals, long-term serving ministers, and those who were associated with the royal court, had been removed from their posts by order of the Shah himself, and some were detained in prison. Meanwhile, people around religious circles were demonstrating against the unreligious establishments in the country: casinos, clubs and cabarets.

We still did not think there was any real threat to the regime. After all, this was the Shah we were talking about. He had the most powerful army in the area along with the notorious SAVAC. During all these years we had not allowed ourselves to criticise the regime in the office, in case some colleague reported us. I started asking myself, 'Why was there so much discontent and hatred?' Until then I had sincerely believed that reforms would work, partly because they had worked within the small scope of my own authority. On the other hand, I often thought of the barriers and discriminations against those who did not have access to power, the working class, women and those living in the rural areas. Despite that, I still believed violence and chaos would not bring development. In August 1978 we woke up to the most horrifying news. In Abadan, where the biggest oil refinery was located, a cinema had been burnt to rubble. Almost 700 people were killed inside the building, while watching the film. The doors had been locked from the outside, leaving no chance of anyone surviving. We were shocked to the point of disbelief. The government issued announcements, accusing the 'reactionary forces' for the tragedy while some people blamed SAVAC. The funerals and commemorations that followed disrupted the country. To this day it has never been revealed who burnt Cinema Rex down, killing so many innocent people.

A week later, in September, Dr Amuzgar resigned from the premiership and Jafar Sharif Emami, the senate chairman, replaced him. To cool the heat down, the new prime minister announced the freedom of the press, increased civil servants' salaries and closed down casinos, cabarets and anti-Islamic places. In addition, he reverted the calendar to its original lunar date of Islamic origin.

The course of events, however, seemed like a snowball rolling down a steep hill. I had become disillusioned about what I had done for all these years. Everywhere people talked about corruption, lack of freedom and their hatred of the Shah. I thought that I had not been corrupted and surely neither was Iraj or our friends in middle-management. Corruption existed among those in high positions. I remembered all the generals in Iran Air, who had the ultimate power, the Ebtehajs and Sami'is in the Iranian Bank and those in high society whom I had known at the bank. The seeds of hatred towards myself and those I had served began to grow. The seeds were also sprouting in those people who lived in the shanty towns and poor housing estates. I felt guilty about working in such a system and thus supporting a regime that was repressive.

From the summer of 1978 on, strikes, demonstrations and the burning of offices, cinemas and business establishments caused damage costing millions. On the night of September 7 the government declared martial law in Tehran and 11 other cities. General Oveisi, who had a crucial role in crushing the 1963 upheavals, was appointed military governor and issued warrants for the arrest of a number of opposition leaders. Martial law was declared, while people were asleep. On Friday morning a group of people, unaware of the decree, were gathering in Jaleh Square in the south-east of Tehran. The army blocked the square, ordering the crowd to disperse. No one obeyed. After a few more warnings and more defiance by the crowd, the sound of machine guns filled the air. The frightened crowd, consisting of students and youths, panicked and tried to flee. Moments later the square was littered with bodies, shoes, trampled banners and the screams of the wounded. We never knew how many were killed. The foreign press estimated 500, some estimates went up to four thousand. That was 'Black Friday', and the beginning of a long, bloody battle in the months to come.

The following day the oil refinery workers in Tehran went on strike. A few days later the rest of the refineries in Abadan, Isfahan and Shiraz stopped work, paralysing the country. Queues in front of petrol stations became longer and longer. The government was forced to order the importation of petrol from abroad. On 12 September print workers, who numbered about 4,000, walked out in protest against General Oveisi's censorship order issued under martial law. Gradually the rest of the workers in the public and private sectors joined in.

The emergence of a short-lived democracy

When in September Mr Sharif Emami, the prime minister, declared the freedom of the press, hundreds of magazines and books flourished. I almost abandoned all my other hobbies and read constantly. I seemed to have missed a big part of the intellectual thought of the day and was keen to catch up. I would often go to the bookshops opposite Tehran University and return with tens of new titles; Marx, Lenin and all the forbidden names.

During the upheavals numerous political groups which had mushroomed suddenly, publicised their ideas through the leaflets they distributed during the street demonstrations. Apart from the Mujahidin and the Fedaian, who had a considerable force behind them, others such as the Workers' Path, Paykar, Ranjbaran, Trotskyists, all with leftist ideologies, and Hojatieh, Forghan, and some others with Islamic views emerged on the political scene.

The loss of my mother, 1978

A few days before Black Friday my mother's condition had deteriorated. In desperation we took her to several doctors, who all refused to operate on her. She was losing her balance rapidly and we barely understood what she said. Finally, one doctor suggested that he might possibly be able to remove part of the tumour so we agreed to the operation.

The day before she was due to go to hospital I bathed her with much care and attention. Her body was still firm and in good shape, although she could not keep her balance. She thanked me and prayed to God for my health. Personally, she was against the operation and was taken to hospital almost by force. She hated hospitals and was frightened of them. We almost dragged her to the car. I have thought since that we should not have taken her against her will. Maybe we wanted to satisfy our own consciences, so that we could think we had done all that we could.

Before my mother left home for hospital she talked of Massoud, who had recently returned to London. She still loved him like a small baby, although Massoud was almost nineteen years of age. I would never forget her last look around the house she so much loved. The last words she spoke to me were, 'Give Massoud all my silver. I have not been able to leave him anything.' I promised I would do that and was able to fulfil my promise, fifteen years later. She was taken to Jam Hospital, where the doctor took her to the operating theatre. Two hours later he called us into the room to inform us of his futile effort. He had opened her brain and stitched it back. She never regained consciousness and I never stopped blaming myself for the part I had played in taking her to hospital. Doctors had already told us that she would die within two months. She was in hospital for two weeks, while we all stayed with her, taking turns, sometimes two at a time. I talked to her, touching her face, kissing her, in the hope that she would know we were around.

On a Friday afternoon I was at home when I received a call from the hospital informing me that my mother's condition had worsened. I went there in haste. That night we knew she was going to die. I asked every one of my family, including my father, not to stay in the hospital. At the time, my sister Simin had a newborn baby and Maryam was nine months pregnant. I insisted that I alone would remain at her bedside. Nevertheless, my brother Mehdi stayed with me.

The whole night we watched her in desperation. At four in the morning, while we must have dozed off, I felt a chill and the silence of death. I jumped to my feet and rushed to her bed. Her last sigh filled the air. Warm as she was, she was free of all the pain of years of unhappiness, the unwanted marriages, the husbands she did not want, the villages and the mountains she hated. Will I cover her with the jasmines and tuberoses she had planted in her garden, or the orange blossoms? Will I hold her tight, still warm and tender, whispering how much we all loved her? Mehdi and I hugged, motionless. The nurses came in, taking us away.

I was not with my grandmother when she died. To me, her death was still a remote incident and I deceived myself by pretending that she was alive in Bam. This was different. My mother died while I was with her. It was real. With us Iranians death of a beloved is hard to accept. Being very sensitive and emotional, we mourn for long periods. My mother's funeral and ceremonies went on for a week. Although my mother had been ill for almost sixteen years and we all had trouble taking care of her, part of us was buried with her. Part of a deep love was lost forever.

Being swept by the tide

The government of night
Presses its presence
On the corpse of freedom
  Mina Dastgheib, *In the Brightness of Dawn*

Had it not been for the heat of the political events I would have mourned for my mother for a long, long time. However, September was one of the most turbulent months of that year. The Shah's administration was heading towards complete collapse. The Shah, it was now revealed, had cancer, which he had hidden for six years, and was no longer able to take firm decisions. Now when the turmoil developed, he expected others, including the Americans, to dictate to him the course of action he was supposed to take. Although at the time there were about one hundred thousand American personnel and a great number of CIA operatives in Iran, they were not able to analyse the political situation accurately.

In our company, Vigeh Airways, a new director had taken control. Mr Kalhor, a former Iran Air director, was a shrewd, opportunistic man, who had a long-standing hatred towards the former director, Abbas Mir-Rashidi, and had made it his aim to take him to court, accusing him of taking commission on contracts of purchase and hire of aircraft. He pushed the managers, including me, to write reports against the director. We had no proof of such allegations and therefore rejected his accusations.

Mr Kalhor was an anti-revolutionary as well. One day, in a meeting, he talked of the actions he would take against those workers who had gone on strike at Qazvin Airport, our base. He said that he had asked General Ansari, Qazvin's military commander, to take the tanks to the airport to crush the protesters. Being on the side of those who had paralysed the private and public sector to bring the Shah down, I warned him of the consequences and we argued fiercely. He was astonished to see me defending the strikes and called my husband at his office, informing him of the consequences of my action. Iraj told him that he had nothing to do with my business and he'd better deal with me himself. Kalhor did not send the tanks to Qazvin in the end.

The Islamic groups

In early October 1978, in coordination with the Shah, Saddam Hossein ordered Ayatollah Khomeini out of Iraq. The Ayatollah was planning to go to another Arabic country, but instead he went to Paris. Throughout the years after the 1963 upheaval the Ayatollah's resistance had been well organised. Unlike the left movement and the Mujahidin, whose leaders had either been killed or in prison, and hence unable to build up their organisation, the Ayatollah's supporters were well prepared. While in Iraq his supporters built a religious movement which constituted an extensive network of communication and a widespread publicity campaign.

No other organisation was able to recruit 180,000 members with 90,000 cadres (mullahs or low-ranking clergymen), some 50 leaders (Ayatollahs), 5,000 'officers' (*hojat al-islams* or middle-ranking clergy), 11,000 theological students (*talabeh*, seeker of religious knowledge) and a mass of preachers and procession organisers. Apart from these, outside Iran many Islamic personalities worked with the inside resistance. In Germany, Dr Beheshti, an Imam in the Hamburg mosque, and Sadeq Tabatabai, the Ayatollah's close relative; in France, Abol Hassan Bani Sadr and Hassan Habibi; in Lebanon, Jala Aldin Farsi and Chamran; in the US, Sadeq Ghotbzadeh and Ibrahim Yazdi, a US citizen and founder of the Islamic students' union, were actively working to promote the future Islamic state. The inside resistance was headed by Ayatollahs Motahari, Rafsanjani, Khameneni, and Montazeri and tens of Imams throughout the country.

Ayatollah Khomeini's faction became stronger for three reasons as the movement gained momentum. Firstly, the Ayatollah's presence in a Western country with all the mass media was a unique opportunity to strengthen his position and prepare the ground for widespread propaganda. Secondly, religious organisations and their communication network made it possible for the clergy to take control of the movement. Thirdly, the Ayatollah had had one concrete agenda since his exile from Iran: the establishment of an Islamic regime. That made it easy for the followers to make up their minds, although very few were aware of what an Islamic state might be in terms of the economy, and a social, political and cultural system. These were never explained in an explicit programme. Only when the Ayatollah was asked about women's hejab, he answered that 'in an Islamic state, women will be free to dress as they wish'. That was enough to remove some anxieties. On other issues, people never asked questions and an Islamic state in its broad sense was not explained.

At the end of October, however, as chaos spread, the Shah appeared on television with a drawn face and a broken voice, to tell the nation that he had heard 'Their voice of revolution' and he would do what the people wanted. We were all shocked to see the powerful Majesty in such a weak state. Now we were certain the Shah's era was over. What we were not certain of was the type of regime which was going to replace him. Heated debates about a republic of some sort were held amongst the intellectual circles, by the media and in public meetings. Universities, especially in Tehran, had become the centre of intellectual thought. Every week thousands of students and lecturers engaged in these open debates, during which political groups also distributed leaflets and directives to their followers.

The psychology of involvement

Having seen the hatred the populace showed towards all that I considered modernisation and advancement, I began to distance myself from reformist strategies. I had not yet attended any street demonstrations, the way others did, so it was only in early November that I decided to participate in a demonstration which was being held in the Behesht Zahra Cemetery. While driving down through the streets in the south of Tehran with my brother and sister, we saw groups of women, covered in chador, some carrying their babies, were heading towards the cemetery. I had a strange feeling I cannot describe. When we finally got there and saw the huge crowd of hundreds of thousands of men and women, a sense of excitement, of being among those who were united to achieve one goal, invaded my mind. It was one of the rare moments in our history where political electricity had drawn so many people together. I wanted to experience and share it with others, to see the world through their eyes. What was that they were demanding? Was it democracy, freedom of speech, bread, home, or all at the same time? Since my sister and I were among the few women without the hejab, some offered us their extra scarves, which we accepted.

I did not know until then that such a large number of women had been involved in the street demonstrations. Neither had the world witnessed such a spontaneous mass mobilisation and the presence of so many millions on the streets. Women who until then have been confined to their tedious, daily routines at home, suddenly became part of a big force which was unpredictable and uncontrollable. As far as I understood, the bulk of them belonged to the lower strata of workers, the lumpen proletariat, dwellers in the orbital shanty towns around Tehran, who had migrated from their villages in search of better conditions. Once they had built a shelter for their crowded families, their men began labouring in the construction of the city, building modern houses, motorways and skyscrapers, while facing poor wages, deprivation and a lack of basic facilities. They were the voice of oppression and exploitation. The majority had poured on to the streets in search of better conditions as promised by the religious leaders: free electricity, water, health care and education.

A comparison with the French and the Bolshevik revolutions may be relevant in the case of the Iranian masses. The masses who formed the backbone of both those revolutions came from similar backgrounds, with similar expectations and demands. Even their hatred of the ruling class bore similarities. In addition, the Iranian masses spoke the words they had not been allowed to spell out for decades. Words which reinforced their hidden power, denounced their inferiority and deprivation and gave a false hope for the future which they wanted to establish. To me, it seemed that women, with all their contradictions and tensions as a subordinate group, were critical of the power which had silenced them for centuries. No more did they want to speak behind the back of the dominant power, the Shah; although this did not deny the fact that they were oppressed by the patriarchal systems inside their household as well as outside. In any case, I had no choice but to admire them and to support them. I never thought that their interests would later alienate my interests and cut through all classes, causing harm to many. Although other political groups were increasing their power base among the urban poor, political messages in the guise of religion were better understood and conceptualised by these people.

Inside the cemetery hundreds of thousands had gathered. Some estimates went up to three hundred thousand. We joined the oil company workers who were marching across the cemetery lanes. In the middle of the march, I suddenly noticed a mullah being carried on the shoulders of a number of bearded youth, cutting our line, shouting Islamic slogans. It was the first time I had heard slogans such as '*Hezb, Faght Hizbollah, Rahbar Faghat Rouhollah*' (The only

party is the party of God and the only leader is Rouhollah Khomeini).
I did not understand why specific slogans had been chosen. I myself
was not able to shout, yet. In those days, every slogan had a meaning,
and different ideologies and trends of thought had their own slogans.
That was the first time I became aware of Hizbollah, the party of God.

Iraj did not believe in the revolution and change. He was not
interested in politics and the rest of it. The more I became involved
in the revolution, the more our old differences deepened. He
believed that I had gone insane, suddenly becoming involved in the
crazy upheavals in my late thirties. To me, apart from fulfilling a
duty which I thought I had not accomplished, it was a flight from
my internal problems. I was not happy with my marriage and the
more I thought about it, the more I believed that I had married the
wrong person. Although Iraj was a very nice person, our characters
and world views differed tremendously. Even though earlier on I
had considered separation and divorce, there were legal barriers for
those women who initiated divorce and social pressures, beside the
threat of not being able to keep the children. This had always
prevented me from taking any action. So I was caught between my
two children and the mounting differences with Iraj. It all led to
my increasing involvement in the struggle outside my own household.

From November onwards the majority of the professionals –
teachers, civil servants, lecturers, lawyers, television and radio
personnel and the private sector – had brought the country to a
standstill. These groups, which had been badly paid, often shouldered
the burden of inflation and price increases. Intellectuals – writers,
poets, playwrights, film-makers and university students – campaigned
for a mixture of goals, less for their own material gain, more in a
broader sense for social justice, democracy, freedom, and an end to
dictatorship and the increasing foreign presence. Inactive bystanders
were either elements of the Pahlavi regime or conservatives like my
husband, who would not involve themselves in any political
movement under any circumstances.

As a matter of fact, at the Flight Service College in Iran Air, where
Iraj was the deputy principal, there had been demonstrations and
strikes but he would not let the students participate or join in the
street marches. He was frightened they might get shot. Indeed, one
day, while he was watching a demonstration from his top floor office
on Forsat Avenue, while the soldiers were shooting indiscriminately, a bullet burst through his window frame, forcing him to throw
himself on the ground and to remain there until the shooting stopped.

In a situation where everyone felt in danger, a number of people who held high positions left the country in fear of reprisals. Some of these were not even involved in any unlawful acts, nevertheless they escaped in fear. One such person was a friend of mine, who was the director of one of Haji Barkhordar's companies. Haji Barkhordar was among the top entrepreneurs, owning companies, factories and bank shares. My friend took his wife and two young children out, through Zahedan and Baluchistan to Pakistan, facing serious hazards. He believed that he would be persecuted for Haji's wealth.

At home during the day we often saw helicopters flying from the Niavaran Palace, the Shah's residence, which was a mile away from our house, to the airport on daily shuttles. We wondered what their mission was. Later, we found out that they had been taking the royal family's possessions to the airport to be shipped abroad. By then, most members of the royal family had left the country, along with all the wealth they could take with them. In addition, the wealthy Iranians who had sensed danger were transferring their money abroad. Those I knew from the Iranian Bank had left already. Central Bank published a list of people who had fled, along with the amounts they had taken. There were many familiar names among them, with figures of up to $700 million on the list.

Chanting on the rooftops

From November onwards we heard voices on the rooftops chanting *Allah o Akbar* (God is great) during the night. This was a new tactic of resistance by the ever-growing Islamists. Millions could be heard in a harmonious voice, breaking the silence of the night and the curfew. This form of protest quickly spread to other cities. The government was unable to launch a counter-attack against the people who joined at a specific time to form a chain of chanting whose waves pierced every ear.

By then the press had gone on strike and the only means of communication was the state radio and TV, still controlled by the regime. Every night, when the main news was being broadcast on TV, technicians at the power stations cut off the electricity, stopping the regime from broadcasting biased news. Instead, in the shadow of the candles, we often gathered around the battered radios, to listen to the BBC World Service which gave details of the day's events. To attract viewers, the regime had invited a popular retired newsreader (Taghi Rowhani) to join the national television station. In the heat of the revolution, people captured the unfortunate man and cut his tongue. People believed that the only reliable sources of information were word of mouth and the leaflets which were distributed in the street demonstrations from all factions.

In early December, which coincided with the month of Moharram, and Tasua and Ashura, the martyrdom of Imam Hossein, people poured onto the streets. Estimations went as high as two million; women comprised the biggest number. The slogan 'The Shah must go' was heard on these demonstrations. My brother Mehdi and his girlfriend Alex, who were in Iran at the time, attended the Ashura march.

From November to February political prisoners had gradually been released. Many of them were welcomed as national heroes. Among them were many long-term prisoners such as Masoumeh Shademani, a fifty-year-old mother of two Islamist guerrillas, who had been honoured as 'comrade mother'. She had spent years in prison for sheltering and helping the guerrillas. Ayatollah Taleghani and Safar Ghahremani had both spent more than two decades in prison. We were moved by the courage of these men and women who were ready to sacrifice their lives for the overthrow of a dictator. Now I felt humiliation for myself. I had lived comfortably in ignorance while they were struggling for justice and freedom. Now I turned my back against all the reformist ideologies. I attended public meetings which were held to commemorate the martyrs or welcome back a political prisoner. Once I attended a meeting where a woman prisoner, Roghieh Daneshgari, was speaking. Roghieh, a member of the guerrilla movement, had recently been released from years of imprisonment. Having been brutally tortured, she was so weak she could not speak properly.

During these periods interesting incidents occasionally attracted attention. One day in a public meeting, where hundreds were jammed in a basement, I noticed a man looking at the women earnestly, with a mocking smile. I went forward and asked him the reason he was looking at us in such a strange way. He replied: 'Because I will not see any of you unveiled in the near future. You will be covered in chadors once religion takes over.' At the time his remarks were so out of context that I thought he was insane. A few months later his prophecy came true.

While the Islamist groups, especially Ayatollah Khomeini, had an organised network, and were able to use the mosques for their propaganda, leaders of the opposition groups had the hard task of helping to set an agenda for a new government, to formulate and to publicise their strategies and gain public support. These required time and hard work. The pace of developments was far ahead of all the political groups.

Now chaos, lawlessness and disruptions at all the public and private institutions had become a part of our daily life. Suddenly, at the end of October, we heard that General Khademi, the long-serving director of Iran Air, who had been removed from his post a few months earlier, had been assassinated at his home. Some rumours said that he had committed suicide when an order had arrived for his arrest. The mystery over this general whom we knew and respected for his endeavours to build a big airline was never solved.

By early November, the Americans, who had sensed that their long-term interests were in serious danger, dispatched Mr Brezjinski, the US National Security Adviser, to Iran. As a result of his negotiations the Shah replaced the civil government of Sharif Emami with a military government. General Azhari, the new prime minister, brought six high-ranking generals into his cabinet. Now the Shah, reassured of America's support, wanted to show a tough fist to restore 'law and order'. The army was confronting the defiant people on the streets every day and killed and wounded many. The military government planned to put a complete end to the disruptions. This was a decision which was doomed to fail from the start. General Azhari, unable to cope with the pressures, resigned from his post after only a month. He was aware of the futile killings on the streets by the army. Soldiers had gradually begun to defy their commanders and were deserting their posts in large numbers.

A month later strikes and demonstrations had brought the country to a standstill and the Shah, desperate to stay in power, consulted the old statesmen whom he had removed from politics years ago. Dr Amini, a pro-American and an influential politician, and some members of the old National Front and friends of the late Dr Mosadeq, Sadighi, Sanjabi and Bakhtiar were all summoned to a meeting to agree between themselves the election of a civil prime minister and the formation a government which would restore public confidence. As a result of this meeting, Shahpour Bakhtiar was appointed as prime minister and his assignment was ratified by the still remaining parliament and the senate. From among the religious leaders the moderate opposition led by Ayatollah Shariat Madari declared their support for Bakhtiar's government, but Ayatollah Khomeini, uncompromising and defiant, declared that this government was illegal because the Shah had ruled the country illegally and therefore his decrees had no validity.

Now very few offices functioned properly. I sometimes went to
my office to see how thing were developing, so did the other
directors. The director, Mr Kalhor, who by then had become hostile
towards those of us who had disobeyed his orders, threatened to
dismiss us all. We had challenged his policy of forcing the employees
to come to work regularly. I did not know how he was able to dismiss
his top managers but one day he just did as he had often threatened.
The letter to me read: 'You have been dismissed because you
disobeyed the directives and encouraged the employees to go on
strike.' I left my job without any regrets. I had a lot to read and a
lot to do.

After Mr Brezjinski left Iran, General Huyser, deputy to the
NATO commander, arrived in Tehran. Without visiting the Shah,
as was customary, he began negotiations with the army commanders.
According to some analysts General Huyser had three agendas.
Firstly, to ensure that the top-ranking generals stayed behind Bakhtiar.
Secondly, to assess the feasibility of a final bid to crush the revolution;
even by means of a coup. Thirdly, and as a last resort, to encourage
both Bakhtiar and the military commanders to reach a compromise
with the Ayatollah, in order to keep the Left movement out.

As the Left movement gained more support and increased in size,
the old fear of a leftist regime gaining power had spread through
the White House and the Pentagon. A week after his arrival General
Huyser, accompanied by William Sullivan, the US ambassador, met
with the Shah and possibly informed him of their decisions. Huyser
stayed in Iran until after the revolution. The G7 conference at
Guadeloupe in early January decided Iran's destiny. By then the US,
disappointed by the Shah's weakness, withdrew its long-term support
for him. That was the time the Shah, frail and depressed, decided
to finally leave the country.

A mighty king leaves his empire in tears

Far, far away tonight
The gates of houses open
And all the stars suddenly fall.
    Shadab Vajdi, 'Hope'

On January 16 I had invited the former director of Vigeh company,
Abbas Mir-Rashidi, and some of my colleagues for afternoon tea at

my house. I waited for some time but no one showed up. Since we did not have a telephone line I went to the public telephone and called one of them. My colleague told me of the impossibility of reaching Shemiran because of the crowds on the streets.

The Shah and Queen Farah had left Tehran from Mehrabad Airport in the early afternoon of that day. We watched their departure on the TV later that night. Some of the army generals, the new prime minister Bakhtiar and a few statesmen, had been present at the Royal Pavilion. It was a melancholy scene. The Shah and the Queen had both been crying. To keep the situation under control and to give a chance to the government of 'reform', a Regency Council had been appointed to take the Shah's place while he went on an 'extended vacation'.

A few minutes after their departure millions poured onto the streets, celebrating. Cars blew their horns, people distributed sweets and newspapers with the words 'Shah went' printed in the biggest type size possible. The Shah's and his father's statues were pulled down and smashed by the angry mob. Iraj was on his way home when he faced the crowd in the middle of Mohseni Square in the north of the city. He was pushed by the mob a few miles further down before he managed to separate himself and come home. I went to Shemiran Square to see what was happening. There were no crowds there. The Imperial Guards and the Immortal Corps, who were the Shah's personal regiments, had arrived in time and had washed the streets and the people with a water canon. The Shah and Queen Farah arrived in Egypt unaware of the events back home.

Between the day the Shah left and the day of the revolution on February 12, Bakhtiar tried hard to keep things in order. By then Ayatollah Khomeini, who had already dismissed any negotiations with what he called the 'illegal' government, had formed a Revolutionary Council. During these weeks three-sided negotiations had continued. General Huyser and Sullivan, with constant advice from the White House and the Pentagon, negotiated with the army and Bakhtiar. Bakhtiar negotiated his position as the legitimate prime minister with the Ayatollah's aides and explained his worries to them of an army coup taking place if the Ayatollah returned. The US, on the other hand, negotiated directly with the Ayatollah to reach a compromise. The Ayatollah was still in Paris and had free access to the world media. Now he had a powerful position and repeatedly demanded Bakhtiar's resignation and his own return to Iran. Rumours were spreading of possible sabotage and the assassination of the Ayatollah once he returned. None of these negotiations between the different groups bore any fruit. Finally, Mehrabad Airport, which had been closed for some time, reopened for the Ayatollah's return.

The Ayatollah returns

Tehran prepared itself for the historic welcome. An Iran Air flight which was scheduled to bring the Ayatollah home was replaced by Air France at the last minute. The Revolutionary Council organised a committee to oversee the proceedings. Most of the political groups, outside the Islamists, prepared to welcome the Ayatollah and show their solidarity with the movement. From the airport to Behesht Zahra Cemetery, some 30 kilometres away, where he was due to deliver his first speech, millions of people had formed a human line. The Mujahidin personalities, such as the Rezai family whose four children had been killed by the Shah, formed a separate contingent. The Fedaian had their own group of some ten thousand supporters on a corner at Shahreza Street. Members of the ethnic groups, such as Christians and Jews, had formed their grouping with banners and slogans. It seemed as if the whole population had gathered for such an historic event. I walked along the lines for a mile. Everyone was excited and people had broad smiles on their faces, hoping the Ayatollah would bring freedom, prosperity and social justice. Women constituted the bulk of the welcomers. Among the lines I noticed all types of women, the majority in black chadors or head scarf.

The Ayatollah, who had been in exile since 1963, was accompanied by two hundred advisers, assistants, followers, close friends and the international press. Aboard the plane the Ayatollah slept for most of the time and spoke very little. In response to one reporter, who, upon crossing the border, had asked him what he felt, the Ayatollah replied 'nothing'. Among the advisers, Bani Sadr, with his French-style, gentle voice; Ghotbzadeh with his elegant clothes and arrogant manners and Yazdi, with his American-Persian accent, were already known to us. They had acted as the Ayatollah's public relation officers in the last few months he had stayed in Paris. Upon arrival, a group of spokesmen of the ulama went aboard the aircraft to welcome him.

When his car reached Shahyad Square, a mile away from the airport, the crowd made it impossible for it to move any further. A helicopter

was called in to take the Ayatollah to the cemetery, where he made
a speech, declaring the end of monarchy and the beginning of a new
era. Later, he was housed in the building of a girls' religious school
(Alavi), in the south of the city, where millions poured in to see
him and listen to his sermons which went on for two weeks. His
household, including his wife and his daughters and daughter-in-
law had not accompanied him. They arrived privately, a few
days later.

The formation of the revolutionary guards and the Islamic Committees

During the upheavals of 1977–8 members of the neighbourhood
youth were active in the mosques and became the force behind the
street rioting, setting fire to places, destroying state buildings and
functioning as local power centres. Later, these neighbourhood
groups formed ad hoc organisations throughout the country and called
themselves Committees of the Islamic Revolution (*Komiteh*). During
and after the collapse of the Shah's administration some of these
committees had maintained law and order, helped with the
distribution of food and other necessities and set and controlled prices.
These were Islamic militants who were from shopkeeper, retail and
middlemen backgrounds. The majority, however, were the shanty
town dwellers from a backward peasant origin, or lower urban
classes, whose fathers were engaged in badly paid, labour intensive
jobs and their mothers either in domestic labour or factory work.
Funds provided by the merchants were distributed through charitable
organisations to the families of the victims of the Shah, and the local
mosques, which provided financial support for these groups.

In the public and private organisations, on the other hand, ad hoc
councils formed to hear grievances and set demands. These councils
comprised all groups: Islamists, Fedaian, Mujahidin and others. The
councils subsequently transformed into Islamic councils as the general
movement increasingly took an Islamic structure. Central committees
also emerged, with greater powers to coordinate, supervise and
direct the revolution within the urban population. Some of these
committees were armed volunteers, youths, students and guerrilla
activists, and their main tasks were to protect the revolution from
anti-revolution groups such as the secret police and the Imperial
Guards. From the day the Ayatollah arrived these unofficial

committees played a crucial role in securing, defending and establishing an Islamic regime.

Towards the revolution day

The return of Ayatollah Khomeini speeded the pace of developments. Bakhtiar, still in office, wanted to negotiate his position. The Ayatollah, on the other hand, appointed his government in waiting, with Mehdi Bazargan, a religious nationalist and head of the Freedom Movement, as prime minister. Meanwhile, General Huyser was trying to keep the army under control and made arrangements for the safeguard of the sophisticated weapons the US had sold to the Shah. He succeeded in convincing Bakhtiar to cancel some of the big arms contracts.

Within the disintegrating army, insubordination and desertion had increased and although there were still commanders who ordered the soldiers to shoot the people, they would often refuse. People had started building human relations with soldiers; offering them flowers and sweets and explaining to them the regime's crimes. The soldiers, themselves from a humble peasant, lower-class background, were increasingly disillusioned with their task and had gradually sided with the people. Among the armed forces, the air force personnel were the first to defy their commanders. Some of them were initially arrested and allegedly executed.

In early February I went to the Iranian Bank to visit a friend. It was a Wednesday but I saw the bank was closed. I was informed by the guards that the army had ordered the closure of the bank for three days. The Iranian Bank had not been a political centre as, for example, the Central Bank, where most of the employees were highly political. Being surprised at the incident, I made inquiries and later found out what had happened. Most of the high-ranking politicians, bankers, ministers and the wealthy capitalists who had been detained by order of the Shah, escaped from prison in a dramatic act. A jumbo jet, the last to leave Mehrabad Airport before it was closed down, had taken them abroad. Hojabr Yazdani, the bank's main shareholder, who had been detained for months, had paid about two hundred million Rials (the equivalent of $3 million at the time) to factions of the army, to take them out of Iran. They had closed the bank to take that money out. It was alleged the money was being carried in big sacks and placed in army trucks. Most of the regime's top-ranking detainees had escaped in this way. The ex-prime minister, Hoveyda, and General Nassiri, head of SAVAC, had refused to go.

From February 9, the Iranian state apparatus was rapidly falling into the hands of the people. On that morning I attended a demonstration which had been organised at Tehran University. Since I did not expect any danger, I had taken the children with me. We were marching at a slow pace, enjoying the crowd, when a mile further down, under the Hafiz Bridge, we were told that the army had sent troops to attack the marchers. Everyone ran for safety. I ran towards a building and took shelter under a low wall, hiding the kids behind me. That was the first time I had taken them out on the streets and I was already feeling guilty. What will I do if something happened to them? I asked myself in panic. After twenty minutes, which seemed like hours, we saw trucks full of armed people, coming from the opposite side, showing signs of victory. They had friendly faces.

Apparently, the Imperial Guards and the Immortal Corps had taken it upon themselves to discipline mutinous air force technicians and cadets (*homafars*) to keep the rest of the forces in line. Therefore, they had attacked the Doshan Tapeh Air Base in the south-east of Tehran. Some of the cadets had managed to escape from the base to spread news of the assault. While the base was surrounded by the Guards, groups of armed guerrillas, Fedaian and Mujahidin, ran to the base, attacking the royalists troops from behind. It took some six hours of intense fighting to drive the Guards into retreat. The rebellious air force personnel opened the armoury and distributed rifles, machine guns and light weapons among the guerrillas and local activists. When we got to our feet, those friendly faces who cheered at us were some of the guerrillas returning from the air force base. Although the march continued to the base a few miles away, I hurried the kids home.

On Saturday February 10 barricades had been set up on major streets to prevent the army from attacking the people. Factions in the army and the secret police, defying their officers who by then were pulling out from the streets, took it upon themselves to impose law and order. The people, on the other hand, were determined to take control of the city and by Saturday most of the south-east of Tehran had come under their control. In the early afternoon I told Iraj that I was going to drive into town to see what was happening and to offer help to the revolutionaries. Unable to convince me not to go, he suggested that we take the children to his parents' house, which was in the south of Tehran where people had taken over the military bases. He was very frightened and angry at my decision and when I dropped them off he said he wished I would never return.

I drove towards the Nezam Abad area in the east, where I knew people had attacked the army bases and had confiscated arms. This was a working-class area with crowded streets. I was astonished to see children as young as twelve carrying Uzis and Kalashnikovs, guarding the streets. Thousands of women, accompanied by small toddlers, also stood on the pavements. I was being stopped every now and then at the barricades for my car to be checked. I had to explain that I had come to help. Some looked at my car, a Ford Cortina, with suspicion.

At a roundabout a group of bearded young men, carrying Molotov cocktails asked me to take them to Abbas-Abad Army Base, where the fighting continued. We drove at a slow pace, because every once in a while they had to explain to the armed youth on the street where we were heading. When we got close to the base, the fighting and shooting were so intense that I became frightened and told them that I could not drive any further. They thanked me and left. I took another group to the Eshrat Abad base and it was not until late that night that I returned, tired and horrified by my experience. At my in-laws' house Iraj's father looked at me in amazement and said, 'Why you, Rouhi Khanum? How come you support the mullahs, with your education and experience?' It took me some years to understand what he really meant.

The next day started with the collapse of the police stations, and more army bases. Early in the morning General Rahimi, Tehran's military governor, announced martial law at 4.30 pm, instead of the usual 6.30. At that time, we were at my brother's house in Aryamehr Street. At 3 pm two of my brothers and I went out to see what the situation was. Crowds had gathered alongside both pavements of the main street. I asked the women who had young children to go home because we did not know what would happen after the curfew hour. The women refused and stayed.

Rumours were around that the last of the army generals who had not agreed to withdraw had decided to put up a fight. We decided to barricade the street to prevent heavy army vehicles from advancing. The three of us called on the other youths to help gather tyres and lamp posts. We spread the tyres alongside the street and set them alight. The wooden lamp posts made a good barricade. We left a narrow way in between for small cars to pass.

By 6.30, when the crowd was growing in size, we saw a white Peugeot driving through the barricades, announcing through loudspeakers that the Ayatollah had ordered the people to stay on the street to defy the martial law. We had been doing that on our own initiative. As night fell the crowd reached several thousands. By then, some elements, who had appeared out of the blue, separated men from women, against our wishes, putting the women behind the men as was customary in all Islamic rallies. At this time Manuchehr went on a tour around the city to see what was happening elsewhere. He returned to announce that the whole of Tehran had become a chain of burnt tyres and barricades. We went home late at night, all covered in black smoke and dust.

On the Sunday the Mujahidin and the Fedaian, who each had occupied parts of Tehran University, were busy teaching the youth military techniques. Thousands had gathered to join the action. At this time Evin prison was everyone's main target. Crowds had already surrounded the prison building, trying to cut through the electric doors, wires and barriers. Once in a while we heard over the loudspeakers the guerrillas asking for skilled technicians, welders, tank drivers, doctors and nurses. Since I knew some first-aid, I volunteered to use my car as an ambulance.

Meanwhile, among the cheers of the crowd, a tank, confiscated from a base, drove into the university grounds. A few hundred yards away a group of Islamists established a temporary base and had their loudspeakers turned towards where the guerrillas had gathered. This prevented the guerrillas from giving further instructions to their supporters, because the speakers were so high no one could hear a word. Although a spirit of unity was in the air, all were irritated at this unfriendly act.

At Evin prison people were fighting their way through the maze of the notorious building. Later, I heard that even an American, whose wife was Iranian, had been amongst those fighting to open the prison. He was removed by his wife, who was frightened he might be taken as a spy. Once the prison doors opened the remaining prisoners were released. Those guards who had stayed at their posts were detained and the electric whips, torture beds and other interrogation devices found at the chambers were confiscated. An ad hoc Komiteh took over the prison from those who had opened it. There were a large number of women among the prisoners. A list of 300 long-term prisoners had already been published, showing some who had been made nearly blind or paralysed or maimed by the torture devices. There was a call for the prison to be blown up as an end to imprisonment and torture. This idea was abandoned.

On the night of February 12, 1979 the remaining army bases were attacked and their armoury confiscated by the two guerrilla organisations and the Islamic militias. Police stations surrendered voluntarily. An eye-witness saw Hoveyda and Nassiri being taken from their detention centre at one of these bases. Nassiri was shown on TV, beaten up and bandaged. The army supreme command, in agreement with General Huyser, announced its full support of the 'wishes of the people'. At 6 pm Tehran radio and TV station fell to the revolutionaries and Mrs Boroumand, who had once been in charge of the children's programmes, and Mr Hosseini, a newsreader, appeared on the screen, un-groomed and in street clothes to announce 'The voice of the revolution and the voice of true Iran.' They apologised for their untidy appearances, due they said, to having been dragged from the streets to announce the end of the monarchy.

Chapter Nine

The beginning of a new era, February 1979

There is a dark cloud over my mountain
So proud
If it does not rain loud
They insist not to grow
The wild daffodils have vowed.
    Mehdi Shafii, personal thoughts

We woke up to the 'Spring of Freedom', intoxicated by high hopes
and aspirations. Uncensored newspapers, magazines and books
painted a colourful picture on the sidewalks and in the bookshop
windows, promising democracy and freedom. Tehran University,
with thousands of books on display at each corner, was now a
Mecca for the youth, the intellectuals and those who had fought for
the overthrow of the Shah. Heated debates and stories told by the
released prisoners could be heard all around. The next few days passed
in disillusion and a state of waiting as to what the new situation
would be.

Prime Minister Shahpour Bakhtiar had gone into hiding after the
collapse of his cabinet and Mehdi Bazargan had become the first prime
minister of the revolutionary government. He appeared on TV for
his first speech. Two things attracted our attention. First, he said that
'the revolution has now ended and people must go home and let
us do our job.' Second, he declared the country's bankruptcy: 'The
Treasury had been emptied of all its money. The Pahlavis have taken
all they could.' We were surprised that he did not mention any plans
for the future; the unity among the people and those who had
contributed to the revolution. Shortly afterwards, the Revolutionary
Council appointed a committee to draft the new constitution and
make preparations for a referendum. Other political organisations

believed in a holy alliance with the dominant clergy groups, but were ignored by them from the start.

Meanwhile, a sequence of executions began. New words entered into our vocabulary: *Mofsed fi-al arz, taghuti.* Those who held high office during the Pahlavis were branded Mofsed fi-al arz (corrupted on earth) and condemned to death. Those who had a Western life-style were branded taghuti and were dismissed from office, had their possessions confiscated and were themselves detained. Prime Minister Hoveyda, General Rahimi, military governor of Tehran, General Nassiri, head of SAVAC, Mrs Parsa, ex-minister of education and tens of other famous names were executed after summary trials which only lasted a few hours. In these trials, Dr Ibrahim Yazdi acted as prosecution, and Hojat al Islam Khalkhali as the executioner.

In the first few weeks hundreds were detained and many were executed. At the time we were all jubilant that those who had committed crimes against humanity were being punished promptly. Naive as we were, we did not know that summary trials and executions would set a precedent which no one would be spared. We did not know that mob culture and lawlessness would not consolidate the precious, newly grown sprouts of democracy and soon everyone would fall victim.

On the third night after the insurrection we were watching Mr Ghotbzadeh's speech, as the new head of the National Broadcasting Network. His words were authoritative and patronising. We believed that broadcasting belonged to the people and he was not in a position to implement his own plans without consulting the people.

Changing direction

The new revolutionary government asked the civil servants and the private sector to end the strikes and resume work. Workplace associations in the form of syndicates, *shoras* (assembly) or cooperatives, which had bloomed during the two years prior to the revolution, began to reorganise and reshuffle. Each political organisation had a number of supporters, active in one of the political formations of Fedaian, Mujahidin, Tudeh Party, Islamists, Maoists and independents. These new foundations of democracy were vulnerable to influence, infiltration and disintegration. Shortly after the revolution Islamic militants began to either monopolise the existing associations or alternatively formed their own. These steps were in line with creating an Islamic state. The first organisations which were attacked were the radio and television.

Gradually, Islamic councils became the institutions of political and ideological promotion. The first impact of such an autocratic act was felt by those who were non-religious and had until then hoped for an alliance with the Islamists. In my former office, the Vigeh Airways, the anti-revolutionary director changed his mind and declared himself a true Muslim and revolutionary. One day I called in to see my colleagues. Suddenly, one of the managers came to me and asked me politely to leave the building immediately because I was in serious danger. I did not know what was going on but sensed the danger and left. The director, Mr Kalhor, had convinced a few opportunists whom he had gathered around him that I was anti-revolutionary and was sending them downstairs to beat me up. I got out before they reached me and never returned to that office again.

With Iraj, his situation as the deputy to the principal of the Flight Service College was more serious. A week after the revolution some of his employees, whom he had hired and trained, along with a few guards, servants and messengers, began a campaign of terror and intimidation. They mobilised students to accuse him and other directors of being anti-revolutionary and taghuti and demanded his dismissal. The director himself had already left for the US. In horror and disbelief Iraj kept a low profile and stayed home for a while.

At other offices where friends and relatives worked, the mood was changing quickly. It was too soon to know what the future held for all of us. The first official act of control came when a decree called for everyone to surrender confiscated arms to the 'proper authorities'. Identity cards were issued for the Islamic members of the Komiteh. In many provinces, such as Kurdistan, Turkaman Sahara, Khuzistan and Baluchistan, people were already preparing themselves for autonomous rule which they had expected to be granted by the revolutionary regime. They refused to surrender their arms. Apart from the regional forces, the only organisations which could be a potential threat to the Islamic Komitehs were the two main guerrilla organisations of the Mujahidin and the Fedaian and they had become the target of disarmament. They recognised the threat to themselves was serious and advised their followers to hide their weapons. At a different level, the military personnel, in a demonstration which took place on February 16, protested against the composition of the armed forces and demanded 'the formation of a democratic army'. They wanted the dissolution of the existing army structure and the establishment of a Revolutionary Council elected by the rank and file.

By the end of February the breakdown of the holy alliance had become imminent. Groups of street thugs, whose identities were not yet known, began systematic physical attacks on the political activists, apart from the Islamists. The two guerrilla organisations, with hundreds of thousands of supporters, were not in a position to use their potential power. They did not want to alienate the newly established regime, because it had millions of people behind it. Besides, ideological differences began to crack the loose alliance they had made during the revolutionary days.

Although before the revolution all forces had joined against the Shah, after the victory, the Left as a whole split over two main issues; supporting the newly formed government or forming an opposition. The Mujahidin found it in their best interest to distance themselves from the Left and press for a share of power. The Fedaian, although accepting the Ayatollah's leadership, distanced themselves from a religious state and set an agenda for 'Independence, Freedom and a Democratic Republic'. A few weeks after the revolution everyone began to be wary of each other. At the same time the orchestrated policies of Islamicisation and the movement towards establishing an Islamic republic went ahead and other political groups lost ground.

The end of the beginning: women as first targets

Was the Spring of freedom
Our simple hallucination?
    Mina Dastgheib, *In the Brightness of Dawn*

We were still confused by the contradictions and indecisiveness that had begun to manifest themselves in the political mood. At the beginning of March the revolutionary government issued a decree ordering women civil servants to wear Islamic hejab. Secular women who had contributed to the revolution in their hundreds of thousands took to the streets to protest against such a decree. This was in the week of March 8, International Women's Day. For a week women attended demonstrations at the university and on the streets of Tehran. I had attended some of the demonstrations and meetings before the revolution, but this period marked a turning point, with our protests being met by verbal and, most of all, physical abuse by street thugs who called themselves Hizbollah, the party of God. Women did not expect to be ordered to cover their hair by the force of decrees and street mobs.

Ironically, the Left refused to support women's demands and advised their supporters not to participate in the demonstrations. Ideologically, the Left did not believe in an independent women's movement. Marxist ideology believes that class struggle and the struggle against imperialism and capitalism take precedence over all other types of struggles, including the women's movement. Marxism believes that 'once the working class and the proletariat are free of oppression, women will be free as part of the liberation of all oppressed groups.' Strategically, the Left did not want to confront the new regime by defending women. They had concluded that it would harm the alliance, an alliance which never existed in the first place.

The Fedaian and the Mujahidin bear a heavy responsibility for the defeat of the women's movement at its inception. Although both these organisations had incorporated vague declarations, borrowed from socialist manifestos on women's liberation, they lacked the knowledge and the insight to conceptualise the women's movement in its autonomous form. Within the Left, feminism was taboo. No one was allowed to declare a tendency towards feminism. They scarcely had any knowledge of the biggest liberation movement of the decade, where millions of women had demanded their equal place as citizens of planet earth. There was no specific discourse on women, free of the ideological battleground. Being Muslim, the Mujahidin women were wearing a type of hejab they had invented; a long coat with trousers and scarf, mostly in dark colours.

Secular women from all walks of life were left alone to defend their human rights and the limited rights they had gained during the Pahlavi regime. The menfolk in general seemed to be happy with the restrictions placed on women. We did not hear our husbands, brothers and other male family members volunteering to accompany us on the street protests, knowing that we were being attacked and abused. An unspoken, unwritten and unholy alliance amongst all men, the Left, and the Islamists shrouded secular women, pushing them into a corner, where they were left on their own to fight; a fight which has continued to this day.

The assault on women began with the decree on wearing the hejab, but it was obvious that this was just the beginning. The courage women had gained during the revolutionary days and the legitimacy they claimed, because of their contribution to the downfall of the Shah, made them determined to react to restrictive measures in every way possible. Secular women, comprising the bulk of civil servants, teachers, nurses and other professions, had been active in paralysing the Shah's system through strikes at their workplace. The Islamist women had mainly been active in street demonstrations.

Many women, who until then were supporters of the Left, decided to defy the decrees and joined in the demonstrations against the abuse of their rights. However, women were not organised and had no clear strategy. One day, for example, women decided to march from Tehran University to put their demands to the authorities. The marchers, estimated at about twenty thousand, did not know where they were heading. Some proposed going to see Ayatollah Taleghani, the moderate, liberal Ayatollah, whom everyone respected and loved. Others suggested Prime Minister Bazargan's office. An ad hoc committee of a few women decided on the prime minister. After all, he was in charge of the government. By noon, after four hours' walking in the snow, women reached Kakh Square, where the prime minister's office was located. Women, tired, soaked and angry, sat on the ground. After some consultation, ten women were chosen as delegates to take a petition inside. A woman lawyer and a writer were amongst the delegation. They were taken inside, while others waited outside under the falling snow. Guards aimed their rifles from the top of the high walls of the building at them. Two hours passed. The women became impatient and gradually left. Worried for those inside, those who were in the ad hoc committee waited for another two hours. Nobody answered their queries. They had no choice but to leave. By now, all the adjoining streets were full of thugs who threw stones at them and called them ugly names such as whores, agents of the CIA, supporters of taghut.

Later, we found out that the delegates were directed to a room where six women wrapped in black chadors had been waiting for them. They then engaged in a futile argument over the wearing of the hejab and its necessity in an Islamic country. Deputy Prime Minister Mr Amir-Entezam was present at the meeting and promised to discuss the matter with the prime minister. Once outside the building the women delegates were confronted by the mob and verbally assaulted. Afterwards no one ever heard anything from the prime minister's office.

On March 21, we went to Jiroft to spend our New Year with my father. With my mother's death in October and the subsequent turn of events, we had not found much time to contact my father. My brothers Manuchehr and Mehdi also joined us. In a small rural town like Jiroft revolution had not taken root in the same way it had done in the big cities. Nevertheless, people who came to visit us were curious to know how things were going. The wealthy landowners had already left the town and the peasants, with the aid of their Left sympathisers, were demanding land redistribution. In some places they had even confiscated some properties. Those who over the years had been involved in the politics of the town, the mayor and members of the town's council, did not feel safe any more. My Uncle Akbar, who had once been elected the Council Chief, was frightened for his life because he had received threats. My father had called on his tribe to station a number of armed men on Uncle Akbar's household to protect him. Since my father was never involved in politics he was immune from being brandished an anti-revolutionary. He was always critical of all politics and people respected him for his impartiality.

Back in Tehran, the referendum had already taken place. One question was put: Do you want an Islamic republic? No other choices were offered. The result was 98 per cent positive and the Islamic Republic gained its legitimacy.

Islamicising the country

The Islamicisation of the country began not with the consensus of other smaller parties, but with a unilateral strategy based on majority rule. The instruments of implementing these policies were not democratic devices such as multi-party talks or parliamentary debates but mass mobilisation and street mobs. In the days, months and years which followed, people were set against people to implement law and order in its Islamic context. Physical intimidation and orchestrated propaganda against the 'others' soon became a common scene. We woke up to an era which alienated people in their own native land. This meant the negation of the rights of millions of people who were secular. The issue of women, on the other hand, cut across all ideological boundaries, class, faith, ethnic origin and nationality. Women by their sex and gender were to abide by the patriarchal rule.

Islamicisation of the country could not achieve its goals unless the judicial system, based on the secular law, was dismantled and replaced by the Islamic law (Shari'at). This meant that the Shari'at family practice would replace the Family Protection Act. By the same law, men would be permitted to take up to four wives and as many temporary concubines (*mota'a*) as they wished. A man was allowed to divorce his wife without her knowledge. Child custody went to men exclusively and women were reduced to the status of chattels, with few independent rights. The only right women were guaranteed was the right to hold property and keep their earnings. Men were responsible for their maintenance in exchange for their sexual subordination (*tamkin*). Shortly afterwards clerics took up the duties of judges and juries, even before the move was sanctioned by the Islamic constitution. Islamic courts began functioning immediately after the March referendum. Women became a window through which the world would identify the Islamic state. Three fronts opened simultaneously to bring women in line with Islamicisation: first, the laws which gave women limited protection. Civil rights were ordered to be 'reviewed', which included the Family Protection Act (1975) and equal opportunity laws in employment. Second, women were barred from specific professions such as the law, the army, the police force, heavy industry and agriculture. Third, and most importantly, was the women's dress code and the wearing of the Islamic hejab.

Since the 1979 revolution the hejab or veil and its implementation has been the topic of much discourse among women inside and outside Iran, including non-Iranian scholars. I have come across literature that claims women themselves chose the hejab during and after the revolution and the Islamic Republic only sanctioned women's wishes when they incorporated the wearing of the hejab into their policies of Islamicisation. From my own experience and observations, this is not the truth. It is true that the majority of women were using some type of hejab after the first period of unveiling by Reza Shah in the 1930s, but there were millions of women who had not worn the hejab for decades, although their mothers and grandmothers might have done so. I was one of them. We might have enjoyed an occasional use of the chador, when we went to Islamic shrines and holy places, but the idea of a forced hejab and a uniform dress code was against many women's free will and an abuse of their human rights.

Before the revolution there was no hostility between the veiled and the unveiled women. To us, it seemed a matter of choice usually dependent on family background. Lower class and religious women wore the chador, while peasant and tribeswomen and those who lived in the rural areas had their own national dress, depending on their culture. Middle-class, educated women did not wear the hejab. To us, who had lived our lives in a secular era, this issue seemed out of date.

As the Islamicisation of the judicial system developed, women judges and lawyers were expelled from their jobs and trainee lawyers were ordered out of their colleges. It was claimed that in Islam women were not eligible to be a judge because by nature women are weak and emotional and would not be able to pass a fair judgement. After the expulsion of women from the judicial system, a week-long chain of protests and demonstrations began in Tehran. On the first day about 10,000 women marched to the Ministry of Justice on Naser Khosrau Street. Some decided to occupy the building. Single women and those who did not have family obligations were asked to stay overnight. About five hundred volunteered. Others brought them food and blankets. For three days the building remained occupied until the guards stormed in and kicked everyone out.

Months passed in confusion, hovering between hope and despair. Women's street demonstrations continued throughout the spring and summer. Women now understood that the long-term strategy was either to encourage secular women to make themselves redundant from public office, or expel them. Ironically, men, even intellectuals who spoke of equality and liberation, kept a dead silence, leaving women to fight on their own. It seemed that women were aliens, who had invaded a space which belonged to men. Within the period of two years plans to segregate work and public places were introduced. Women were removed from managerial and technical positions and their promotion became limited. Workplace nurseries were closed down as part of the implementation of these policies. In sports, women were banned from many areas and resources were withdrawn from women's sport centres. Beaches, hotels and all areas of public life became genderised and thousands of articles, papers and seminars prepared the ideological justification for these policies. Women continued with their overt protests for almost three years, after which persecution and detention forced them to choose the tactics of covert resistance and struggle.

The situation was worse in the educational establishments. After the dismissal of thousands of teachers and principals, newly religious women and men took over, without having any qualifications or proper experience. The slogan, 'We do not need expertise but dedication' became the official guideline in choosing people for the office. The Islamic shoras, which had been established at every workplace, decided who was a dedicated Muslim and who was to be expelled or made redundant. For example, a friend of mine, who was an excellent, dedicated secondary school teacher, was expelled as part of the purging of the Left from schools. She was accused of being Mofsed fi-al arz because she had helped to build a library and had held reading sessions outside school hours. In line with this school books were rewritten, in which the unequal position of men and women and stereotypical gender attributions were justified.

The spring of freedom which brought hope to the intelligentsia's cherished dreams of a long-lasting democracy, was a short-lived experience. The summer of 1979 was a turning point in all spheres of our lives. The assault on newspapers and democratic organisations began in full force. The offices of the *Ayandegan*, an independent newspaper, was set alight and bookshops were smashed up. We did not understand why a system which we had all helped to bring to power had such intolerance and hostility towards the intellectuals and educated people. By August the new ruling body could no longer tolerate demonstrations, critics, ethnic demands and women's disobedience. An order to crack down on all opponents was issued. This was to end 'Prostitution in the name of freedom'; 'to break the poisonous and corruptible pens'. They closed down all the newspapers which did not follow the popular path, the path of Islam. Foreign schools were ordered to close down and co-education was banned. My children, who were attending the French Saint Luis and Lycée Razi, had to be registered at the local segregated schools.

We spent the summer in confusion and disillusionment. Since my dismissal from the office, and in the light of the new developments, I did not intend to seek any employment. Therefore, I began translating books and articles on social and political issues. Before the revolution I had, once in a while, translated a number of articles for professional magazines. In addition, I had translated two books. Now, I began writing again.

Meanwhile, Manuchehr, who was now lecturing at a number of universities in Tehran, introduced a girl to us whom he had known in Detroit, in the US. I met Shahla on several occasions and we became friends, although she was much younger than me. Both Manuchehr and Mehdi were staying in my mother's apartment now that they had returned to Iran. Manuchehr had now matured into a young man, whose extensive education, insight and political experience made us respect him very much and take his advice on different issues. Once at his house he asked me what I thought of the idea of him getting married. I said it was great and asked him who the lucky woman was. He said it was Shahla. Now I understood why, out of so many friends he had made in the US, he had introduced this particular one to us. Later, we arranged to meet Shahla's family. As a matter of courtesy, as was customary, our entire family, my father, Aunt Iran, my sisters and I, along with Iraj, accompanied Manuchehr to his future in-laws. We arranged for their wedding to take place in November 1979.

Meanwhile my brother Mehdi informed us of his decision to marry Alex, his long-term girlfriend. Although we all liked Alex as a lively, friendly woman, we would have preferred Mehdi to marry an Iranian girl, but he had made up his mind and a date was set for their marriage in late September. Alex, who had come to Iran during the revolutionary months, had by now returned to England. In September we travelled to London to attend Mehdi's wedding. Mehdi and Alex had a flat in Chiswick, where we all stayed. The wedding was simple, but after the events of the last year it was the first time we had enjoyed normality. In November we held Manuchehr's wedding. The religious ceremony was as simple as it could be. Shahla refused to wear the traditional white dress and make-up because she didn't believe in it. Since the Family Protection Act had been cancelled, we offered to add her equal rights to divorce and child custody in the contract but the mullah refused to write them down.

Their wedding reception was held at our house in Niavaran, where some fifty guests attended. In those days, every aspect of our lives was transforming. Neither of them wanted to follow the traditions which had existed during the Shah's regime. For example, I could not get Manuchehr's approval to invite a band of Jewish musicians to play at his wedding. He was frightened they might play vulgar music. Years later, when he was not among us any more, I wished I had brought the band and had held a proper wedding for him, even though he might not have approved of it.

Towards the civil war

From the summer of 1979 the pace of political developments accelerated. After the March referendum differences began to appear between Prime Minister Bazargan and the dominant clergy section who were on the 'Council of Experts in Islamic Law'. The relationship between the secular democratic forces and the clergy had already deteriorated and the grass-root foundations of the short-lived democracy were gradually dying, pushing the country into a state of civil war. The regime had succeeded in eliminating hundreds of royalists, former secret police agents and those who had been branded as counter-revolutionaries. Thousands more had to retire, were made redundant or dismissed; women were the biggest proportion of these.

In these developments the situation of the army was not clear. The aim was to incorporate those who had proved their loyalty to the regime into the revolutionary guard regiments, the Pasdars, which had already recruited some 30,000 youths from among the urban poor and shanty town militias. The Pasdars, along with the Komiteh members, initially had the task of keeping law and order, attacking women's demonstrations against the veil, and attacking the offices of the opposition newspapers and the Left.

At the national level minorities were pressing for limited rights such as autonomous regional economies, the right to use their native languages and regional representation in the political establishment. Among the minorities, the Kurds, headed by the Kurdistan Democratic Party and the Turkamans, headed by a number of intellectuals, comprised the biggest faction. The government's representatives were engaged in negotiations in order to defuse tension but the increasing strength of ethnic demands loomed as a threat to the overall Islamicisation of the country.

Finally, contingents of revolutionary guards were dispatched to Turkaman Sahara and Kurdistan and civil war broke out. The Turkamans' demands were swiftly withdrawn because they were disorganised and, after the first assault, their four leaders were killed, leaving a vacuum in their movement. The Kurds, however, continued fighting for years because the Democratic Party had thousands of *pishmargeh* (armed militias). It took the government years to bring the area under its control.

In Tehran, apart from the existing political forces, a National Democratic Front was established by the writers, poets, lawyers, human rights activists and groups of the intellegentsia who did not follow any specific political line. Women joined the Front in large numbers. By the end of the summer the Left and the Mujahidin had organised tens of demonstrations demanding participation in political power. These rallies were often attacked by the mobs, their banners torn and members assaulted. In August the National Democratic Front held a peaceful rally, which was disrupted by thugs, who hurled stones at the speakers and the participants, injuring hundreds. Objections to the authorities about these callous attacks landed on deaf ears.

In December 1979 the new constitution which had been drafted by the Council of Experts was ratified through a referendum. Personal liberties, freedom of the press, and freedom of association, assembly, speech, religion, with the exception of the Bahai faith, were constitutionally guaranteed, at least on paper. Nevertheless, parts of the constitution contradicted this, because the phrase, 'according to Islamic standards', did indeed hamper the way for a truly democratic constitution.

In early 1980 the first presidential and parliamentary elections were held. Although the non-Islamic political organisations were allowed to participate, none found their way into the parliament. In addition, out of more than three hundred members, only four women Islamists were elected. In the presidential elections, Abol Hassan Bani Sadr, who claimed he had been working on the formation of an Islamic state for 18 years, was elected as the first president of the first republic of Iran. By then factionalism and differences had emerged among the clergy and the liberal-religious elements.

Codifying life

As time passed, we knew that Iran was not heading towards democracy and freedom, the way the guerrilla movement, the socialists and the intellectuals had hoped. Gradually, all aspects of our lives came under codes, decrees and directives. Islam had its own interpretations of everyday life. Music was banned, drinking became illegal, parties, receptions and weddings, as well as gatherings of mixed sexes came under codes of practice. Neighbours were ordered to spy on each other and report any misbehaviour. Night patrols would barricade roads and search cars for arms or means of sabotage as well as for drinks, forbidden books and periodicals. Although at the beginning we appreciated these patrols, because they prevented counter-attacks by the Shah's supporters, shortly afterwards patrolling the streets became the means of controlling people's movement.

Gloomy, dark clouds began to gather over the colourful skies of Iran. Black, grey, and brown clothing covered the streets. Laughter vanished and happiness became a vice. The unity and comradeship of the revolutionary days were replaced by the disintegration of the united movement which had overthrown the Shah. Now the aim was to create a nation of martyrs, mourners and morbid figures. Now people started to walk at a slow pace, head down, looking around cautiously. Women began to lose their self-confidence and self-esteem. The psychology of inferiority was enforced by constant campaigns of terror and intimidation. When in September I returned from my trip to London, after my brother's wedding, the first thing I noticed were the black-cloaked women and the armed patrols with hostile gazes, at Mehrabad Airport.

Women's activities in the period after the revolution

Apart from the women political prisoners who upon their release had joined their mother organisations, independent women had also joined the National Democratic Front and established a working committee within it. These women, in coordination with the Left movement, made an alliance, 'The Women's National Alliance', which published a monthly magazine of the same name. In the course of events, Fedaian sympathisers took over the leadership and the Alliance began to function more like a woman's section of the Fedaian than a democratic alliance. The Mujahidin, on the other hand, had their own women's organisations, which acted independently of the others. Islamists had established women's Islamic societies, charitable organisations and local groups which worked through the mosques.

In Autumn 1979 a number of secular women established an ad hoc group which decided to convene a conference on women's issues. The conference was doomed to failure because it did not have the backing of the Left. About 300 women attended the conference, which was held at a hall at the Polytechnic of Central Tehran. Suddenly, in the middle of the event, the lights went off, leaving the speakers reading their papers in the light of candles. It was obvious that a group had successfully sabotaged the conference. At the time, we concluded that it must have been the Hizbollah, the party of God. Years later one of the main organisers alleged that it had been a faction of the Fedaian organisation who had cut off the electricity, forcing the participants to end the conference quickly, so that they could join in their march, which was being held simultaneously. Whoever the saboteurs, they put a nail in the coffin of women's independent activities. The women's alliance, however, did not take off because most members already belonged to political groups and were following strategies of the mother organisation which contradicted the women's independent movement.

Cultural revolution

Since the revolution political groups which had established their offices in the main university buildings campaigned from inside the university compound. Thousands of students, lecturers and intellectuals usually gathered on the university's grounds, debating current political issues and exchanging ideas. Islamicising higher education and controlling universities was not possible unless these groups were out of the compound.

By 1980 a Cultural Revolutionary Council had been formed and its main architect, Abdol Karim Soroush, appeared on TV, discussing theology, philosophy and political thought in its Islamic version, through which we were being familiarised with the need for a cultural revolution in the educational system.

In mid-April President Bani Sadr announced the culturalisation of the educational establishments. To implement this policy he gave a three-day ultimatum to the political groups to evacuate the buildings. Since the warning was ignored, on the third day fierce fighting broke out between the revolutionary guards and the armed guerrillas, and thousands of the students participated, defending their political groups. During the fighting a number of students were killed and hundreds injured. Large quantities of literature were burnt and in this way the 'Cultural Revolution' triumphed. At this stage, all higher educational establishments throughout the country were closed down until further notice. Instead, Tehran University opened to people for Friday prayers, where people would assemble for the sermons in their thousands.

The universities re-opened only after almost four years of revolutionary cleansing. By then, tens of staff and hundreds of students had been dismissed. A new revolutionary management and the Islamic shuras took over. As a result of Islamicisation women were deprived of the right to attend some sixty subjects. These included all technical, scientific and agricultural, as well as arts subjects. Un-Islamic books were destroyed and the subjects which had revealed contradictions with the official ideology were re-written. Classes, hallways, corridors, laboratories and recreation centres were genderised, men and women segregated.

Bani Sadr himself did not stay in power for long. His views seemed to be too liberal for the newly formed state and differences which had developed between him and the clergy factions intensified.

Americans taken hostage

In November 1980 Mr Bazargan, unable to implement a democratic state, as he had wanted, resigned from his post of premiership. A member of the clergy replaced him. On November 4 we woke up to the news of the occupation of the American Embassy by a group of 400 Islamic students. Students, men and women, had climbed the walls and, before the US marines and guards could defend themselves, they were surrounded by those who had stormed the compound. The staff only managed to shred some of the sensitive documents before they were all captured; fifty three in all.

The American Embassy was a huge compound, with adjoining buildings and gardens with high walls, located on Persepolis Avenue. Although before the revolution approximately one hundred thousand Americans were in Iran, their numbers had dropped to a few hundred after the revolution. Occupation of the embassy was said to have been in response to the admission of the Shah to a US hospital for urgent treatment. The Shah, who was dying of cancer, was accepted on humanitarian grounds after lengthy negotiations with the American administration. No one knew if the high-ranking clergy and the government officials were aware of the students' plan. Nevertheless, all political factions, including the Left, sanctioned the hostage taking.

From then on, all attention was diverted towards the 'Great Satan', America. Anti-imperialist feelings among the whole population superseded other internal conflicts, such as armed conflicts with the Kurds over self-determination, conflicts with the Left and the women's movement. It also diverted attention from economic stagnation and the collapsing of the infrastructure of the country. For a year, every week, thousands of demonstrators gathered around the embassy compound, which was heavily guarded, and manifested their support of the hostage taking and their hatred towards imperialism, Zionism and colonialism. Political groups of the Left, the Right and the Mujahidin issued declarations in support of the action. We were not sure if the hostages were being kept in the compound, or if they had been moved elsewhere. Shredded documents were put together by the students in a painstaking job and were put on sale in twenty volumes entitled 'The Secrets of the Spying Nest'.

Negotiations with the Americans and their threats did little to end the deadlock. On April 25, 1980, the US administration, in coordination with its fifth column in Tehran, launched a military mission to rescue the hostages. The plan was to move the commandos and support personnel through the capital into Amjadieh Gymnasium, a few hundred yards away from the embassy compound. From there, the commandos would attack the embassy and rescue those inside. In the darkness of night, eight helicopters and six C-130 transport planes from the USS *Nimtaz* in the Persian Gulf landed in the desert, 50 miles from Tehran. What the US intelligence had not predicted was the desert climate. A sandstorm, which had began in the early hours of that day, caused the helicopters and the aircraft to crash into each other, killing eight US personnel and destroying a number of the helicopters and aircraft.

The rest of the fleet flew to their bases in haste, in fear of being captured by the revolutionary guards. To our surprise, before the guards reached the scene, the Iranian air force bombarded the already crashed aircraft. It was alleged that some elements inside the air force were afraid that the documents inside the aircraft would reveal the identities of the internal collaborators. The failure of this mission was declared an act of God, who wanted to discredit the Great Satan.

On January 20, 1981, on the eve of the American presidential elections, when Reagan took office from President Carter, the hostages were freed. The terms and conditions of their freedom had been set in the negotiations between the Iranian government and the American State Department in Algeria. In all, Iran didn't gain anything from the act. Instead, we were faced with additional problems. America broke off relations with Iran, all Iranian assets were frozen outside the country and an embargo on arms and other imports was imposed.

Chapter Ten

Iran–Iraq war, 1980

Think of the earth
The winds of horror have poisoned the soil's breath
Have burnt the roots of gardens.
What was the use of so many eyes
Just to witness the death agony of a generation?
                                    Shadab Vajdi, 'Why'

My sister-in-law Alex was expecting her first baby and had asked me to travel to London to be with her. At the time, Mehdi was working in Tehran. We flew to London in July. By then, Iraj had long been removed from his position as the deputy principal of the Flight Service College and was demoted to a job in Iran Air's legal department. The college itself had been Islamicised before the cultural revolution and eventually closed down as part of the cultural revolution.

I intended to stay in London until October but in mid-September the media reported that Iraq was about to launch an attack on Iran over border disputes which had existed for a long time. In disbelief and horror I decided to return quickly. Alex was disappointed, although she understood my anxieties. Back in Iran, the mood was even more sombre. We could not believe that among all the social, cultural and political turmoil the country was also threatened by foreign invasion.

On September 18 Iraq announced that it was taking control of Shat al-Arab estuary, abrogating the 1975 pact with the Shah. On September 22, 1980 I was at my sister-in-law's house when we heard the unexpected news. In broad daylight, Tehran Mehrabad Airport had been the target of an air raid by the Iraqi air force. There was damage to the buildings and all the flights had been cancelled. Iraqi fighters had penetrated deep into Iran, attacking civilians and military targets and bombing the Iranian radar system. The invasion started from the western and southern borders, targeting oil pipelines, refineries in Abadan, Khark island, Dezful, Mehran, Ghasr Shirin and the port town of Khoramshahr. The attacks on oil refineries suspended the oil export immediately.

Although Iraq occupied the desert border lands easily, once it approached the cities and towns the Islamic revolutionary guards, the army and the people fought them fiercely, and eventually the Iraqi war machine was halted. Because of the ill-preparation of the Iranians, Iraq managed to capture tens of small towns and hundreds of villages. The battle over capturing the port of Khoramshahr was a heroic one. The populace, along with a handful of the guards, resisted and kept the invaders out for almost three weeks.

The government had to react quickly in organising the revolutionary guards and the army, as well as mobilising the youth to fight on the battlefronts. President Bani Sadr, as commander-in-chief of the armed forces, travelled to Khuzistan province to supervise the organisation of the Iranian defence. At the same time, he was under attack from Ayatollah Khomeini and the high-ranking clergy over the policies which contradicted their views. Iran now faced simultaneously the hostage crisis, the Iraqi invasion and the internal conflicts with opposition parties.

Split among the old comrades

As hostilities towards the non-Islamic groups intensified, differences over supporting the Islamic government or becoming an opposition party deepened within the largest political group, the Fedaian. Among bitter arguments the old comrades split into two factions. The Tudeh Party, the pro-Soviet communist party, was partly responsible for this split. Having no experience in politics, and the complexities of the Islamic regime, the biggest section of the Fedaians was attracted to the Tudeh Party's politics of supporting the regime. These were considered as a big brother with political expertise. The expertise had, in fact, long-since perished, though it is doubtful that it had ever flourished in the first place. However, the majority of the leadership and many of the supporters of the Fedaian organisation sided with the faction which accepted the Tudeh analysis of the Islamic government as 'an independent, anti-imperialist regime'. A minority who did not agree with this analysis called for opposition to the regime. After the split, each of the Fedaian factions claimed to have inherited and represented the glorious past of the Fedai movement against the Shah's dictatorship. A few months later another split in the majority section of the Fedaian created a further crisis within the Left movement. These splits had dire consequences for the Left as a whole.

By March 1981 President Bani Sadr's differences with Ayatollah Khomeini had intensified. He was accused of 'incitement to riot' by the newly established Islamic Republic Party which held key positions and was the real power behind the government. Bani Sadr's life was threatened by the Hizbollah, the party of God. Ayatollah Khomeini denounced Bani Sadr's policies and, under threats from all sides, he was forced to abdicate his presidency and went into hiding. Later, he and Massoud Rajavi, leader of the Mujahidin organisation, escaped to France with the help of their army supporters. All these developments increased pressures on public liberties, especially women's. By 1981, the wearing of the hejab had become almost universally enforced, although women were resisting it fiercely and clashes with the guards often took place.

During 1981–2 the war continued in the western provinces with some success on the Iranian side. By then, millions of refugees had emigrated to Tehran and other big cities. In some areas the government had built special camps to house the people. In Tehran the houses and apartment buildings which had been confiscated at the beginning of the revolution were allocated to these people. The war had the worst effects on women and children. Becoming refugees without much support forced many young women into prostitution. Those who were optimistic that the war would soon end waited for some time before they settled elsewhere. The war increased shortages and inflation. Rationing of essential goods was being enforced and the black market expanded. As the result of the embargo and the black market some merchants and retailers became millionaires overnight while the majority suffered.

We believed that America was behind Saddam's invasion of Iran and the immediate consequence of such feelings was a mass mobilisation against American policies in the region. Anti-imperialist feelings increased even among those educated in the West. We blamed America for the unexpected and the unwanted war. So we stopped buying American goods and tried to economise in order to save the country's resources. Sentiments were running so high that many people, including women, began to attend military courses in order to go to the front if necessary. In the winter of 1980 I registered at a training centre, along with many other friends. Military training was run by the revolutionary guards throughout Tehran. Confiscated buildings were used as military schools. At our school almost all the instructors were women. We found out that women Muslim revolutionaries had been active in the hostage taking, at the front and even among the revolutionary guards. One woman, Mrs Sedigheh Dabegh, was appointed commander-in-chief of a brigade in Hamadan, a city in the west of the country. Later she was elected to the first Islamic parliament. But in general women Muslims were mainly engaged in support units, not the army itself.

Our training lasted about two months. Every afternoon a group of thirty women, mostly educated and middle-class, attended the two-hour sessions to become familiar with combat tactics. We spent the last week of training in the hills outside Tehran, practising shooting and the use of grenades. At the time, our patriotism closed our eyes to who the real winners of the war would be.

The childcare centre, 1981

After the revolution I was almost certain that I would not take up employment in the public or private sector again. Hence, I began translating books and articles. I translated three books within a short period. Translating and writing, however, did not satisfy me. It was a tedious job which segregated me from society and kept me to myself for most of the time. Needless to say, a great number of men and women who had been forced out of work did nothing at all and spent their time in a state of 'waiting to see what future lies ahead'.

Meanwhile, a number of my women friends who had also been made redundant, suggested that we do something useful. Among us there were doctors, educationalists, teachers, managers and many other professions. Finally we concluded that establishing a childcare centre would be best. Throughout Tehran public childcare centres, which had been available at workplaces, had been closed down as part of the drive to get women back into the home. Now very few were functioning and that was due to the efforts and persistence of the working mothers, who would not give in to the orders. To get permission from the authorities for an activity which was already ending was almost impossible. Besides, licences were only issued to those with sanction from the local mosque. We decided, however, to open the centre without such permission.

A group of four of us began to study the childcare systems throughout the developed world, in order to write a curriculum which would offer quality childcare. By the beginning of October 1981, through voluntary donations and the sale of our clothes and valuables, we had raised enough funds to start our centre. One of my gold rings paid for a library of 500 children's books. We rented a six-bedroom building in a prestigious area north of the capital. The building accommodated around one hundred children. Women volunteers helped to paint, decorate and furnish the place. We decided to run the establishment as a collective. We selected a board of directors which comprised eight women. I was appointed principal with two other women as assistants. They supervised the educational programmes, while I managed the administration of the centre. We began with seven children of friends and relatives. By the end of the first year the number of children had increased to twenty-five. Gradually our centre became known for the quality of the service it offered. We regularly evaluated our work in weekly meetings and discussed our achievements, weaknesses and overall performance. Our collective work was a valuable experience through which we learnt a lot. However, after a while, the lack of hierarchy and the non-profit making approach that we had chosen became problematic. The ministry which was responsible for the childcare centres, having heard of our existence, sent inspectors around. I pretended that we did not know of the licensing procedures and promised that I would apply for one, being certain that we would never be issued with one.

By then the political situation had worsened. Some of the children's parents who were allegedly involved in political activities did not feel safe any more and went underground. We were not allowed to have their addresses or even phone numbers. Some decided to leave the country. They came to take their children off the register under false pretences. We were aware that we could be accused of political activity. Many establishments had been closed down and their directors detained by such accusations. Now, we were more careful over the selection of the children, although it was difficult to refuse toddlers for their parents' political ideas. Unfortunately all aspects of our lives, even our infants and toddlers, had gradually become politicised.

To find a way out of our anxieties we decided to register the children of some of the revolutionary guards, although they often were not able to pay the fees. These were often poor labourers who had found upward mobility through joining the guards or the street mob and now wanted their children to attend an educational establishment from a young age. The problem this tactic created was a change in our curriculum. We now had to pretend that we were following the official guidelines. By the beginning of the second year, however, our children had increased to fifty and the centre was known to many parents who were looking for quality childcare.

At the political level after Bani Sadr was ousted from power, Mr Rajai, a religious fanatic, was first appointed prime minister and then became president. The spring of freedom had now turned into a gloomy winter. Fear, violence and the battle of power between the government and its opponents had intensified. Although the war had consumed most of the human resources there were still enough youths to enforce law and order through intimidation and terror. Demonstrations, rallies and strikes had long been outlawed, though there were sporadic acts of defiance.

In March 1981, for example, we were informed of a big rally at Shahyad Square, near the airport. A group of us decided to attend. My sister-in-law, who was nine months pregnant, and my son, who was ten years old, came along as well. The crowd was estimated at about 60,000, comprising the supporters of the Left movement and independent people like us. We were standing in the middle of the crowd when we suddenly noticed mobs approaching from the far end of the square. Before we could decide to get out of the crowd, a hail of stones began to pour down on us. We escaped quickly into the safety of the side streets, while observing the efforts of the organisers to drive the mob out. At this point an explosion deafened our ears. We did not know what had happened, but just a few yards from where we had been standing, a grenade had been thrown, killing and injuring tens of people. We were lucky to have escaped in time. Near where we had been a young boy of ten was selling ice-cream on a mobile cart. I had in mind to buy some after the rally ended. I will never forget his innocent face and have often wondered what happened to him after the explosion. The mob attacked indiscriminately, tearing down the banners and placards and injuring many more people. That night on TV the organisers could not convince the authorities to condemn the violence and nobody took any responsibility for it.

On June 20, 1981 the Mujahidin guerrilla organisation, angry at the government's hostilities, decided to bring all their supporters out on to the streets and demonstrate against the government. An estimated 500,000 people poured into the city centre. A battle broke out between them and the revolutionary guards and as a result thousands were detained. The number of those killed has never been known. Prisons became overcrowded with youths as young as ten. Many were executed on the spot or within a short period. That was the bloodiest day in the history of the internal conflicts between the main opposition group and the government. The Left, especially the Fedaian, had advised their supporters to avoid that demonstration. Their analysis, right or wrong, was based on the fact that the majority of the people supported the Islamic regime and it would be suicidal to rally their supporters just to get them killed in a futile street battle.

After the June incident all political groups went completely underground. Thousands changed their addresses and moved from their neighbourhoods. Children had to be left with grandparents so that parents would escape persecution. Thousands more left the country in haste. A week later, on June 28, an explosion at the offices of the Islamic Republic Party headquarters killed the entire leadership of 72 members. The Mujahidin took responsibility in retaliation for the atrocities against their organisation. A month later, on August 30, another explosion killed President Rajai and his prime minister Bahonar. From then on a semi-civil war between the government and the Mujahidin began.

The closure of the opposition's offices and the clamp down on the regional parties, such as the Kurdish Democratic Party, the detention of thousands of people and the ban on newspapers and bookshops, resulted in a mass exodus. Over a period of six years more than three million Iranians left the country. The bulk of the migrants were intellectuals who saw their lives as being in danger. This was the first time in living memory that educated Iranians had left home in such large numbers. The only time Iran had experienced a similar exodus had been after the Arab invasion (640 AD), when thousands migrated to India. Now everyone we knew had a family member in exile. Shortly afterwards most of my friends at the childcare centre emigrated, leaving me on my own.

By 1981 everyone felt the changes in their life-style. My children had almost forgotten their French, on which I had spent so much money. Now Parastou went to a girls' school with the Islamic hejab, which often irritated her skin in the summer. Physical punishment, which had been banned years ago, had returned and children were severely punished if they disobeyed.

In the New Year of 1981 we went to Jiroft to keep my father company. The town had changed to a great degree. The properties of Mr Ameri and Mr Shahpouri, the two big landowners, had been confiscated and divided among the peasants who had worked for them. In the south of Jiroft, which stretched to the Bander Abbas port, Baluchi clans and a few warlords had clashes with the revolutionary guards. Elements of the Left, the Mujahidin and other political groups, and educated individuals, had been dismissed from office. A number of them were detained in Kerman prisons. Now, local revolutionary guards and those in charge of government offices were mostly the children of gardeners, labourers and landless peasants. The effects of the war had even reached such a remote area as Jiroft. There were refugee camps outside the town where some twenty thousand people, mainly women and children, were kept. Hostilities had developed with the locals over rations.

In 1982 Iraj retired from the airline at the age of forty. He could not endure the pressures and the changed environment. At Iran Air hundreds were made redundant or retired. They ranged from pilots, through cabin crew to technical personnel. A large number of them emigrated to America. Islamic elements were being recruited quickly to replace them.

Because of shortages and inflation our consumption patterns of food, clothes and other goods had also changed. I did not care any more about what I wore. In fact I had not bought a new dress for years. A pair of jeans and baggy tops were all I cared to wear. In a garage sale to raise money for different purposes, including the childcare centre, I had sold most of my fashionable clothes, costume jewellery and make-up. We did not need any of these any more.

The war was dragging on. By the second year of the war Iran had made some advances and had recaptured a few miles of its land from the Iraqis. The turning point was September 1982, when the port of Khoramshahr was liberated as a result of the sacrifices of thousands of young people and the revolutionary guards. The Iraqi soldiers fled in haste, some even leaving their boots behind. The whole country was jubilant. People were celebrating and hoped that the war would soon come to an end.

In fact some of the wealthy Arab countries, fearful of Iran's victories, which they thought might threaten them, proposed to pay Iran substantial compensation to end the war. Saddam Hossein was in a weak position and declared that he was ready to sign a peace pact. Despite Iran's upper hand at the time and the international efforts at mediation, the Iranian regime did not approve of a ceasefire and ordered offensive attacks. From then on, until the end of the war in 1988, hundreds of thousands were killed on the battlefields. During the eight-year long war, the culture of martyrdom for Islam took form. People were sent to the front to compensate for the lack of machinery Iran had over Iraq and eventually the country was drained of its resources, both human and material.

Another dramatic development affected women Islamists. Four women were elected to the first Islamic Parliament. At the lower levels women became active in all areas. Hundreds now worked as nurses, workers and support groups at the war front. As a result of mass dismissals and redundancies, there was a serious shortage in the civil servant section. Vacancies were filled with these dedicated, religious women. Ironically, the very ideology which sent one group of women home, brought others into the labour market. The difference was that this latter group lacked education, expertise and the experience of the former.

As with art, television, radio and cinema, Islamisation continued. No one knew what the Islamic entertainment was. The only programmes worth watching were censored cartoons, wildlife and survival programmes. Women were not to be shown unveiled and, needless to say, strict moral codes had to be observed in film-making. It was difficult to produce films and observe all the restrictions.

The year 1982 began with war and more exodus. Nobody was sure of the future. My sister-in-law Alex, who had come to stay in Iran after she gave birth to her son Darius, decided to return to Britain. Manuchehr was dismissed from the university for his alleged political views. My sister Simin was the only one determined to stay at the Central Bank, despite being demoted and the growing pressures on her.

By 1983 many of those who had originally contributed to the formation of the Islamic republic had either been killed by the Mujahidin, or at the war front, or by the regime itself. For example, Sadeq Ghotbzadeh, who had acted as the spokesperson during the Ayatollah's stay in France, and had been appointed the head of broadcasting and later foreign secretary, was accused of treachery and of plotting a coup. He was detained and executed shortly afterwards. Ibrahim Yazdi, who was the chief prosecutor in the initial phase of the revolution, issuing Prime Minister Hoveyda and other top-ranking officers' death warrants, was ousted from power altogether. He was lucky not to lose his head.

As for the childcare centre, our children had increased in number. We celebrated the end of our first year before we broke for a short summer holiday. By then we had enough money to pay some wages. Until then, apart from the cook and the cleaner, almost everyone worked as a volunteer. My financial situation was worse than other partners. Not having much savings, the money I received as compensation for my dismissal from the company had long since run out. I did not get any help from Iraj except for household expenses and for the children. Since I had lived independently for so long it was hard to accept any offers from him. Fortunately, I did not have to pay for private fees and nannies any more. My new way of thinking romanticised being poor and that helped me psychologically to cope with the situation. Reflecting, I sometimes thought the type of society we had wanted to materialise was not dividing the wealth among all but dividing poverty to make all equal. This has been indicated in some writings and poetry of our renowned revolutionaries. Khosrau Golesorkhi, for example, wrote; 'I see the day when people, all in one body march on Tup Khaneh Square. Bread and hunger, divided among them, equally.'

The loss of my beloved brother

A heart born of love
Is immortal, never dead
In the book of life
So it is written, so it is said.
                              Hafez

After the summer break we opened the centre with more children. Manuchehr's son, Arash, who was one-and-a-half years old, was among our toddlers. Now Shahla worked at a private firm and I often took Arash to Manuchehr on my way home. On a Wednesday afternoon in late November I called their house to see if Manuchehr was there so that I could drop Arash off. I had not seen Manuchehr since the previous Saturday. The phone rang for a long time but no one answered. I thought he might have gone out, something he rarely did because of security reasons. I dropped Arash at his grandparents' and went home, not knowing what was waiting for us.

On Thursday morning I went to the centre as usual. Suddenly the phone rang. It was my cousin Zarin, whom I scarcely saw. She told me that Manuchehr had been taken ill and was in hospital. Since we did not have a phone at home there was no way I could have been informed the night before. I asked one of my colleagues to take over and rushed to the hospital. Manuchehr had contracted meningitis. In the last few months he had had constant headaches but no one, not even himself, had paid any attention to them or thought they might be serious. On the Wednesday morning when Shahla had left for work he had complained of a fever and pain but she thought it was a cold and returned home late at night only to find Manuchehr in a very bad condition. It took them several hours before a hospital accepted him. Many hospitals were not prepared to accept patients with such a serious condition. By then he had gone into shock and a coma. When I saw him in the morning his condition had deteriorated.

After a few days, when the team of doctors told us that his situation was not improving, we called Jiroft to inform my father and Mehdi, who was there at the time. They arrived the next day. For the next ten days the hospital was full of specialists, his many friends and relatives. He had got the disease twice before but had recovered quickly. He was now beyond help. During the days at the hospital we watched him, talked to him and begged him to fight. He was a good fighter. He did his best but the killer disease was stronger than his will and our efforts. To our horror and disbelief on November 28 he died at the age of 36, leaving all his dreams of a future for Iran, his young wife and son behind. That handsome young man, whom we loved so much and respected so much, was not there any more.

In the ambulance which took him to the cemetery I embraced him all the way to keep him warm. Amidst the shock and remorse we did not leave him alone. At the cemetery Shahla and I held him tight to protect him from the cold and the look of strangers. A mullah came around and told me to pull my hejab down while I was holding his body in my arms. The smell of camphor powder they used after washing him according to Islamic custom still reminds me of the young, handsome body we let the earth take away. We lined up to sing a song for him. Alas, we were not allowed to raise our voices. He would not know any more how much love he left behind. I remembered the teenage boy I had brought with me from Jiroft and accompanied to school those first days in Tehran. The teenage boy who became one of the best political scientists and economists of his generation.

We partly blamed the group of intellectuals he worked with for his death. The culture of sacrificing the personal for the political had a deep root in the movement. Political activists were not allowed to have normal family lives, take holidays or rest even if they were ill. Manuchehr was so busy with his work that he did not pay any attention to warnings and continued his work, regardless of constant colds and headaches. However, apportioning blame did not reduce our agony.

It took me a year to stop crying and accept the fact that he was not there. My sisters and brothers were in the same situation. I lost interest in everything, even my children's education whom I cared about so much. I could not manage the centre on my own any more, although I still went there. One of our group members was appointed to run it with me. Eventually, my father had a heart attack and I went to Jiroft to stay with him until he recovered. I had enough time to walk through the garden of our house where we had all spent our childhood. I talked to Manuchehr and planted his memory in every corner of the garden. I had enough time to mourn his loss and cry as much as I wanted and stretch out my hand to hold him in my arms. When spring came and swallows returned to Jiroft, I knew that he would never return. I left my father in Jiroft only to return years later after he was gone as well.

Spring of freedom turns into a chilly winter

By summer 1983 hundreds of thousands had left the country. There came a time when we were all frightened for our lives and that of our families. Although we had not done anything wrong, it did not matter. Possessing a wrong book could send you to the gallows. I had thousands of books in my library. In those days of horror, every morning piles of books were often dumped at the rubbish collection centres. In the shadow of the night people put their precious books in sacks and threw them into the rubbish. Out of fear I did it several times but still I had many more books at home.

One night, while Iraj was out, I began to burn my books in the basement. It took me until four in the morning to burn all those I thought might jeopardise our lives. By the time he arrived here, at five in the morning, I had already cleaned the house of the traces of knowledge we were forbidden to acquire. I pretended that I had been asleep throughout the night, having sweet dreams. In our unusual circumstances we learnt quickly to deceive, even our closest ones.

Now it seemed that all signs of pleasure or happiness had gone out of our system. Now I felt that I had become like those people who walked with heads down, fearful, and frowning most of the time. I did not see a path to happiness any more. To me, all hope was gone, withered away with the cyclones that swept us around and crushed us under its dreadful power. In the early winter of 1983 Iraj planned to go to the US and stay there for a while. Over the years I had constantly refused suggestions to leave Iran. Although I loved travelling abroad my roots were here, in the rivers, mountains and deserts and the orange gardens of my home town. How could I leave my mother and Manuchehr behind? I visited their graves regularly and talked to them. I still loved the people the majority of whom had turned their backs on us. I still hoped I would be useful some day, some time. I thought it was a good idea for Iraj to go. At least one of us might find happiness on some other soil. Finally, he left for the US and I busied myself with the centre. The first week he arrived in Dallas he called me and cried for a while. I asked him the reason. He said he could not stand the colours, the plentiful goods in the supermarkets and the happy-go-lucky people. He had almost forgotten that people had normal lives in some parts of the globe.

The war with Iraq was in its fourth year now. All the country's resources were diverted to the war. We had driven Iraq from most parts of Iran. It was the expansionist ideas which took the war onto the Iraqi soil. Hundreds of thousands of youths were constantly being killed in the battlefields, on mines or under heavy Iraqi artillery. Boys as young as twelve and thirteen. Most streets and alleys in Tehran were renamed after a martyr. Every week hundreds of corpses were carried into Tehran and other cities, buried in lengthy processions.

I sell the childcare centre

By December 1983 suspicion was building about our centre. We felt we were being watched. Although most of those who had originally helped to establish the centre had already left the country and many politically minded parents had taken their children away, we did not even trust our workers. Could anyone accuse us of something ? Did we have to apply for a licence? Fear invaded our minds. Every knock at the door or an unexpected phone call made us jump to our feet.

Finally, we decided it was time we closed the centre, like many other establishments which bloomed and died in the coldness of fear.

Packing my life in cardboard boxes, 1985

It took me two months to prepare ourselves for the final journey. Apart from the big pieces of furniture which I sold, the rest of our belongings were packed in boxes and left in the basement, hoping we would return soon. Although I had disposed of many of my books I still had many left. I shipped some to London and I was careful in my selection. At the post office all the books were examined before I was permitted to pack them. I still had a certain number of books which I wanted to leave with a friend. The last act of terror happened when one morning I put the books in the car to deliver them to the friend. I was stopped on the way by a police motorcyclist, who asked me to accompany him to the station. Giving me no explanation, I panicked to the point of collapse. If I went to the station and they inspected the car, which was the first thing they would do when one was stopped, I would be detained immediately. Carrying books in those days meant asking for trouble. I wished I had hugged and kissed Parastou when I dropped her at school. I wished I had said goodbye, left a note. Did I water the flowers this morning? So many untold words, so much unfinished business. I might be gone so easily. We reached the station after a few minutes. I parked the car further down the road, to avoid inspection. I went to the station to find only that my rear number plate was lost. I left my licence with them with a written promise that I would get the plate immediately. For three days my mind would not function properly. Was this the land of Hafis and Sa'adi and all those great poets who preached eternal love for human beings and happiness ever after?

A week before we left my father came from Jiroft to say goodbye. The day before we were due to leave we went to Iraj's parents. His mother cried for the grandchildren she might never see again. She said she was always sure I would not leave Iran and she would be near her son and grandchildren. Tears were swelling in Iraj's father's eyes but he did not let them flow. When we left the house he stood at the door, his eyes following our car until we disappeared round the bend of the street.

In July 1985 the heat was intense even in the early morning. We said goodbye to my sister and her children, whom I loved very much. None of us cried at that point. The door closed behind us when the taxi moved away. Crowded streets, noisy cars, the early morning bakeries and the dusty trees of Pahlavi Avenue were lost among the swell of my tears.

At the airport the woman custom inspector in her black chador went through our belongings for two hours. At last, tired and disappointed at not finding any valuables, she asked the reason I was taking so many unimportant things with me, for example, my son's ragged teddy bear. I looked at her for a moment and asked her if she knew what *kooch* (migration) meant. She went silent. Later, there was a misunderstanding about our reservations and we almost missed our plane. Parastou insisted that we leave our hejab on board the plane when we landed at Heathrow. Here, we joined the already three million exiled Iranians who had already left the country.

Chapter Eleven

Exile, 1985

I am a breed of trees
Breathing stale air
Brings me to my knees
A dead sparrow told me
Just remember the flight
Otherwise, the birds will always cease.
Forough Farokhzad, Rebirth

From above, London seemed green and peaceful. Clouds were
scattered in the sky and I could see the Thames and the rush of traffic
on the motorways. Upon approaching the runway I could even see
flowers blooming in the small gardens. When our plane landed I
looked at Heathrow differently. A group of young girls in fancy dress
attracted my attention. Tears filled my eyes. On the same planet,
six thousand miles away, people had forgotten about colours. Broad
smiles on some faces drew my attention. The scarf and the long sack
which distinguished us Iranian women as forbidden, untouchable
creatures were no longer there. My daughter was right. It was good
to leave the symbols of our enforced womanhood behind on the
aeroplane seats. Parastou's face was shining, her long, brown hair
dancing with the breeze.

It was nice to see Mehdi and his family among the crowd; hugs,
kisses and countless words poured out. They had recently moved
to a two-bedroom maisonette which they had bought in Hayes,
Middlesex. We were given one of the bedrooms for the time being.
The first thing I did was grow some vegetable seeds I had brought
with me in the rear garden. We did not know what to do next. For
the first two weeks friends and relatives came to visit. We bought
a small car to become mobile. We listed our priorities.

Just a month before our departure from Iran Iraj had been offered a job to take over a company whose owner had moved to Germany. While in Tehran he had not been sure if he would accept the offer. Now, after a month in London, he decided that it would be best if he returned and took up the job. The salary was being paid in sterling, which would help us in London until I got a job. Deep in his mind he preferred to be with his parents, rather than us. By August we were left on our own to make something of our lives.

The first thing I had to do was to find a place of our own. Living with my brother's family was becoming harder by the day. I began to look at the properties and before long I secured a mortgage and bought a flat in the street nearby. To move to the new flat, however, took us to the end of October. It was difficult at first to register the children at school. When school started they were still at home. Finally, I managed to register them at Barnhill in Hayes which was a few minutes from where we lived. I bought them uniforms and accompanied them on the first day. I could see anxiety in both their eyes. Back home they were familiar with everything. Now the environment seemed alien. Although their knowledge of English was fairly good, for the first two weeks they could not understand what the teachers or the kids said. Colloquial language was different from the English they had learnt. Parham often came back soaked in perspiration and filled with anxiety. Parastou was by nature a more relaxed and sociable person, so it was easier for her to adjust. New concepts entered their vocabulary: whites, blacks and Asians. The children didn't know where to place themselves. I did not know either.

I was beginning to learn a new identity. I discovered that we were no longer part of a 'big nation'. The status that had been accorded Iran in the early 1970s, exhibited by the London cabby, no longer existed. We were categorised as an ethnic minority. I also found out that I was in the category of single mother; having two teenage children by myself. Now Britain began to open its true self to me. I began to learn that I had some rights as a single mother but I was restricted by the unwritten rules as I belonged to the minority and not the majority. Fear began to swell inside me. I realised that I was not even respected as the big sister by my brother any more. Rather, I was a woman who was confused and sad most of the time. 'Why don't you take it easy? You are in Britain, safe and sound' my sister-in-law wondered. I was worried about the country and the loved ones I had left behind and the unknown path I had taken. With all the familiarity with London, smells, people's gestures, the way they looked at us seemed unfamiliar. How long would it take us to make London home?

Living in London was very different from visiting it on short trips. It was like rewriting a story to make it ready for a film. Gradually, I noticed that my living standards had dropped. Although after the revolution I was living on a limited income, still we had the big house, two cars and enough money to live on. Now the three of us had to shrink into the tiny bedroom of my brother's house and later into one tiny apartment. Apart from my student years, I had never had to worry about bills, taxes and expenses. Now I had to go on a tight budget, with few friends and, above all, had to stand on the sidelines, marginalised from the society at large.

No one in Hayes, Middlesex was interested in knowing my story, although I had lovely neighbours; an old woman painter who gave advice to Parastou on her drawing and a young man who had just got married. Nevertheless, they were more interested in our kitten and her welfare than us. I could not blame them. These were people with few complications in their lives. Well-protected by the security of their peaceful country and content with their TV, electricity and gas stamps and the pennies they could save in their daily shopping. At the beginning I used to explain myself to people I met. Soon I found out that I bored them. These people could not understand the complexities of my life. Even the few intellectuals whom I happened to know soon had their interest diverted. Nevertheless, I happened to like these people. I could learn a lot living among them. I could learn to make peace with myself, to experience normality, to walk through a different path, away from dust and noise.

We moved to our flat on a cold early evening in November. It was on the first floor with two bedrooms; in total, the size of two rooms in our house in Tehran. Immediately, after we had put things in order, I began looking for a job. Having much pride in my diverse experience, I was certain that I would find a good job. After a few months of filling applications and waiting, I understood that life was not going to be as easy as I had first thought.

Iranians in exile, shadows of the past

One of the problems facing exiles lies precisely in how to resolve the acute tensions between being uprooted, of which they are the victims, and the need to put down new roots, which can only be within certain limits. If you put down roots too deeply in your new environment, then you run the risk of denying your origins. But if you put down no roots at all in your new environment, then you run the risk of being annihilated in a nostalgia which it will be difficult to free yourself from.

Paulo Freire, *Learning to Question*

I soon began to socialise with the Iranians whom I knew and who had already settled in London. We all belonged to a generation who had high hopes and unfinished promises. We spent hours debating, discussing and analysing the events. What went wrong? we wondered. It seemed that everyone blamed someone else and no one was prepared to take any responsibility for the defeat of our ideals. I began to learn of the growing hostilities among the once friends and allies of the revolutionary days. The group of politically minded intellectuals who now lived in exile had more hostilities towards their own comrades than towards those who had forced them to leave. The public meetings, social gatherings and special events were often disrupted by hostile arguments and even physical attacks. Until then I had believed that physical attacks were the culture of street thugs. It seemed that we all had something of it in our psyche. Hatred among the defeated was showing its ugly face even in a foreign land. Surprisingly, the number of women who acted as mob activists was considerable. Until then I had considered these intellectuals as respectful, cultured people. To my surprise, many were no different from Zahra Khanum, the leader of a gang of thugs, who was famous for her attacks on women and her use of strong language.

Fragmentation was the by-product of the defeat of our ideals. Periodicals which were published by different political factions were full of articles, analysing the Iranian regime, the defeat of the secular movement and predictions about the future of Iran. Seminars, conferences and debating societies were plentiful within Iranian circles. It took years before Iranians, realising they would have to remain in exile, possibly for good, decided to divert their attention from politics to art, culture and literature in order to preserve their identity in the increasingly hostile world.

The first winter in London was cold. Our flat did not have central heating and the gas fire was not enough to warm us. I made thermal curtains to keep the frost out. The curtains stuck to the windows until March. After sending out tens of applications, I finally got a job at the British Council as information assistant. Although it was a part-time, low-paid job, I was happy that I did not have to stay at home for most of the time.

The British educational system and the openness of the society was teaching the children things they would not have learnt otherwise, so this was a contradictory time for us. On the one hand, I wanted them to be brought up free and independent and to learn to stand up for themselves. On the other hand, I was frightened that they might step into the wrong path and be misled by the sudden freedom they had found. I tried to give them as much information as possible on the ethos of the schools: bullying, drugs, intimidation, racism and how they should stand up for themselves.

To keep in touch with events in Iran we listened to the news broadcasting from Iran in the coldness of our tiny flat. I subscribed to the Iranian daily papers. Back home the war had intensified after our departure. Saddam was bombing the cities indiscriminately. Shortages and inflation were on the rise. I wrote many letters to relatives and neighbours. No one ever bothered to reply. I could understand. They were so busy dealing with the hardships of daily life that they could not afford the luxury of writing me letters. I began to search for the friends who were scattered all over the globe and soon managed to find almost everyone. They all had a story to tell: their departure from Iran, their life in exile, their children and the problems they were facing or the successes they had made.

Apart from the US, which had the largest Iranian population, the rest were scattered throughout France, Germany, Sweden, Australia and many other countries. In France the financial situation had put everyone under much pressure. Since the French government had banned the employment of foreign nationals by its administration, exiles had to turn to low-paid, low-status jobs. For the bulk of exiled Iranians, who were highly educated, this was very hard.

Britain, on the other hand, had the toughest immigration laws of all EC countries and the lowest number of Iranians. Those who arrived at the entry ports and asked for asylum were detained and treated as criminals. To help these Iranians I volunteered to work for a number of refugee organisations. Unfortunately, Iranian refugee organisations were also polarised along ideological lines and one had to be careful in approaching them. Sometimes these organisations were used as the battleground for ideological differences. The more I became familiar with them, the more I came to the belief that we intellectuals and our movement for democracy had yet to grow out of infancy.

Living in Iran, a country which had been under arbitrary rule for centuries, made it difficult for us to grasp the concepts which were the topics of our endless debates: democracy, freedom, liberation, tolerance.

In January 1987, when my contract with the British Council expired, I was employed at the National Childcare Campaign as a part-time officer. This was a voluntary organisation which worked as a collective. I was glad to be working in a place with a good cause. The organisation was located at Wesley House, London Women's Centre. This gave me a unique opportunity to become familiar with the women's movement. I came to know many organisations and become familiar with their activists.

The more we settled down, the happier we felt. In the summer of 1988 I decided to sell our apartment and buy a bigger place. It was the housing boom of 1980s' Britain and I made a good profit on that tiny apartment. I bought a house not far from where we lived. We were all very excited and spent time in painting, decorating and repairing the house. It had a big rear garden which let me do my favourite hobby: gardening. Our neighbour Ken was a nice old man who advised me on plants and flower beds. I grew lots of vegetables and border flowers. Our blackberries were harvested and we had the space to entertain friends. Some of our relatives came to visit from Iran and we had a nice time after our initial hardships.

The horrors of war and Saddam's increasing atrocities

We were a green forest
With roots entwined
We are a bunch
Alone and no more Divine.
   H Ebtehaj, *Mirror in Mirror*

In 1987 the Iran–Iraq War entered its seventh year. Saddam, desperate to force an agreement on the Iranian regime, began to attack Iranian cities with missiles. Missiles were not like bombs. Once they hit a target, they would destroy a large area. We began to get extremely worried for everyone. I could not convince Iraj to get out. He did not want to leave his parents behind. My sisters were telling me of the frightful nights they had driven out of Tehran to the outskirts. For some time Tehran was almost deserted, while the majority of the six million population swelled the outlying towns and villages. Missiles were sent indiscriminately. Thousands were killed and many others developed nervous disorders. In the political arena there seemed to be no end to the war. It was stated that millions of people should be sacrificed for victory over Saddam and ultimately Zionists and Imperialists. The West had decided to keep the war in balance to let us destroy ourselves.

The year of 1988 was a turning point in the Iran–Iraq War. Missiling the cities was coupled with new atrocities. Now, in full view of the world, Saddam Hossein's forces threw chemical bombs on Halabcheh, a Kurdish town in the west of Iran, killing approximately 5,000 people. People worldwide watched the aftermath on television in horror and dismay. Although chemical warfare had already been used in the war, this time it was on an unprecedented scale. Saddam, however, got away with this crime and threatened to bomb Tehran with the same chemicals. Now many, including the families of martyrs, mainly women, became disillusioned with the aims and the 'holiness' of the war and made sporadic protests demanding an end to it. This was a serious warning to the government. These women were not the 'anti-revolutionary' elements who wanted to disrupt the revolution, as was usually alleged. These were the backbone and the providers of human resources for the war machine.

Although throughout the eight-year war the United Nations had issued several resolutions, asking Iran and Iraq to end the war, none was accepted by the Iranian government. The war was a blessing for the newly established regime to strengthen its power base. The constant mobilisation of people in the name of fighting the 'holy' war established a contingent of trained fighters whose experience could be used for diverse purposes. Apart from the first phase of the war, which brought chaos and disorder, the culture of sacrifice and martyrdom for the cause of Islam changed the course of the revolution.

The theory of Muslims belonging to one nation, without any boundaries, developed, and Iran declared itself the centre of the Nation of Islam. For this reason hostility towards Iran increased from other conservative Islamic states, who were threatened by this new form of Islamic militancy. The spread of Islamic radicalism throughout the Islamic world posed a threat to Western 'interests' in these countries as well. With the failure of the socialist ideology and the collapse of Soviet Union, Islam began to fill the gap and in many countries, including in the West, the youth turned to Islam.

The Iran–Iraq War was one of the longest and most destructive wars of the twentieth century. Whatever the underlying purpose, the damage, human and material, inflicted on both countries was enormous. Now it was time the war ended. Advisers to Ayatollah Khomeini convinced him to accept the UN Resolution. On 18 July, 1988 Ayatollah Khomeini announced that he would accept the Resolution 598 of the Security Council, which established a ceasefire in the war with Iraq.

The war left both countries in ruins. In Iran about one million were dead and maimed, twenty thousand had been taken prisoner and ten thousand had disappeared. About two million were driven from their homes. Some 54 cities, 3,096 villages and 118,000 commercial-industrial units and homes were destroyed over a period of eight years. The Irangate affair, which was exposed in 1986, revealed the scale of arms deals with the US, the same country Iran had denounced as the Great Satan and the enemy of the Nation of Islam.

On June 3, 1989 Ayatollah Khomeini passed away, at the age of 79, leaving a country which was now an Islamic state.

Experiencing the dark sides

In 1988 my son Parham was about to finish his O Levels. My daughter Parastou was starting her GCSEs. By then she had firmly established her reputation as the best student in her class and the envy of others. Bullying at her school, Barnhill, was rife. Children, especially the Asians, often kept quiet about being bullied and harassed. Parham talked about his observations of children being beaten in the corners of toilets. Parastou was not the type to keep quiet if she was being harassed and this created hostility with her peers. On a winter night in 1988 she attended a school party at Barnhill. Parastou argued with a group of girls from her class at the party and on their way back from the party they began beating her, 'to teach her a lesson.' When I arrived at her friend's house, where she was taken after the incident, I saw Parastou covered in blood. Her face swollen and full of bruises. The ambulance was about to take her to hospital. Her best friend Alison and her mother stayed with me until two in the morning, disgusted with what had happened. This was the ugliest face of London I had seen so far.

I did not know what to do or how to help Parastou to cope with her mental suffering. I did not want a permanent scar on her mind. She was not to be frightened of the environment she now lived in.

I had to convince her that this was an isolated case. The police took action. The children involved were suspended for a few days and cautioned by the police and the school gave reassurances this would not happen again. But these were not enough to heal the mental wounds. Did she have to put up with the abuse and harassment which was inflicted out of jealousy or racism? I had brought her out of my country so that she would not have to put up with harassment and abuse. I did not believe she should put up with it at all. I decided to change her school but the principal convinced me that it was best if she stayed until the end of year. It took Parastou a long time to forget the incident. She was frightened of being attacked once more and had to be accompanied to and from school for the rest of the year. Nevertheless, at the end of the year, she got the best grades in her GCSE exams and proved that she had the courage I had expected of her.

Our life, 1989–96

In August 1988 Iraj's father died of a heart attack. Now he was left alone with only his mother to take care of. I proposed that he should come and live with us. He said he would, provided he found employment and I promised to think of something. Back in Tehran the tenants in our house in Niavaran were war refugees and wanted to confiscate the property. Iraj managed to evict them through a lengthy court procedure, after which we agreed to sell the house. So our dream house was gone and the contents were given away, leaving no trace of us behind. Eradicated.

By 1989 my sister Simin, who had worked in the Central Bank for twenty years, made herself redundant and left the country, arriving in London in the summer, four years after we had arrived. We were thrilled to see her and her daughters Saviz and Sanaz, who were now adolescents. Only my sister Maryam and my father remained back home. Maryam was not the type to leave Iran. Her husband had become a successful businessman with factories in Tehran and Qazvin. In 1989, my father, whom we had not seen for years, came to London and stayed for the summer. He promised to return if my brother Massoud decided to get married. Massoud had now grown up into a young man.

Since I had promised Iraj that I would prepare the ground for him to come, I remortgaged the house and bought a business which was a building with a shop in a parade in Hayes, near where we lived. We cleaned and decorated the building. The shop changed name, and 'under new management' we opened it as a mini-supermarket and newsagent. In November 1989 Iraj arrived in London, bringing his mother with him. We were glad to see Gilan Khanum after so many years. She had grown older, especially after the death of her husband. By the time Iraj arrived I was working at two places. I had my part-time job at the National Childcare Campaign and was also teaching a part-time course in Childcare and the Community at one of the London colleges. Although the pay was not good I received much satisfaction being back in the classroom after all these years.

Unfortunately, things did not go the way we had planned. Iraj could not cope with the business on his own. I had to spend all my spare time in the shop. Gilan Khanum became frustrated living alone in a house which did not have much space for manoeuvre. Besides, it was winter and she could not go out. The children found it difficult to cope with the new situation and instead of having a peaceful time, tension filled our house. After three months, we decided that it was best if Gilan Khanum went to America to stay with her second son, Jahangir, in Oklahoma. Besides, her daughter Mehri lived in the nearby state of Texas with her three children. Finally, Iraj took her to Oklahoma, where she settled temporarily. By March 1990 we had become very busy with the business although it was a depressing time and our finances were getting worse. Now I was working almost eighty hours a week. Finally, I decided to resign from the NCC and just concentrate on the business, despite the fact that I had never been a businesswoman and hated everything about business.

During the two years that we ran the shop we began to get to know the community around us and saw a side of the society we had not appreciated before. We came to know more of the working class and the poor who lived in the neighbourhood in miserable conditions.

Now I knew what was happening to these people in a recession which was gradually creeping up. Until then, our conception of Britain had been very different. Although both Iraj and I were very frustrated at running that miserable business, we found no way out. All our resources were invested in it. Some advised us to let the rooms above the shop to earn extra money. Our lodgers were among the most deprived people. Some did not even have the money to pay for rent and stole food from others. Drug dealing and prostitution were widespread in the area. We would have never learnt about the effects of poverty in Britain if it wasn't for the shop.

By summer 1990, however, Parastou had finished her A Levels and was preparing herself for university. Parham was slower in getting his A Levels and was not sure what he wanted to do. It was important to all of us that they studied for a degree which would lead to a profession. I was very optimistic about them both, although I knew that it might be a long time before they found their own way separate from us. Now I could see that the second generation of Iranians in exile were doing well. Their parents did not want them to end up like themselves, whose work experience was not relevant to this country and who therefore often ended up with jobs unrelated to their past. Fortunately, in September 1990, Parastou got an offer from King's College London to study pharmacy and in October she moved to the Halls of Residence to begin a new life.

By the end of 1990 I became disillusioned over whether I had made the right decision in persuading Iraj to join us. Our old differences began to surface and he became very depressed. Unfortunately, in October 1991, his mother had a heart attack in Oklahoma and he went there in haste to see her. She died before Iraj got there. It broke his heart. She was buried in a green cemetery, far away from home. We were all very sad and held a simple ceremony for her. Iraj loved his mother very much and her death added to his depression. The children began to distance themselves from him. They did not see him as the loving father they remembered from old times, but rather as a person who made all of us very miserable.

Eventually our business was collapsing, the few lodgers we had could not afford to pay us, and we could not balance our budget. Mortgages had gone up and the recession began to bite. By June 1991 we could no longer continue and I was made bankrupt. All we had was in my name; the house, business, credit cards and the bank accounts. We were partly hit by the depressed economy and partly by our own mismanagement. I was not a business person and Iraj would not run it on his own. We returned to the point where I had started six years before when I arrived in this country.

After the initial phase of depression and confusion, Iraj decided to return to Iran for a while. I did not do anything for about a year. Slowly, with hesitation, I began writing and translating once more. I decided to study a course which I hoped would help me to get the job I wanted. I applied to do an MA at London University.

In the summer of 1992, my father, accompanied by Maryam and her family, arrived in London to attend Massoud's wedding. He had met an Iranian girl and decided to marry her. We were glad to see Maryam and her daughters, Avid and Azin, who were now adolescents, full of life, despite the harsh conditions at home. That summer was one of the happiest of our times in London. We were all together. My father's wish for Massoud to marry had now materialised. Having raised him during his childhood while my mother was ill, I regarded him more as my son than a younger brother and I helped with the wedding preparations as I would have done if Parham was getting married. My sister-in-law Shahla and her son Arash came for the wedding as well. Shahla never married after Manuchehr's death. Although her marriage lasted only three years, she has never lost her contact with us and we remain close.

In October 1992 I began my course in Women's Studies. By then Parham had started a degree course in Law and Parastou was doing well on her pharmacy course. I began a survey on the situation of Iranian women in Britain. Surprisingly, most of us had similar experiences. Men found it difficult to cope with life in exile and it was the women who had to give support to the family, work outside and run the household. Women found it easier to adjust. Life in a liberal society gave them opportunities they were deprived of at home. They stood up for themselves and helped the children adjust to the adopted society. The tensions of being uprooted were sometimes coupled with men refusing to give them support. My MA gave me much insight into women's struggles worldwide, although it did not take me into the job market as I had wished. I had to settle for jobs I did not find interesting.

In August 1994 my father died of a heart attack in Dalfard. None of us were at his bedside at the time. Being old and away from his children, he had often said that he had no wish to live any more. He was buried in Jiroft, near his sister and two of his stepbrothers. The whole town attended the funeral of a man who was respected by them.

Iraj came to stay with us for some time and we faced the same problems once again. Finally, he returned to Tehran for good, leaving us behind. I would have loved to resolve our differences and reach our old age together. How impossible I found it, now that my eyes were opened to the harsh realities of life. Parastou finished her pharmacy course and is currently doing a Ph D. Parham has become a lawyer. Both of them have grown up to be good human beings, the way I wished them to be.

We are now in the mid-1990s. Our ideals and ambitions have shrunk. The group of Iranians who once believed they would rock the foundations of our rotten, old society has now disintegrated into small particles with no identity. The world has changed to a great extent. The young generation of Iranians in the Western world are integrating well into their adopted countries, though they are drained of any philosophical ideas of how to change the situation in Iran.

Iran has moved on since the revolution but there is no specific direction in which she is heading. On the one hand, we witness a return to the past, a past which was rejected by the industrial revolution and other revolutions and liberation movements of the contemporary world. On the other hand, the modern world, especially modern technologies, are opening up a road to progress. The struggle for social justice, democracy and equality drove us into exile. It will be left to the next generation in Iran to begin from where we left off. One day we must learn to do away with the vicious circle of arbitrary rule, to de-romanticise our repressive ancient cultural mores and step into the universal village of humanity. If human beings are of 'one body and one mind', as Sa'adi wrote, our thoughts, words, and even silences will bear fruit for all.

Epilogue, October 1996

To do or not to do
Calls the eternal priest
So long, so old
That heavenly list
I whisper to the tavern mist
Let the wine flow
And carry on the feast
  Mehdi Shafii, 'Inspired by Omar Khayyam'

It is an early morning at the end of October 1996. I draw the curtain and sit back in the dark. I feel as if I have been Shahrzad, the storyteller in A Thousand and One Nights, having begun a story, now ending one, having taken you to the unknown lands, now taking you back to your safe and secure home, having involved you in bizarre events and the heat of tormented upheavals and now bringing you back to the end of the twentieth century. I was at times overcome by emotions and immersed in love, remorse, hatred, forgiveness and nostalgia. At times I thought my storytelling would be therapeutic to my injured heart and if I touched the pain which had sank into me it would go away. At times I built bridges of hope between generations, cultures, nations; past, present and the future.

I told you two things at the beginning of my story. I have been brought up to observe the rules and be self-restricting. All through my story, I lamented that I found myself unable to move beyond those rules imposed on me. I have unveiled myself superficially but the veil still exists inside me. Once, I prided myself for breaking the rules of traditional society, only to find now, at a mature age, that there are covert rules which keep me in place. The shield of secrecy, the veil of the personal, controlled me throughout the story. I understood to my horror that my textual self-representation cannot be divorced from cultural factors. Walls, veils and harems are still well-placed in my blood.

Mystic representation and *half the truth* were all I could afford. Unveiling myself and the others to *namahram* needed much courage, which I lack. Still, I refuse to stay in anonymity, and walk through a channel to pave the way for others. If our mothers told their stories through lullabies and inside a closed circle, mine is a step forward. I wish I had found the courage to tell you *the whole truth*. But *sharm* (consideration) and self-censorship confined me to tell the parts which will not bring harm to those involved. The cloak of secrecy that confines me physically and verbally has not been confined to any one genre or era. It is as old as the ancient history of the Persian plateau. It is as strong as the pine trees of my father's homeland. However, now that I see that I have climbed a mountain and seen many sides of life, I am optimistic that the hands of females, so oppressed, so confined and so restricted are beginning to shake the foundations of the old, rotten roots. Once one of our famous poets, Owhad ed-din Owhadi (b. about 1271), frightened by women gaining access to writing, wrote:

> The shroud her paper, the grave her inkpot
> They should suffice if they insist on knowledge.

And Forough Farokhzad in her first collection of poems, *The Captive* (1955) wrote of her sense of limitations:

> I think about it and yet I know
> I'll never be able to leave this cage
> Even if the warden should let me go
> I've lost the strength to fly away.

Well, I have distanced myself from both these notions, as did Forough herself. Optimistically, I believe that I have left parts of me in the two lives who will continue after me and for me and on behalf of me. The two lives who gave me much love, affection, aspiration, hope, torment, limitation, and restriction. Had it not been for the role of mothering which I embraced with much love and pain, I might have gone a different path. Had it not been for the sake of the man I promised to share my life with and the complications that promise brought, I might have been in a different position. Had it not been for the necessity of hiding and keeping appearances and holding secrets and veiling the private and glossing the public, I might have written the full account of an unfinished business.

My mother, Afagh Khanum, pushed me forward into a better future and I built a few steps. It is up to the next generations to build up the ladder. The veil is rotten and will soon tear off. The eyes will see then the depth of the skies. The scribbles in this book are an effort towards that ultimate goal. As Susan Griffin said:

> There is no end to any act. The rock thrown into the water is followed by waves of water, and these waves of water make waves in the air, and these waves travel outward infinitely, setting particles in motion, leading to other motion and motion upon motion endlessly. And in every particle every act lives, and the stars do not frighten us, starlight is familiar to us.

Notes

Prologue, 1995

1. According to Fatima Mernissi two theories exist in the Islamic perception of women's position in the social order. The implicit theory, as seen by Imam Ghazali's interpretation, is that women are considered by Allah to be destructive elements, powerful and dangerous. They have the power to deceive and defeat men, not by force but by cunning and intrigue. The explicit theory, with an antagonistic, machismo vision of the relationship between the sexes, is epitomised by Abbas Al-Aqqad who sees female power in a negative way, wanting to be overpowered and subjugated.

2. A Thousand and One Nights, known in the West as the Arabian Nights, is based on the power of women's storytelling. According to myth, King Shahriar, who was once betrayed by an adulterous wife, came to believe that the only protection against women's unfaithfulness was to destroy them before facing the danger of intimacy. He married a virgin every night, murdering her in the morning, never allowing a woman to deceive him. Shahrzad, who had the magic of storytelling, reversed the relationship of domination and subordination. Every night she told a story for the king, always stopping before the denouement, thus delaying her death by a thousand and one nights. These stories are written in thirty volumes, depicting the power of women in controlling their own destiny.

3. Sa'adi, the prominent, didactic, thirteenth-century poet who travelled widely around the world, putting his observations and world views in two books *Bustan* (The Orchard) and *Golestan* (The Rose Garden), both a rich source of Persian literature to this day.

Iran, a brief history

1. The Hammurabi Code is the legal decisions of the Babylonion king, which at the end of his reign, was inscribed on a stone rock set up in Babylon's Temple to the god Marduk.
2. Persepolis and Pasargadae: two cities, the remains of which are located in the Fars province near Shiraz. Both cities had their monuments and historical sites burnt down by Alexander of Macedonia after he conquered Persia. The ruins are now preserved as part of Iran's national heritage. Interestingly, the tomb of Cyrus the Great remained intact and saved from invasions and destruction throughout the centuries.
3. The Arab tribes, who lived in black tents in the Arabian deserts, kept their primitive life-style, away from urban civilisation.
4. Caliphas were the Prophet Mohammed's successors. After the Prophet's death, there were four Caliphas before a dynasty was established in the Arab countries.
5. The Umayyed were the first to establish a dynasty after succeeding to power (661–750 AD).
6. Shortly after the Prophet's death his followers split over his successor. The group who believed that Imam Ali, the Prophet's son-in-law and his descendants up to the twelfth Imam, were the Prophet's lawful successors were called the Shi'ats. Shi'aism was a radical movement at the time, opposing the ruling elite of the Arab dynasties. The majority Sunnis accepted the rule of the Prophet's close allies, Abubakr, Omar and Ottoman and the rest of the Caliphas.
7. Mujtahids are the Shi'at clergy who have reached the height of religious knowledge and expertise and have written treatises. They can sanction fatwas on their followers.
8. *Shah Nameh* (The King's Letter) is the title of books of poetry written by Ferdousi in the tenth century AD, reviving the ancient history of Persia. It took Ferdousi thirty years to collect the documents and historical evidence and to put them in a recollection of events in a poetic language. Not only did *Shah Nameh* preserve Persian history from further destruction, it revived the Persian language as well.
9. Although both women became queens and ruled Persia for some time, I do not believe this meant a return to the matriarchal eras. The two sisters were appointed to the post only because there were no males left in the Sassanid dynasty at the time.

10. Madrases or religious schools had been established in Persia since the eleventh century AD. Their main curriculum consisted of religious sciences but some taught other subjects such as maths, geometry, astrology and philosophy.

11. The ulama (plural for a'lem), the learned men, are the high-ranking clergy, who usually study at the religious madrases for a number of years and become masters of Islamic laws and inter-pretations (*hadith*). Among the ulama, some are promoted to the rank of mujtahid.

12. Sheikhi, a branch of Islam which the Bahai faith sprang from.

13. Qurratol'ayn, a woman poet who lived in the mid-nineteenth century in Qazvin. She was educated by her father from an early age and became master of theology and many other social sciences. Married to her cousin she had three children, but left them when she turned to Babibm and started to preach the new faith. She became its leader after Bab died. Later, she was murdered by her opponents.

14. In Islam one can trade with goods but charging interest on loans (*raba*) is forbidden.

15. Teghyeh is an act of secrecy performed by the Shi'ats, once they are in danger of being persecuted. By the act of teghyeh they are allowed to cover their identity in order to protect themselves from harm.

16. Since its arrival in Iran many politicians and influential people are alleged to have become members of the society. Although before the revolution the identity of many was revealed in two volumes of books by a writer (Ismael Rain), who himself was later murdered, the names of many more became public after the revolution.

17. Avizenna was a philosopher and physician (980–1037 AD) and his medical books were translated into Latin and taught in the European medical schools as the basic books until the mid-eighteenth century. He was also master of many arts including music.

18. Imam Hossein was the Prophet Mohammed's grandson. His martyrdom by Yazid, the Umayyed Calipha, is commemorated by the Shi'at Muslims every year.

19. Sofreh or tablecloth is a white fabric made in a rectangular shape. It is laid on the floor in the same way that a tablecloth is put on the table, for food to be served on. Sofreh is also used on occasions such as feasts, weddings and funeral services.

20. Shari'at are the laws and decrees of Islamic jurisprudence.
21. Morgan Shuster wrote his observations in a book (*The Strangulation of Persia*, 1912), exposing foreign interference and describing people's lives in Persia.
22. Chador, literally means tent. It is a full-length loose cover which is made of crepe, cotton, or muslin, usually in black, and envelops the body from head to toe. It is normally held in place by a band under the chin or, if the woman is very strict, under the eyes. Women wear it on top of their dresses when they are out of the house.
23. Dervishes are members of a Muslim religious fraternity, resembling in some respects a Christian monastic order.
24. Hejab (hijab) literally means partition or curtain. It refers to the cover which protects women's body from the eyes of men who are forbidden to her.
25. Namahram refers to men who are not women's close relatives. By exposing themselves to namahram women commit a sin and they are often warned of the consequences.

Chapter One

1. According to the Shari'at, women cannot give themselves in marriage. When the mullah performs a marriage ritual, he asks the bride's permission to act as her attorney to wed her. In asking her permission, the mullah reads out the terms of the contract and the amount of *mehr* (alimony which should be paid to the bride before the consummation of the marriage). The amount can be from a few coins to millions of Rials, in the form of cash, property or gold or any other item depending on the agreement between the two families.

Glossary

a'al	evil genie
abanbar	water reservoir
ab-baz	professional river crossers
Allah o akbar	God is great
Ashura	tenth day of the religious month of Moharram
badgir	wind-turret
bazl	present given at weddings and celebrations
Behesht	Heaven
caravanserai	a staging post
chador	a long, engulfing dress cover
chadorshab	large, thick woollen square
chang	harp
dalak	women masseuse in the hamam
dasteh azadaran	group of mourners
dohol	big drum
doroshky	horse-drawn carriage
eidi	present given in the form of cash at New Year festival
faloudeh Kermani	a cold sherbet which is served in the coffee shops
ghanat	an ancient system of underground water in the Middle East
ghari	mullah who recites the Quoran at cemeteries or religious events
ghelian	hubble bubble pipe

hadith	sayings of the Prophet Mohammed
haft-seen	a collection of items which symbolise growth and fertility at Nowrooz
hamam	public bath
hejab	the Islamic term for a woman's veil
hejleh	bridal room
hojat al Islam	middle-ranking clergy
hojreh	a shop that is used for trade and money transactions
homafar	air force cadets
howzkhouneh	large, cool room used in summer
Imamzadeh	holy shrine
kavar	square cottage made of reeds and wild almond branches
khanum	Mrs; Miss; lady
kharabat	a remote, rundown building
khazineh	hot pond in the hamam
Khoms	Islamic tax which is one fifth of one's income
khorjin	saddle bag
Komiteh	Committee of the Islamic Revolution
kooch	migration
korsi	a traditional means of heating in winter
kotook	oval cottage made of reeds and palm tree branches
lowng	loincloth
madrases	religious schools/universities
mafrash	first aid kit/herbal pharmacy
mambar	staircased pulpit
mashk	sacks made of sheepskin to keep water in
mehr	bride price
Mofsid fi-al arz	corrupted on earth
Moharram	first month of the Islamic calendar
mota'a/moteh	concubine/temporary wife through a short unofficial contract
motreb	amateur musical band
mujtahid	a high-ranking clergyman
mullah	clergyman

myrubalan	herbal root
najis	impure, not to be touched
namahram	a man who is a stranger to a woman
nazem	school deputy principal
Nowrooz	Persian New Year
ojagh	fireplace made in the ground
ormak	grey fabric for school uniform
pardeh	veil/curtain/big piece of cloth used for covering
Parsis	Persian immigrants to India
pashuyeh	borders of a pond
payab	narrow stairs leading to an underground water system
pishmargeh	armed militia
raba	interest charged on a loan
Rowze khun	mullah who eulogises in religious ceremonies
sabji–polo	rice dish mixed with vegetables
saghi	girl servers
samanoo	custard
shameh ghariban	mourning procession on the third day of Imam's martyrdom
shora	assembly/association
Sizdabedar	the thirteenth day of the Nowrooz holidays
sofreh	a piece of cloth spread on the floor to eat off
sorna	musical pipe
taghuti	wealthy/leading a Western lifestyle
talabeh	theological student
tamkin	sexual subordination of women
tar	an Iranian musical instrument similar to an Indian sitar
Tasua	the ninth day of Moharram, which is the mourning day
tazieh	religious processions in the form of sacred street theatre
teghyeh	hiding one's faith
tekyeh	town square where tazieh is performed

ulama	learned clergy
yakhdan	wooden case used for storing valuables
zakat	money given to Islamic charities
zangir	metal chains for self-flagellation

Works cited

Afkhami, M. *In the Eye of the Storm: Women in Post-revolutionary Iran*, I. B. Taurus, London, 1994

Ahmad, L. *Women and Gender in Islam*, Yale University Press, New Haven & London, 1992

Alamuti, M. *Iran During the Pahlavis: Chronology of Events*, Vol. 15, Peka Publications, London, 1990

Ansari, A. M. *The Pahlavi Dynasty and I: Untold Parts of Pahlavi's Life, Before and After Their Downfall*, Tooka Publications, San José, Ca, 1992

Aryan Pour, Y. *150 Years History of Persian Literature*, Franklin Publications, Tehran, 1969

Aryan Pour, Y. *From Nima to the Present Time: History of Persian Literature*, Zevar Publications, Tehran, 1995

Bamdad, B. *Iranian Women from the Constitutional Revolution to the White Revolution*, Ibn Sina Publications, Tehran, 1969

Bargshad, J. *Babak*, (translated by I. Rais Nia & R. Anzabi), Thunder Publications, Tehran, 1986

Behnoud, M. *Iranian Cabinets from 1921–79*, Nima Publications, Tehran, 1987

Dastgheib, M. *In the Brightness of Dawn*, edited by Owji, Navid Publications, Shiraz, 1991

Ebtehaj, H. *Mirror in Mirror*, Cheshmeh Publications, Tehran, 1990

Fallafci, O. 'The Mystical Divine Shah of Iran, Interview with the Shah', *Chicago Tribunal*, 30 December 1973

Farokhzad, F. *The Captive*, as quoted in F. Milani, *Veils and Words*, Syracuse University, 1992

— Rebirth, Morvarid Publications, Tehran (undated). English translation by Mehdi Shafii.

Fazel, M. K. 'The Politics of Passion: Growing up Shia', *The Journal of Iranian Studies*, Vol. XX1, No. 3–4, Sheriden Press, Hanouver, PA US, 1988

Ferdowsi, A. *Shah Nameh, Collection of Works*, in *Literary Work of Eastern Nations*, edited by Y.A. Bertles, Moscow, 1966

Franco Vene, G. *Uccidente Lumumba* (translated by M. Pejman), Faryab Publications, Tehran, 1973

Freire, P. *Learning to Question: A Pedagogy of Liberation*, Continuum Publications, New York, 1992

Griffin, S. Women and Nature, Women's Press, London, 1978

Guppy, Sh. *The Blindfold Horse*, Penguin, New York, 1988

Hafez, Sh. *Collection of Poems*, as quoted in Shusha Guppy, *The Blindfold Horse* Penguin NY, 1988

Hall, Nor *Mothers and Daughters*, Rusoff Books, Minneapolis, 1976

Ismailzadeh, M. & Farshchi, M. *The Incident of Unveiling: Unpublished Documents*, Organisation of Cultural Studies of Islamic Revolution, Tehran, 1992

Ivanov, M.S. & Grantovesky, A. K. *Ancient Persian History* (translated by S. Izadi & H. Tahvili), Donya Publication Press, Tehran, 1980

Kar, M. *Women in the Iranian Labour Market*, Rowshangaran Publication, Tehran, 1994

Keddie, N. *Iran; Religion, Politics & Society: Collected Essays*, Frank Cass & Co., London, 1980

Khayyam, O. *Rubaiyat of Omar Khayyam*, Eqbal Publications, Tehran, 1968

Maki, H. *Amir Kabir*, Bongaheh Targomeh va Nashr Ketab, Tehran, 1981

Mernissi, F. *Beyond the Veil*, Al Saqi Books, London, 1975

Milani, F. *Veils and Words: The Emerging Voices of Iranian Women Writers*, Syracuse University Press, US, 1992

Mosadeq, Gh. *Oil Documents: A Compilation of Concessions, Historical Letters and Speeches*, Rastin Publications, undated

Najmabadi, A. *Women's Autobiographies in Contemporary Iran*, Harvard University Press, 1990

Neruda, P. *Selected Poems* (edited by Nathaniel Tarn), Penguin Books, 1975

Owhad ed-din Owhadi, as quoted in Aliakbar Dehkhoda, *Maxim*, Amirkabir Publications, Tehran, 1982

Petrochevsky, I. P., *Iran in the Middle Ages* (translated by C. Izadi and H. Tahvili), Donya Publication, Iran, 1980

Ramy, N. *The Wrath of Allah*, Pluto Press, 1983

Sa'adi, M. *Golestan (Rose Garden)*, edited by Sa'id Nafisi, Foroughi Publications, Tehran, 1962

Safari, M.A. *Constitutional Makers (Mashruteh Sazan)*, Elmi Publications, Tehran, 1991

Scott, J. C. *Domination and the Art of Resistance: Hidden Transcripts*, Yale University Press, 1990

Shirazi, M. *Seige of Azadi Square: A Novel of Revolutionary Iran*, The Women's Press, 1991

Shuster, M. *The Strangling of Persia*, T. F. Unwin, London, 1912

Tabari, E. *Iranian Society During Reza Shah*, Tudeh Party Publications, 1977

Tehrani, Kh. *The Left Movement: An Examination from Within*, Bastabverlag, Germany, undated

Vajdi, Sh. *Closed Circuit: Selected Poems*, Forest Books, London, 1989

Zinoviov, A.A., *Constitutional Revolution and Iran Between 1905–1911* (translated by A. Etesami), Eqbal Publications, Tehran, 1983

Also available from Scarlet Press

Daughters of the Dragon
Women's lives in contemporary China
Christine Hall

Packed with information about education, careers, politics, and religion, *Daughters of the Dragon* is the first book to document comprehensively the concerns of contemporary Chinese women. Here, women speak openly about their attitudes and ambitions, from sex, relationships, marriage and motherhood, to living conditions, leisure, fashion and beauty. This book provides invaluable source material on the status of Chinese women and is an indispensable guide to both scholars and travellers.

ISBN Paperback 1 85727 068 1

Stolen Lives
Trading women into sex and slavery
Sietske Altink

The trafficking of women for prostitution is one of the most shameful abuses of human rights. It is also a fundamental economic and development issue for Third World and East European countries. Driven by extreme poverty, women are forced to migrate in search of work which very often results in their exploitation either as prostitutes or domestic slaves. This important work reveals the way in which women are spuriously hired in their country of origin, transported, left without money or resources and are trapped into prostitution by organised crime syndicates. Sietske Altink has interviewed many women from the Far East, Latin America and the more recent recruits to the trade, women from the East European countries. Their stories tell us of their motives, the routes and methods the traffickers use and how the gangs control the women through blackmail and violence.

ISBN Paperback 1 85727 097 5